DEFINING FEMALES

THE NATURE OF WOMEN IN SOCIETY

Edited by SHIRLEY ARDENER

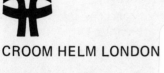

CROOM HELM LONDON

In association with the

OXFORD UNIVERSITY WOM

D1429232

©1978 Shirley Ardener, Kirsten Hastrup, Renée Hirschon, Caroline Humphrey, Judith Okely, Wendy James, Helen Callaway, Freda Newcombe, Graham Ratcliff and Hilary Callan
Croom Helm Ltd, 2-10 St John's Road, London SW11

British Library Cataloguing in Publication Data

Defining females.
   1. Women — Social conditions
   I. Ardener, Shirley
   301.41'2   HQ1121

ISBN 0-85664-746-2
ISBN 0-85664-822-1 Pbk

The Oxford Womens' Series

This volume, the first in a new series, derives from papers presented at a seminar convened under the auspices of the Oxford University Women's Studies Committee, during Michaelmas Term 1977.

Other volumes

FIT WORK FOR FEMALES

Edited by Sandra Burman

WOMEN WRITING AND WRITING ABOUT WOMEN

Edited by Mary Jacobus

Printed in Great Britain by offset lithography by
Billing & Sons Ltd, Guildford, London and Worcester

CONTENTS

1 INTRODUCTION: THE NATURE OF WOMEN IN SOCIETY

Shirley Ardener

The Volume

The Topic

This book is concerned both with the *nature of women* in society, and with the nature of *women in society*. On the one hand it considers the facts of, or more precisely, society's identification of the inherent biological properties or natural endowments of women, and how these have been used by society. On the other it looks at the structural, or social position of women, and asks how the category 'women' is defined, and is related to others in society. It suggests that perceptions of the *nature* of women affect the shape of the *categories* assigned to them, which in turn reflect back upon and reinforce or remould perceptions of the *nature* of women, in a continuing process.

Genesis

A brief preliminary digression on the background of this volume may be useful. The study of women at Oxford has been carried out until recently through the personal interest and the individual initiative of workers whose numbers and influence upon their respective fields have varied. Certain academic supervisors have especially encouraged research on women in recent years, and as a result there have been more theses dealing with women. Some seminars have been held. The most extended series of papers has been that organised unofficially by a number of female social anthropologists, who have between them read a new paper each week throughout every academic term since early 1973. Many of these have already been published (in, for example, *Perceiving Women*, 1975, and in various issues of the *Journal of the Anthropological Society of Oxford*), and more papers are expected to appear in print in the future. In its most recent phase, some colleagues with other disciplinary interests, not all of whom are formal members of the University, have joined the seminar. The Ruskin History Workshop has also given attention to the study of women, and has published papers in the *History Workshop Journal*. Various small discussion circles have also sometimes met to concern themselves with feminist issues.

9

Despite all this effort, there was no formal interdisciplinary programme explicitly concerned with the study of women. In the autumn
of 1976, however, a small group met to consider ways to pool efforts
to promote work on this topic. A special task was to advise on how best
to allocate a small University fund, made available through the welcome
financial generosity of Keith Hope. In passing on money to the University, he had thoughtfully suggested that it be allocated to women's
studies. If the suggestion for a women's studies fund had not met with
the approval of the University, the Hebdomadal Council would have
been asked to devote the money to the purchase of some dinosaur
bones needed by the University Museum. Fortunately for women, on
this occasion, the prehistoric monsters did not win. So precariously do
academic concerns advance!

As more interested persons were swept into the net of discussion, a
programme emerged. Some small grants were made to graduates to
meet special research costs. A little money was used to support a bibliographical exercise designed to locate existing resources in Oxford. One
aim of the programme was to put those interested in the study of
women in touch with one another, by providing an additional forum
for discussion. The major part of the fund was therefore allocated to
meet the costs of an interdisciplinary series of seminars, to run throughout the academic year 1977/78.[1]

The project was arranged with three themes in mind. The first was
treated in a series of papers drawing upon the human sciences, called
'Women: Some Biological and Cultural Perspectives'. The second (the
seminars are still in progress while this is being written) draws on historical and socio-political research and is called 'Woman's Work', while
the third, forthcoming series will be concerned with feminist literary
criticism. It is hoped that other themes will be taken up in future years,
financed in part by some of the royalties from this volume. Among the
audience for the first set of papers, now made available in this book,
were some who were specialists in their own fields; others were newly
arrived undergraduates; while some had a personal rather than an academic interest in coming. In view of this broad spectrum, contributors
were asked to avoid obscure technical terms where possible, or to
define them when first introduced. We hope that readers will understand that we are addressing ourselves to a wide audience, and will
make due allowance for this in their assessment of our efforts.

The Task

It was decided that a useful task for the first part of the programme would be to examine certain basic assumptions relating to the definition of our data. Later seminars would, inevitably and justifiably, tend to be more ethnocentrically based. It seemed helpful, therefore, before being immersed in this 'local' material, to be reminded that we tend to think of the category 'women' as some kind of universal, with a place in a cross-cultural frame of reference. We should not be allowed to forget that our own cultural model of women, and the adventures of the beings who realise that model, are very special examples from a wider category called 'women', which has many other possible realisations. Clearly an English model has no ultimate theoretical or moral primacy, although it may legitimately command our interest. It follows, of course, that any *general* conclusions about women which we may wish to draw from English historical, literary and other material, need to be viewed in the light of such awareness, and of experience in other parts of the world. Although we do not yet have the data or the techniques to do this adequately, even some hints as to the problem are likely to be useful. The papers which follow here provide us with new examples of data which deviate from those which deck our ideas of women, and remind us that a range of other possibilities is available. At the same time the analyses of other cultures might reveal to us aspects of our own whose significance we have not noted before.[2]

This expectation might well seem self-evident to social anthropologists and others who are used to giving thought to cross-cultural data. The relevance of such material is not, however, always obvious to everyone. After one paper based mainly on nineteenth-century English documents given in the second series of seminars, a young woman contrasted its approach, and also that of others in the 'Woman's Work' group, with the studies on the 'Nature of Women in Society' represented in this book. She said that the latter 'take us back in time' and are therefore less relevant to her. She could not assimilate the fact that while the 'Woman's Work' papers had indeed taken us back in ('English') time, on the contrary all the papers in the 'Nature of Women' series are more or less concerned with the present day. The idea that in these we are being 'taken across space', but not 'back in time', seemed hard to grasp. The women studied who are remote from her in space she placed in some, presumably mythical, past. The nineteenth century in England was, in contrast, part of her 'present'. I do not, of course, dispute the value of discovering history, or its place in our present; far from it. We may also, very cautiously, attempt to apply the lessons of other spaces to our own nineteenth-century past.[3] Here, however, I particularly recommend those who have not tried it to see what understanding we can gain of our present from studying other spaces, as well as other times. We may not be very good at this yet, but the effort is worth making.

Definitions of women usually include some physiological and psychological criteria. Some Hageners in Papua New Guinea, for example, say that 'the female's mind' is innately endowed with 'more compartments' than the male's (Strathern 1976, p. 53). It seemed appropriate, therefore, that work by scientists dealing with the brain should be among the first papers. Another contribution at the seminar added a valuable psychological perspective: this has subsequently been published elsewhere.

The Contributors

Of those who have contributed to the series represented by this volume, Wendy James is currently an Oxford University lecturer. Renée Hirschon teaches at the Oxford Polytechnic, and Freda Newcombe undertakes medical research in hospitals on behalf of the Medical Research Council. Judith Okely, Hilary Callan and Kirsten Hastrup, when first invited to contribute, were all working for doctorates at Oxford, while simultaneously holding University teaching posts at Durham, Kent and Aarhus Universities respectively. Caroline Humphrey is a lecturer at Cambridge University. Susan Lipshitz, of the Tavistock Institute in London, kindly came to participate in the series, but since she had the opportunity to include her paper in a book with an earlier publication date which she herself was editing, it has been omitted from the present collection to avoid duplication. Helen Callaway, who is currently working for a research degree at Oxford, allowed us to include in this published collection a paper which she gave to the independent women's social anthropology group during the period covered by our interdisciplinary series of seminars. Her topic was one that demanded some attention in this volume, and we are grateful to her for supplying a statement from her work in progress. Graham Ratcliff kindly collaborated with Freda Newcombe in the preparation of her talk for publication. It will be seen that together the authors represent a wide range of scholastic centres. All of them already have substantial publications in their fields of enquiry, some of which are referred to in the various bibliographies below.

The Papers

The book starts immediately with our main concern: the semantics of biology. Kirsten Hastrup has the avowed aim of reinstating biology as an important element in the comprehension of the position held by women in society, but not simply as facts of nature. She sees a mutual dependence between nature and culture such that 'biological facts are always transformed into meaningful categories, which are defined by their relationship *to*, and interaction *with*, other categories of society'. To this we might add that biological facts which have no meaning are unlikely to be perceived at all. The perception of the biological body and its 'natural' divisions, as Edwin Ardener and Drid Williams, among others, have shown, is not the same in all cultures, nor indeed within all socio-linguistic registers within the same ethnicity.[4] For, as Kirsten Hastrup says, 'biology and culture are mutually affecting spheres of reality'.

Hastrup's paper shows us how the biological properties of women may be used as 'markers' of social categories in a way that does not so often happen in the case of men. The penis is one outstanding male attribute, and has often been regarded as a symbol of power and authority. But compared to the case for men, the potential physiological changes in women are more various and more discrete. The physical boundaries of female virginity, for instance, can be more easily defined, and any particular case is, theoretically, easily open to proof or disproof. Societies have therefore found female virginity to be a useful symbol, one that can be made to carry a variety of connotations, of concern to persons of both sexes and all ages. Hastrup illustrates her argument here by examples from the Zulu and the Tewa Indians, showing at the same time that virginity can only be fully understood by reference to all the conceptual categories of the system of classification of which it is part.

Renée Hirschon points to another biological difference between males and females. The effect of sexual stimulation on a man is clearly observable, while that on a woman is not easily detected without secondary signalling. From this differing visibility, conclusions as to the different force of inherent sexual feelings of men and women, and their control, have sometimes been drawn. Such assumptions have given rise to complex social orderings. Hirschon takes the perceptions of a modern Greek community to illustrate her argument.

The conspicuousness of the biological role of the mother in the production of a new child is another fundamental difference between the sexes which has complicated repercussions in the social field. In their different ways Helen Callaway and Wendy James, as well as Renée Hirschon, show what some societies have made of this asymmetry. A few cultures give no social recognition to the physiological contribution of a father in procreation, as Hastrup notes when she considers the special case of virgin birth in her paper here.[5] Callaway usefully draws our attention to the fact, less often noticed, that not all societies equally recognise the creativity of the mother. James carefully examines the different ways that various societies have reflected the role in human generation of the mother, in their ramifying systems of kin relationships.

Judith Okely concentrates her analysis upon the way one group of female virgins are taught to think about themselves, their bodies, and their future place in society. All the actions of the English schoolgirls whom she describes are mapped for them in advance. The degrees of freedom allowed them are few. As few, perhaps, as those permitted to the category of women under the scrutiny of Caroline Humphrey — Mongolian daughters-in-law. The old adage that 'little girls should be seen and not heard' might well be extended to read 'females should be neither seen nor heard' — except in certain carefully defined spaces. We shall return to this question below, linking the data from several of the papers.

The first five studies are each concerned in various ways with different 'folk' perceptions of female biology. The papers at the end of the book, on the other hand, all give attention to specialist or 'scientific' models of women. Helen Callaway's paper acts to some extent as a bridge by discussing certain non-Western and 'lay' attitudes towards childbirth and its management, as well as 'medical models' of this socially meaningful physiological event. Callaway points out that surprisingly little attention has been paid to childbirth itself by social anthropologists. The omission is surely striking when one considers that kinship, a central concern, is, as Hastrup notes, 'a way of representing biological facts'. Evans-Pritchard wrote one of the best ethnographic papers on pregnancy, in 1932, but even he broke off his account before it reached, as he said, 'the final phase of birth'.

Helen Callaway examines the role of men in childbirth practices, and the attitudes surrounding them, and disputes the theory that there has been a 'recent' male 'takeover'. 'Childbirth', it is suggested, has *always* lain within the embrace of dominant, male-generated, social orderings. The midwives at a birth are under their influence and perform in accordance with them, as does the mother herself. Callaway agrees with the view advanced by Hastrup that medical models are not culture-free — any more, we may add, than the models social anthropologists present of the societies they study are free from their own cultural, including academic, traditions. Edwin Ardener has shown elsewhere (1972, 1975) that the so-called 'problem of women' may be an artefact of the anthropologists' model no less than of those of some of the lay observers whom they study. Wendy James's critical analysis of theories of matriliny, below, provides another case where subjective bias has possibly influenced their interpretations. Hilary Callan also gives examples in her study here of cultural influences upon the models advanced by specialists, in this case by ethologists who study animal, including human, behaviour.

Freda Newcombe and Graham Ratcliff, who are medical specialists themselves, start their paper by alluding to a number of cognitive tests designed to probe the capacities of the human female brain compared to those of the male brain. They approach the problem by also examining the evidence derived from measurement of the brain itself. They gather together data produced by normally functioning male and female brains and combine them with those generated by brains which have been damaged, to determine possible sexual differentiation. The work which they describe is still continuing, and we are grateful to them for giving this progress report. The relative newness and consequential fluidity of their field, as a subject of study, makes it all the more fascinating.

Newcombe and Ratcliff end their paper by commenting upon certain achievements and lack of success of women and pose the question as to how far these are biologically determined. They appear to lean towards the expectation that there must be an organic or neural explanation. While not wishing to deny the possibility of this, I confess that I expect the more powerful explanations in the cases cited to lie in the social dimension. I am more easily persuaded than they say that they are, for instance, that young Russian girls might be discouraged from playing chess (or may not have the incentive to do so) and that this alone could account for the absence in Russia of female masters of the game. The value of interdisciplinary exercises is, of course, to reveal just what the different attitudes may be. They would agree, I am sure, that attempts to predict possible variability based upon actual past achievements are fraught with theoretical dangers. At one time females were absent from the higher levels of the medical profession. We can see that this absence had no predictive value, since today some women doctors have now achieved distinction (even in the neuropsychological field!).

The perils of predicting *variability* from the study of *variation* is helpfully elucidated by Hilary Callan. Her general stance is ecumenical. She does not deny the possibility of the influence of some biological factors, but sees them as predispositions which may or may not be transformed into manifestations through the mediation of culture. She has been given the final word in this book because she brings us back to a theoretical discussion of this relationship, which is one of our central concerns. In the seminar series her position was in fact the reverse of that in which she now finds herself. She was asked to open our programme, and she addressed the issue of the interdependence of biology and culture with this in mind. Like most of the contributors, when writing her paper she could not anticipate the line of argument the rest would take. Her general theoretical approach is nevertheless in tune with others here, although she teases out the relationship in her own characteristically delicate analytical manner. The scientific field which she was asked to consider, biosocial explanations of women, is a ground on which some anthropologists and some zoologists meet. Her argument starts by pointing out the 'unwarranted assumption' of some theoreticians of the 'categorical equivalence of biological and cultural femaleness', that is, the assumption that they are the same *kind* of category and hence stand in a 'straight-forwardly knowable mutual relationship'. Her paper is particularly fitting for its place, because she proceeds to lead us through certain analytical complexities and misunderstandings towards some valuable suggestions, tentatively expressed though they may be, as to how we may proceed with our investigations in the future. Thus we finish our effort with a glimpse of a way ahead.

When new papers are to be specially written, some idea of the themes to be addressed and the general intention of a book can be provided, but authors require maximum possible latitude, and it can happen that when the papers appear they are found to be totally disparate. Fortunately, while each of the studies here has its own independent data and outlook, the contributions are generally harmonious. Not only do several of them share the same theoretical approach, but, in addition, certain specific motifs recur. No attempt is made to recapitulate the various arguments, but a few of these common motifs will now be considered, together with some hints as to how they might be brought into potentially fruitful association.

The Importance of the Unimportant

Quite trivial items, with no apparent general significance, can take on a different meaning when seen alongside material drawn from other cultures. What may seem to be an incidental, arbitrary event of limited application, which has been generated from a unique and unrepeatable set of circumstances, may appear differently when a larger view is taken. It may even be seen as a manifestation of a pervasive pattern which occurs with greater elaboration elsewhere.

Consider a recent comment made by a woman in the *Sunday Times* newspaper. Glenys Roberts describes the breakdown of her marriage in an article whose title represents an exchange between herself and her husband: ' "Why are you so late?" "Where's my supper?" ' After describing her choice of various activities while waiting for her laggard husband to return home to the supper she had cooked for him, she states (interestingly enough, in a parenthesis):

> (I always planned to show the judge my time-consuming tapestries when the chips were down, as proof of womanly virtues when mine were called into doubt. 'When did I have time to stray, Your Honour?' I planned to say.) (*Sunday Times*, 12 February 1978.)

Compare this 'one-off', perhaps puzzling, parenthetical statement with Renée Hirschon's analysis of Greek women in her section *Time and Temptation* below. Hirschon discusses the significance given to the provision of food and to its eating,[6] as well as the value placed by Greeks upon handwork such as crochet, embroidery and knitting. An important feature of these female occupations is shown to be their consumption of time. The restrictions they impose by using up a woman's time reduce her exposure to certain supposed dangers. Hirschon leads us to see that many of the domestic preoccupations of a Greek woman, which otherwise purport to be a great focus of attention for their own sake, are ultimately linked to cultural perceptions of her sexuality, of her biological predisposition.[7]

Time is also given consideration by Judith Okely. At her English boarding-school, it was 'subjected to a changeless grid. An electric bell rang at half hour intervals or more often. No way to decide for ourselves the next move . . .' There was no unorganised time. We are reminded in this account of the omnipresent clock and the consciousness of 'real' and 'conceptual' time in the convent of nuns described by Drid Williams (1975). Caroline Humphrey also shows below that even far away from Europe, in Mongolia, a young woman has little control over her use of time. During Humphrey's field research she noted that the young wife

> was required to rise first in the morning and go to bed last at night, to be always occupied and never be seen to rest, and always to be ready to perform any task required of her . . . She was subject to an extraordinary number of regulations . . . A second range of prohibi-

tions forbade the slightest hint of her sexuality . . .

Note here the requirement that she *be seen* working – the result of her work is not of itself enough. Such restrictions were more relaxed for Mongolian women in later life, when their sexuality was deemed of less importance. Further material, on Muslim women, confirms the pattern. In the Lebanon, for instance, women are also given time-consuming tasks which, according to Aida Hawila (personal communication, 1978), are explicitly designed to pre-empt the possibility of the women being engaged in freely expressed sexual behaviour.

Clues drawn from modern English life, taken together with those from different cultures, can open our eyes to new interpretations of other events in our English society, or reinforce earlier tentative implications. We may, for instance, now reconsider the way the Brontë sisters were kept by their Aunt Branwell, for hours and hours, at 'hand work'. Their aunt's training focused upon two subjects: religion and sewing. The Brontë girls prepared all the household linen and clothes for themselves and their father and brother. In addition each daughter completed a sampler and other decorative work. They were also expected to make saleable objects for the 'Jews' Basket', the proceeds of which were put to charitable use (Gérin, 1967 pp. 20-1). As for the aunt, 'bent on doing her duty by her nieces, she prepared them for a life devoid of pleasures, rather than for a life of self-expression . . . she saw the "wildness" in their eyes, and even confided to the servants that she was alarmed by what she saw . . .' (ibid., p. 34)

Charlotte Brontë's frustrated energy was later fuelled by her incomprehension of and fury at the way governesses were kept from morning to night in tedious repetitive occupations. Her employer, Mrs Sidgwick, rarely entered into conversation with her.

> I now begin to find that she does not intend to know me, that she cares nothing in the world about me except to contrive how the greatest possible quantity of labour may be squeezed out of me, and to that end she overwhelms me with oceans of needlework, yards of cambric to hem, muslin nightcaps to make, and, above all things, dolls to dress . . . I see now more clearly than I have done before that a private governess has no existence, is not considered a living and rational being except as connected with the wearisome duties she has to fulfil . . . this burden of sewing . . . is too bad for anything. I never in my whole life had my time so fully taken up. (Letter to her sister Emily, dated 18 June 1839; see, for instance, Gérin, 1967,

pp. 143-4).

Having considered the evidence of the contributors to this book, perhaps we should seek for an explanation of the aunt's rigorous training,
and Mrs Sidgwick's constant demands, in the implicit ideas of their time
concerning the sexual nature of women. That the training was asymmetrical and tied to gender differentiation was all too clear to Charlotte.
She found the close supervision of young women compared to the freedom of young men ironic, in view of their respective social records. She
may have been more aware than she felt able to say that ultimately it
was sexuality itself which was at question. It was the way she later permitted the passion of her heroines to be discerned in her novels (and
one a governess!) that brought unwelcome criticism from the pens of
some of her literary critics. Charlotte and her sisters were considered by
many to be 'unladylike', and their novels unfit for young girls to read.
Among Charlotte's critics was the emancipated Harriet Martineau, who
was appalled at the prominence given to 'love' as the driving force for
the heroine of Charlotte's novel *Villette*, perhaps because such emotion
is 'anti-social' (see below) or because it implies dependence upon men.[8]

Seen in this wider context, the isolated personal comment from the
English Sunday newspaper takes on a new potential significance. Judith
Okely, discussing the customs of her English public boarding-school,
expresses well why we should not overlook the importance of such
detail. In school the 'focus on minutiae demanding all our concentration impeded the thought of, reduced the possibility of bolder action
. . . What counted as crime may seem petty . . . But its very triviality
affirmed the pervasiveness of control.'

A point to note is that it is the pettiness of certain activities itself
which may give them their force. Those who, while pursuing them,
come to enjoy them for their own sake are kept in happy and harmless
occupation. Those who, in performing them, come to regard them as
unworthy of the time and effort they consume may by that come to
consider *themselves* as unworthy and incompetent in other fields, and
they may submit to the humdrum tasks from humility. For, as Hirschon
points out, there is often a close correlation between what is thought
fitting for people to do and what they are thought to be *capable* of doing,
and the doers may implicitly concur. People like Charlotte Brontë who do
not make this evaluation are, of course, condemned to a life either of
frustration or of rebellion. Thus does the unimportant come to have
importance, and come to merit our scrutiny.[9]

On Being 'Tongue-Tied'

It was fitting to open this book by a comment on the meaning of its title since discussion of naming, and of the use of words generally, re-curs within its covers. Of those who treat this subject, Caroline Humphrey explores the field in greatest depth. There is, of course, a wide interest in the analysis of women's language and speech. Much work has been done, in the United States in particular. One discussion from closer to home, which is part of the theory of 'muted groups' first proposed by Edwin Ardener, has been set out in *Perceiving Women*. The gist of this is that there are dominant modes of expression in any society which have been generated by the dominant structures within it. In any situa-tion, only the dominant mode of the relevant group will be 'heard' or 'listened to'. The 'muted groups' in any context, if they wish to commu-nicate, must express themselves in terms of this mode, rather than in ones which they might otherwise have generated independently.[10] Women are usually (though not always) the muted group when sexual polarity is pertinent. For example, the dominant mode may provide a style for them such that, if they are perceived as 'birds', when angry they may be required to 'roar like doves', while the men emulate the King of Beasts. Thus may their voices be unheard, even when they con-form.

When the discussion of 'inarticulateness' and 'mutedness' was intro-duced a decade ago, it was intended to encourage anthropologists and others to pay more attention than they did at the time to spheres of communication and modes of expression of women, and of groups defined by other criteria than sex, which might otherwise be over-looked. The 'mutedness' of one group may be regarded as the inverse of the 'deafness' of the dominant group, as the 'invisibility' of the former's achievements is an expression of the 'blindness' of the latter. Words which continually fall upon deaf ears may, of course, in the end be-come unspoken, or even unthought. It has never been suggested that there is a biological correlation with 'mutedness', quite the contrary, for it is seen to be a phenomenon of structural relationships and a product of society. Any particular group of persons which stands in a relationship of structural mutedness with another category may be dominant in relation to a third group, as shown in the case studies in *Perceiving Women*. The two 'universes' would, of course, redefine the group (as we suggest below). It is because most individuals are also likely to experience (if not identify) various conditions of mutedness and of dominance, in different conceptual contexts, that individuals are some-times able to empathise with others who are in a different structural position at the given moment.[11]

The theory of mutedness, therefore, does not require that the muted be actually *silent*. They may speak a great deal. The important issue is whether they are able to say all that they would wish to say, where and when they wish to say it. Must they, for instance, re-encode their thoughts to make them understood in the public domain? Are they able to think in ways which they would have thought had they been responsible for generating the linguistic tools with which to shape their thoughts? If they devise their own code will they be understood? Of one muted group described in the present volume Judith Okely writes:

> Children cannot articulate their experience in the language of adults, only after childhood can it be thus expressed. When young we found the school world the reality, the norm, the only rationality. That was its power. My mother has often said since: 'But why didn't you tell me?' We, my sister and I, could not discriminate that which now seems bizarre. Whenever I inwardly questioned aspects of this education, I thought myself mad, and identified with the mad and isolated.

The supposed tendency of women to 'nag' (which in our culture men are not perceived to do), or 'to prattle on', may just be a matter of definition. If, on the other hand, these propensities, by whatever name, do occur, then perhaps they are a form of displacement activity deriving from women's supposed greater verbal fluency combined with an inability to express their thoughts adequately in the appropriate forms and forums. Surplus frustrated verbal energy is thereby consumed. Perhaps repetition results from an awareness that the utterances are having little effect, and the hope of the message being reinforced. For those with poorly defined self-awareness, perhaps continuous speech helps to confirm personal identity and existence. The practice of talking to oneself (and the 'silent monologues' drawn to our attention by George Steiner) may be worth considering in this context.

Discussion of 'mutedness', then, is concerned, among other things, with distortion of modes of expression. It has been suggested in *Perceiving Women* that the insertion of an 'extra step' may be required of muted groups after a thought is conceived before it is realised in speech. This process usually operates at an unconscious level and may be so rapid as to be collapsed into a 'simultaneity'. The effect is to stifle statements which have no acceptability in the dominant field of discourse. Caroline Humphrey's detailed presentation of the complicated speech requirements of Mongolian daughters-in-law gives us an unusually explicit example of this. Instead of thinking of a name, then saying it, these women must think of a name, then think of a rule-bound substitute, then say that. In Mongolian society many other members of the community make name substitutions, but none more constantly nor more convolutedly than daughters-in-law, who thereby become a 'marked' category. Another interesting mode of indirect speech is described by M. Wolff (1974). It seems that in China women commonly speak 'through' their young male charges and sons, attributing their own views and needs to them, as interpreters may slant the words of those for whom they translate.

The right to be addressed, and the way you are addressed, are important determinants of a person's place in the structure of any society. In Greece, as elsewhere, 'the most effective way of indicating disapproval and of dealing an insult is to "cut off the 'Good morning' greeting" . . . The strongest sanction is to ignore one's opponent and thereby effectively deny his social existence' (Hirschon, below). We have already noted that Charlotte Brontë said of her uncommunicative employer: 'she does not intend to know me . . . a private governess has no existence . . .'. The actual choice of name or title in a system of address also has great significance, as suggested by the Mongolian material here. A name may not only acknowledge personal existence but also continuity of personal and social definition. Thus we find schoolboys being addressed by the family names which they will keep throughout their lives, while schoolgirls are addressed by their first names (Okely, below). A girl's private persona may be constant throughout her life, but her social persona is discontinuous. An English girl is by tradition given her father's family name until she is married, after which it is replaced by that of her husband's family. She may move from being 'Miss Smith' to being 'Mrs Brown'. Should she be divorced she may perceive a problem: she is obliged to continue to bear her former husband's name, or face the tiresome and possibly embarrassing process of informing those around her of a change and thus of the meaning and status of her personal, jural and domestic relationships. She may well find that Rose, by another name, is not regarded as so sweet. This is a predicament which men do not have to face. Hirschon reminds us that our schoolgirl's Greek counterpart has her relationship to men even more clearly indicated by the use of the possessive form. She moves from being 'Smith's Miss' to 'Brown's Mrs', the latter usage also being found in England. Callaway cites below the case of the Angas women who are known by their sons' names (as if 'Jack's mother'), rather than by their own.[12] That modern feminists have singled out the symbolism of prefixed titles in address systems is not surprising. It is not of small consequence.

The right *not* to be addressed in particular ways, or not to be addressed at all, is also important. The use of a personal name may proclaim an intimacy with the person addressed, as Okely notes. If the intimacy is considered undesirable or is not acknowledged by the addressee, the use of a personal name may represent an invasion of privacy, or imply control, as shown later in this volume. It may be attention-demanding, as Humphrey suggests. It is not surprising, therefore, to find that in both the English boarding-school and in the Mongolian family tent personal names are not always used reciprocally.

The regulation of women's nomenclature, and their use of language, may go so far as the suppression of speech; thus 'muting' becomes total to the point of silence. Greek women who persist in talking when society does not wish to listen are regarded as a threat to its structure. Charlotte Brontë (to invoke our previous case) possessed a high degree of competence in handling words yet she felt herself unable to comment on many things. The dominant religious philosophy of the time was probably an inhibiting factor, just as supernatural beliefs command Mongolian daughters-in-law to observe language taboos. Charlotte wrote: 'Certainly there are other evils – deep-rooted in the foundations of the social system – which no effort of ours can touch: of which we cannot complain; of which it is advisable not too often to think' (Gaskell, 1975 edition, p. 422). Ritual silence may be imposed on women: in synagogues, for instance, and in Greece after weddings, as Hirschon shows. 'A frequent injunction to Greek women is "Don't say anything at all." ' Thus the requirement for some categories of women to be 'tongue-tied' is well illustrated in various papers, and becomes a recurring motif in this volume. The effect of this prescription upon women's power to *think* is one of the interesting aspects of the process of muting.

The material summarised below by Newcombe and Ratcliff is very interesting in this context. Some of the tests they quote, as they indicate, present many methodological difficulties and traps in interpretation. Language, that quintessential cultural phenomenon, is used in setting up and interpreting the experiments and they cannot be as 'culture-free' as they might appear to be to some. Newcombe and Ratcliff have themselves provided necessary words of caution regarding some of the findings which they quote and, it must be said, some of the other contributors to this book would be even more hesitant in drawing conclusions from them. There is considerable evidence to show that males and females do perform differently taken as groups. This should not be surprising because, as I have noted elsewhere, women certainly experience society differently, whatever their genetic similarities to men may be. Work on the topic must be taken seriously for *actual* performance is obviously as important as *potential* performance, in the practical affairs of life. Where we must proceed cautiously is in the methodology of the tests; in the language we use for discussing the differences (some uses of the word 'abilities' are likely to confuse, for instance); also in extrapolating from the results of laboratory tests lest we injudiciously assume that they directly predict performance in other contexts; and further, in assuming that differences are genetically based, or immutable, without reliable evidence for this. A good critical review of some experimental data has recently been provided in Lloyd and Archer, 1976.

The results of the tests considered by Newcombe and Ratcliff here suggest that females have superior executive language skills and are more fluent verbally — at least when they are engaged in the tests. Yet they are reported to do no better than males in those tests requiring 'verbal reasoning'. At the end of her paper Hilary Callan quotes a nurse who is attempting to define herself. Perhaps, if the tests have any extrapolable validity, Callan's example may be significant. It shows how a woman may have a striking command of vocabulary, yet still feel frustrated in her attempts to present her thoughts coherently, to the point of stuttering 'inarticulacy'. Since Callan stopped to listen and allowed herself to understand, the nurse's words were nevertheless heard to mean something. They might have passed unnoted or as incomprehensible, perhaps, in a public forum or in less attuned company.

If, as has been suggested, linguistic skills play a larger role in the 'general intellectual ability' of girls, in their 'thinking and problem solving' (see Newcombe and Ratcliff, below), this could be a manifestation of biological advantage. On the other hand, as many have suggested elsewhere, girls may perform differently as a result of their upbringing. For example, in this case their closer contact in early life with adults of their own sex, whom they could more easily copy, could influence the results. Maybe girls or adult women upon whom they model themselves have to depend upon language to achieve their ends while boys, and the men they emulate, find it easier to satisfy their wants without the need for language. The old joke about the boy who had not spoken until he was six years of age because 'up till then there had been enough salt in his dinner' may have some truth in it in a male-oriented world! If societies should demand special skills from females, as the theory of mutedness implies, then these skills may allow them to perform better in the relatively more simple tests employed by analysts. Another explanation might be that at certain stages, and in certain classes, there is a disincentive for boys to show literary skills.[13] There is no need to give further possible social explanations here.

Women are capable of talking a great deal, and often do in certain circumstances, as we know. What is significant is the way that society has failed to allow them to use their verbal abilities to full advantage. Women are rarely the orators of society. As we have seen, they are often silenced. If it could be proved that women have *inherent* verbal superiority, this would further demonstrate the power of *culture* as the overdetermining force, for 'muting' must have occurred. The superior muscular gifts of men, in contrast, have been capitalised upon in many societies. Even where women do much of the hard work, the group superiority in strength of men is normally given social recognition and respect, whereas female eloquence is rarely promoted and admired.

Newcombe and Ratcliff comment upon the presence of female creative writers in English society, in contrast to the absence of musical composers and mathematicians. This may, of course, be a result, as they imply, of biological determinants. They would agree, however, that it might be possible to find many other, cultural, explanations.[14] One of them might go as follows: writing was part of a woman's domestic and family duties. To be seen to be occupied with these duties was acceptable for educated women in England in the eighteenth and nineteenth centuries. Painting and music were termed 'accomplishments' (and were advertised as such), to be monitored by those around who would hardly fail to see or listen to the results. The great difference with writing was that, as culturally defined, while the mode was public, the product was private. The confidentiality of the written word was much greater in the novel-writing period of the nineteenth century, when women novelists became established, than it is now. It seems almost impossible to us these days that the Brontë sisters could write their poems and novels and get them published without their brother Branwell and other members of the household being fully aware of the implications of their activity, as the sisters in fact did. Their proud father admitted later that he probably would have stopped it had he known (Lock and Dixon, 1965). It is still harder to understand how Charlotte Brontë could have sat silently correcting proofs of her novels in the presence of her bosom friend Ellen Nussey, whose discretion kept her in ignorance of what was taking place. Such secrecy may have enabled women to develop their thoughts, to experiment without question, and, if need be, to publish their works under male pseudonyms.

It is just conceivable that Charlotte Brontë and Jane Austen (if they had had access to the right books) could have sat among their families concentrating upon mathematical problems, but it is less imaginable that they could have painted or composed within the family circle with the creative freedom that would be required to place them among the masters. That 'room of one's own' needed by writers, so well attested by Virginia Woolf, was surely all the more required by potential composers. For conductors there were even more difficulties. Like architects who depend upon clients, they could not remain unseen by musicians and pseudonymous, and learn their craft in obscurity. Social explanations for the presence of novels written by women and the absence of these other female achievements have, I believe, greater power than genetic explanations. If the latter are valid (and this has yet to be conclusively established) they are masked by the former.

It is important to note that the theory of muting is not concerned only with oral 'utterances'. Language is but one of many systems of communication in society, all of which have to be considered. Further, as already noted, mutedness is a phenomenon connected ultimately with structural relationships. There is no place to explore this further here; it has been treated elsewhere by Edwin Ardener, who first opened this discussion in 1968. In her paper at our seminar, now published as 'The Witch and her Devils', in *Tearing the Veil* (1978), Susan Lipshitz clearly appears to misinterpret Edwin Ardener's position. There is no need to go into this now since his direct statements can be referred to elsewhere (Ardener, E. 1971, 1972, 1973 and 1975). Notwithstanding her comments, some of her own views almost mirror the discussions which have been associated with 'muting'. We read, for instance, that 'Women's entry into the cultural order and into language then differs from that of men in some ways.' Further, she writes that 'Since both sexes acquire this culture they will share categories but their positions in relation to those categories will differ depending on their sex . . . when the individual subject does not locate herself (or himself) in the culture, they fall ill.' One of Lipshitz's tasks in her essay is 'to show that this is not accidental but depends partly on unarticulated standards of health and adulthood that measure women against a "masculinity" as an ideal in comparison with which they are always found lacking' (cf. Okely below).

Clearly, Lipshitz's remark that, since 'the language under discussion includes symbolism and does not reject it, and since all subjectivity is constructed meaning, there can be no meaningless natural realm to refer women to' is one that is in tune with other studies here. Her paper goes on to discuss the question of female hysterics, women who are possessed, and witches. Their activities are to be understood as 'women's imaginary representations of their psychic condition to themselves'. 'If we recognise that these forms of illness, possession and witchcraft are not simply attempts to seize power in the face of powerlessness, not simply illicit orgasms or rationalisations of desire, but are women's attempts to speak of the psychological limitation of their sexuality in its subordination to genitality and reproduction, we see them as ideological.' Ardener wrote (1972, pp. 140-1): 'The study of symbolism uncovers certain valuations of women . . . I here contend that much of this symbolism in fact enacts that female model of the world which has been lacking.' The paper by Susan Lipshitz is a welcome attempt to unpack and present in psychological terms one example of such symbolic patterning.

Rebellion

After the Mongolian material was discussed at our seminar, some people who thought the situation of daughters-in-law was beyond toleration asked why they did not rebel. The reason why women have been 'subordinated' so constantly over space and time, and have not found a way through to the top, is a puzzle of particular importance to those who think in terms of 'oppression' and 'suppression'. The discrepancy of muscle power must play its part, but as is noted in *Critique of Anthropology* (1978, vol. 3), the direct use of force has many social limitations.[15] The presentation of economic explanations by Marxists and some others is very helpful. It locates the predicament of women within a larger system of asymmetries. The theory of muting is not incompatible with such a presentation. It, likewise, sees the case of women as part of a more general phenomenon, but places emphasis on a society's multi-faceted system of communication, which it sees as an over-determining instrument of authority, perhaps once acquired by the possession, if not the exercise of, superior strength, but like some weapons, when obtained thereafter no longer dependent upon it. It should not be forgotten, for instance, that where gerontocracies command the dominant mode of communication, the authorities may themselves be relatively physiologically weak.[16]

Muting stems from relationships between groups. It is concerned with their ideas of 'reality', and how they are expressed. The members of these groups do not have to be seen as *actively* 'dominating' one another, nor is any one individual's structural position in a society constant. It depends upon the sub-system, or particular universe, of relevance at any one time, and its components. Charlotte Brontë saw herself within a domestic universe as 'a wild romantic enthusiast' who would 'laugh, and satirise, and say whatever came into [her] head first' (letter to Ellen Nussey, 12 March 1839, Gérin, 1971 ed., p. 127). Yet in the public domain, in 'Society', in contrast, she was muted, she could not 'come out of her shell', despite the endeavours of those of its representatives around her. She could not easily enter its discourse. Her 'shyness', Gérin notes (p. 406), 'was a physical as well as a psychological disability, which she deeply regretted.' Indeed, as Charlotte explained to her distressed publisher, over and over again, 'my occasional silence was only a failure of the power to talk, never of will' (letter to Ellen Nussey, 18 December 1949).

Some reasons why muted groups do not always take steps to alter their circumstances have been discussed in *Perceiving Women*. We may note here that, according to Humphrey, despite the taboos, Mongolian women do not appear socially paralysed in everyday life. 'To the casual observer it would be difficult to tell that the prohibitions exist and he might simply note that women seem to have their own way of doing things.' Members of muted groups may thus come to an accommodation with the social structure in which they are placed, and find their own satisfactions in its interstices or outside its dominant structure. Their alternative systems of value, which may be rich and complex, should be respected and should receive greater attention than they sometimes do.

Members of muted groups, instead of ignoring the dominant group, or of merely tolerating its demands, may even go further and accept the burden of maintaining or 'policing' a system which to onlookers appears to disadvantage them. Thus, as described in detail below, it is Zulu virgins who take steps against breaches of virginity. It is gossiping women who act as lip-servants of their society and keep their sisters off the streets of Athens. It is midwives who endorse the taboos surrounding childbirth. Having learnt their way about a system, they have a vested interest in preserving respect for their expertise and achievements. They may also be rewarded in other ways, both abstract and tangible, for their rule enforcement. The power of the conceptual 'underdog' to threaten the ideological security of the dominant group has been noted (cf. Filomina Steady, quoted in S. Ardener, 1973). This may also give a well-based intuitive sense of personal importance (see Hastrup, below).

Another aspect to be considered is that, as we have noted, self-perceptions may become blunted. The triviality of the occupations and restrictions placed upon members of muted groups, as already noted, also may play a part in ensuring their submission. Further, the importance placed upon small concerns and minutely detailed forms of control enables correspondingly great personal satisfactions to be got from small scale pleasures. Thomas Hardy, when referring to the heroine of his novel *The Mayor of Casterbridge*, cogently describes this accommodation:

> The finer movements of her nature found scope in discovering to the narrow-lived ones around her the secret . . . of making limited opportunities endurable; which she deemed to consist in the cunning enlargement, by a species of microscopic treatment, of those minute forms of satisfaction that offer themselves to everybody not in positive pain; which, thus handled, have much of the same inspiriting effect upon life as wider interest cursorily embraced (Hardy, 1974 edition, pp. 353-4).

If close attention to small pleasures can cumulatively have such an 'inspiriting' effect, so minor deviations and rebellions can nurture the confined soul. Simple acts like taking a lift instead of using the stairs can become charged with emotive force, as Okely describes, and can have greater expressive effect than some grosser confrontations. The novels of Barbara Pym well exemplify how the narrowness of the stage can endow the most minor of acts with great symbolic weight and make them of absorbing interest to the humble characters (some of them social anthropologists) who people her worlds, and who remind us of what we are. Such small gestures are the vivid language and satisfactions of some muted groups.

Among all the different mechanisms which 'keep women in their place' perhaps the most effective is the notion that the place is designed for their own good and that of their families. Thus infringement of a boundary may be thought to expose their own 'vulnerability' to danger, and as Renée Hirschon shows, they may even come to regard *themselves* as a threat to themselves and to their families. To complicate matters, the latter, paradoxically, may be the groups to whom they would have to turn for help in their rebellion. Okely explains that those girls at her boarding-school who were unhappy accepted their positions out of care for and dutiful submission to the parents whose financial contribution to their incarceration was 'translated as love and sacrifice

for the child's greater good . . . public-school children dare not think
through the ultimate blame upon their parents.' 'Running away from
school can only be an emotional appeal to the parents' who might well
send them back 'for their own good' in a similar way as do Mongolian parents of a bride who runs away from her husband.

Out of Sight, Out of Mind

In English society, as in some others, romantic love has been highly
extolled. Further, the nuclear family composed of two young parents
and their children has been much admired, and often recommended as a
necessary basis for a happy community. But elsewhere, many societies
regard the young heterosexual couple, even after their union has been
sanctioned by marriage, rather equivocally. Humphrey's material suggests that the young Mongolian wife is seen by her husband's father and
those around him as a source for the potential disaffection of his son,
and for the dispersal of the joint family group. In her interesting book
on 'male-female dynamics' in Islamic society, Fatima Mernissi concludes likewise that the Muslim system is opposed to the heterosexual
unit. 'What is feared is the growth of the involvement between a man
and a woman into an all-encompassing love, satisfying the sexual, emotional and intellectual needs of both partners.' She goes on to state that
such an involvement is seen to constitute 'a direct threat to the man's
allegiance to Allah' (1975, viii). Yet Mernissi also says that Islam does
not see women as 'inferior' to men, nor are they seen as 'passive' partners; women of the modern feminist movements, she states, are not
concerned to 'equalize' the sexes therefore. It is the 'fate of the heterosexual unit' which is their main interest. These remarks, however, rather
contradict her conclusion elsewhere: that the conception of the individual's task on earth (devotion to Allah alone in the form of know-
ledge-seeking, meditation, and prayer) is enlightening 'in that it reveals
that, in spite of the beauty of the Muslim message, it considers humanity to be constituted by males only' (ibid., p. 14).

Mernissi contrasts her view of Islamic philosophy and practice with
a Western Christian sexual dynamic. While not disputing that there are
indeed discrepancies between the two views, they are not always as
wide as she sometimes implies. It is interesting in this context to note
that the Brontë sisters also perceived that the love of two people could
run the risk of eclipsing their duty to adore God above all others —
although they referred in particular to the religious obligations of
women. Fear of sexuality may be why the expression of affection, even
between man and wife, is so widely frowned upon. Perhaps it is the

exclusiveness of deep passion which makes it seem out of place in social gatherings, as well as in religious contexts. Perhaps the more explicit public sexual activity of young people today in the West may seem more acceptable to them, than it was thought to be formerly, because a lesser degree of exclusive commitment is implied by it than was once thought inevitable.

For another Christian group, Hirschon shows below how wives in Greece are taunted should they show a passionate interest in their husbands. As for peoples of other religious persuasions, similarly in Africa, marital affection and passion are rarely socially displayed. Further, for respectable African women, sex may be thought to be acceptable only as a means for satisfying their husbands or for begetting children (Wambui Karanja-Diejomaoh, personal communication, 1978). This is not necessarily true of all parts of Africa, but certainly where clitoridectomy is practised, sex is often regarded by women as a duty rather than a pleasure (especially where its most extreme pharaonic form is found, which includes, besides excision, the permanent sewing up or pinning together of the genitals in a way that can make sexual intercourse and childbirth difficult; cf. I. Clarke, 1978).

Mernissi notes that in Islamic philosophy, woman 'is a dangerous distraction which must be used for the specific purpose of providing the Muslim nation with offspring and quenching the tensions of the sexual instinct' without being an object of emotional investment (ibid., p. 14). The female is seen to be potentially *more* aggressive than the male, whose will is easily eroded by her attractiveness to the point of his passive acquiescence. He has no choice: she has (cf. Mernissi, p. 11). Compare this view with those of the Christians of Athens reported by Hirschon below. Like these Greek women, the unfettered Muslim woman is seen as the symbol of disorder, she has a 'rampant disruptive potential' (ibid., p. 13).

To curb such powers, wherever possible, the Muslim woman is kept out of public sight. She becomes the prettily fleshed-out skeleton in the public cupboard. 'The Muslim wariness of heterosexual involvement', writes Mernissi, 'is embodied in sexual segregation and its corollaries: arranged marriage, the important role of the mother in her son's life, and the fragility of the marital bond' (ibid., p. 14). Mernissi sees this as peculiarly Islamic and in its specific and extreme forms, it is. But there is much material from many other societies which seems to reflect very similar ideologies. Modern Greeks do not tie their sailors to the masts to prevent them from succumbing to the allure of females, as in their ancient myths; today, however, as in the Athens of ancient days (see

O'Faolain and Martines, 1973, pp. 16-17), Athenians still confine their women by controlling the spaces they may enter. The Mongolians treat young wives similarly. The freedom of movement permitted Branwell Brontë compared with that of his sisters shows that England has not been without its parallels.

It should also be noted here that it is often the presence of men that defines a space as 'public,' and out of bounds for women. Further, space is not, of course, to be defined only by tangible location. Also, a place can remain constant while the definition of its space changes. A good illustration is provided by the Doshman-Ziari people of Mamsani village in Iran, who are Shi'a Muslims. Among these people the traditional tent was conceptually subdivided. This division was often physically marked by a screen. On one side was the hearth around which the women congregated. The other side was reserved for male visitors and was vacated by the women when the latter appeared. Now that tents have been abandoned in favour of one-roomed rectangular houses, with a fireplace in one long wall and a doorway at the end of the opposite wall, there is but one physically undifferentiated space. Yet at any given time, the area between the four static walls embraces one from among three discrete and mutually exclusive conceptual spaces. Type A is associated with females only, type B with females and certain of their close male kin, and type C with males only, including unrelated men. The 'atmosphere' of each is different. There is also a priority such that the space which is deemed to be of type A, in which women move freely, gives way to type B when, say, the head of the household appears. The women then move to the draughty side of the hearth, leaving the place of honour away from the doorway to him. But space type B is reclassified as type C on the entry of male guests. The women then abandon space C entirely and retreat outside into the yard. The senior guest moves into the best position near the fire, away from the door, and the rest of the company arrange themselves according to their statuses. The types of space may be given some markers by the spreading of luxury mats in the more prestigious seating places when those with superior status enter. I base this analysis on material kindly supplied by Sue Wright (1978, and personal communication). It can be compared to the seating in Mongolian tents, as described by Humphrey (1974). And in Morocco,

> When a man invites a friend to share a meal at his house, he knocks on his own door and asks with a loud voice for the women to "make the way" (*'amlu triq*). The women then run to hide in dark corners,

leaving the courtyard free to be crossed by the stranger (Mernissi, p. 51).

It seems then that, ideally, Islamic public space and women should not coexist. When they cannot be kept out of sight, cloistered behind the walls of the harem, and must intrude into the public sphere, they are made as invisible as possible, behind veils. There are near parallels in other communities too, including in England. It is hoped that out of sight, women will be out of men's minds. That this fails is all too clear from accounts of Arab friends (personal communications). Mernissi notes that 'paradoxically sexual segregation heightens the sexual dimension of any heterosexual interaction . . . seduction becomes a structural component of the culture.' When only eyes may be seen they come to be regarded as an erogenous zone 'as able to give pleasure [to men] as the penis' (p. 83). The connection between veiling and sexuality is apparent to Mernissi, who notes that 'Elderly women (supposed to be unattractive) can go unveiled' (p. 84). She notes that even though the mother seems to be favoured as a woman in Moroccan society, she does not escape being viewed negatively. 'Great pressures are put on the menopausal woman to regard herself as an asexual object and to renounce her sexuality as early as possible.' Jokes are made at her expense. 'It is only by understanding the pressure on the aging [sic] woman to renounce her sexual self and her conjugal future, that one can understand the passion with which she gets involved in her son's life' (Mernissi, pp. 71-2).

In her chapter below, Wendy James compares the status of women in such Muslim societies with those of Africans. She adds new insights by analysing the distinction between matriliny and matrifocality and the interplay of the two concepts, in contrast to the case where patriliny is found. She comments on differing attitudes to female freedom of movement, and public visibility and awareness. Her general conclusions gain support from Mernissi's description (in her Chapter 3) of the changes which occurred for women in the pre-Muslim matrilineal social order of ancient Arabia, when Islam was introduced. Some of these women concluded that they had lost certain freedoms, and other abstract and material benefits, as Islam set the trend towards patrilineality. Some of them even rioted as a result.

It should, however, be said that life within the walls of a harem is not always without its attractions for all women. And Greek women do not necessarily find their home-bound lives undesirable, given the alternatives available. The positive (as well as the negative) aspects of any

institution should, perhaps, receive more of our attention than they
sometimes do, if we are to understand their perpetuation. This is also
advisable should we wish to try to improve upon structures lest we in-
advertently fail to include elsewhere their advantages. Judith Okely's
chapter below shows us how a so-called 'privileged' status may carry with
it great individual pain. In some 'socially deprived' conditions there
may be pleasures which we may equally overlook. Nadia Abu Zahra
has illuminated the manner in which, *ideally* the cool fountains and
ordered life within an enclosure can be seen to approximate to the
Muslim idea of paradise, when compared to the hot, dusty and disordered world of labour outside (1976). Older women within the
Islamic domestic circle, as many have noted (among them Joan Arney-
Ebeid, 1978, and Mernissi), may have an important status. We get a
picture of the mature mother dominating domestic affairs (and her
daughters-in-law) rather as is the case in Mongolia. Philip Slater (quoted
in Mernissi) places the mother-son relationship at the end of a theoretical pole, at whose other extremity is the marital bond. And we find
that, according to Mernissi (p. 69), in Muslim societies

> not only is the marital bond actually weakened and love for the
> wife discouraged, but his mother is the only woman a man is allowed
> to love at all, and this love is encouraged to take the form of life-
> long gratitude . . . It is not a process with a beginning, a middle and a
> ritualized end, indicating that now the adult male can engage in a
> new heterosexual relationship with his wife.

Thus, as Wendy James also shows us below, even patrilineal systems do
not necessarily exclude a degree of matrifocality. Unlike in the African
societies she describes, however, its field of operation in Muslim societies elsewhere is often hidden from gaze, and its structural or jural
expression is limited or absent.

The interesting analyses by James and others in this book of some of
the problems associated with the category of 'mother' and of 'woman'
can be pressed a little further, especially with regard to the dimension reflecting the effects of time or age upon these categories.

Sexual Mismatch

It is not true to say that *Woman is to Female* as *Man is to Male*. Nor is
the relationship *Female to Male* the same as *Woman to Man*. We are
dealing with four categories, none of which duplicates or is a mirror
image of another. Further, the asymmetry of any pair of these cate-

gories must be recognised. Yet clearly the sets are to some extent related: for instance, every woman is a female, and every man is a male. Some of the defining properties of one category may be among the defining properties of another. But the exact relationship between these categories has yet to be teased out. And the relationship is likely to be different in each society.[17]

We have noted that, as Hastrup states, no one category can be fully understood without examining the other categories of the system or subsystem in which it is embedded. *Woman*, for instance, may belong to the binary pair *girl/woman*, on the one hand, and also to the pair *man/woman* on the other. The universe of the first system may be *all females* (from birth to death); in the second case it might be *all adults*, all who have passed puberty. The meaning attached to the category *woman* is clearly different in each case, because of the value we give to the category paired with it. This is true even though they have a common label in this case. Confusion can easily arise, therefore, if, in a linguistic exchange between two persons, the communicants do not make clear from which universe a term is lifted. Context will usually help. It is possible that the meaning associated with a label in one universe may (with greater or lesser effect according to context and the like) cast its reflection over or interfere with its *de jure* meaning in another universe. We can also imagine that categories in diverse universes may shape each other, even when they do not share a common label. There may be an inherent human tendency to draw parallels, to try to assimilate concepts. For example, there may be a tendency for us to see some kind of *de facto* equivalence between the category 'wife' and the category 'woman', though we know them to be *de jure* different, such that a husband may even refer to his wife as 'my woman'. We know that when he does this he means something different from when, say, a bachelor refers to his domestic cleaner as 'my woman' (as in 'leave the dishes, my woman will do them'). Among the Ashanti of Ghana, a girl is addressed as 'mother' on completion of her initiation rites, even though she has not conceived (Sarpong, 1977, p. 75), while another Ashanti girl may be denied this appellation sometimes, even after giving birth, as shown below. Some of the dangers for analysts of transferring labels from one set of categories to those in another universe are considered below by Hilary Callan, who cites in particular the two universes of *humans* and *other primates*.

If we try to match one universe with another, some interesting effects may occur. Suppose we take a set of adults who have passed puberty on the one hand (A) and try to match it to a set of adults who have experienced sexual intercourse (B): there is incomplete correspondence. An 'empty slot' appears in one set where we would find ourselves placing 'virgins' in the other. If a conscious or subconscious attempt is made to synchronise the way the two universes are divided into sexual categories, we may come to think of the 'empty slot', the virgins, as like a third sex; see Hastrup's chapter, below.

Figure 1.1

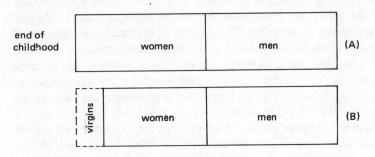

But what, you may ask, of sexually inexperienced young males? In many societies it appears as if there is no logical status for sexually innocent men, even though they may exist *de facto*. Again and again we find that young men are expected to chase women, and if they can to seduce them; the women being classed as 'fair game'. 'Any Asaba adult male must chase, and no one is going to stop him,' one informant said to Patrick Isichei. It seemed to Isichei that for youths,

> running after adult girls and women, and even trying to seduce them was instituted, more or less, as a mark of 'manness' (and not simply maleness). 'Manness' was a status achieved by sexual exploits: it could not be ascribed from the mere possession of male physical characteristics (Isichei, 1973, p. 688).

The inconsistency of requiring women to be chaste while chased, and at the same time requiring men to prove themselves by defeating the women's success, is obvious. One way of resolving this dilemma is to have a category of females who are kept outside the recognised universe — perhaps prostitutes, 'women of the streets' who belong nowhere, or strangers from other universes, who are not fully women — for males to use to complete their 'manness'. Quite often, however, the *myth* that youths are sexually experienced, or would be if they got the chance and are *seen* to be trying to take it, is enough to support the ideology that all adult males are sexually active, who *'would* if they *could'*. Ideally manhood may begin where boyhood (which may be prolonged) ends. Womanhood, on the other hand, may not begin where girlhood ends — sometimes a space exists between them. This may be filled by Hastrup's 'third sex', the virgins.

Among some African peoples, in contrast, females become women as soon as they have been ceremonially initiated. Wambui Karanja-Diejomaoh (personal communication) states that among the Kikuyu uncircumcised women as well as not being 'fully mature' are considered to be dirty. Young girls often pleaded with unwilling Christian parents to be permitted to undergo clitoridectomy. What seems to some of us a horrifying ordeal was generally anticipated eagerly by Kikuyu girls in order that they might become complete and pure women. This ceremony (which in view of the biological marker of female virginity almost seems in one light to be a redundancy) may perhaps be a 'back-formation' from male circumcision. The presence of the former ceremony is rarely found without the latter, whereas the reverse often occurs independently (cf. the Jewish case). The removal of offending pieces of anatomy may represent a 'tidying up' of the categories male and female, making them more discrete. At the same time the ordeals associated with male circumcision may be seen as an attempt to provide the male with a physical and moral experience of such pain and power as childbirth, thus reducing the unique status of the latter (compare Callaway below).

Among the Ashanti, as among many other African peoples, pregnancy before female initiation is regarded as particularly atrocious. This is an area where we see how a system of social classification can have an overdetermining effect on definitions of biological facts. By tradition such a pregnant girl was driven out into the forest to bear her child alone as best she may.

Women denounce her for her intrusion into their territory; girls reject her for her treachery. She is without status: [and now we see biology denied, for] no-one calls her *eno* ('mother') and so she is not a woman, and she is not a girl because girls do not become pregnant. It is after giving birth to a child who formally can call her mother that she demonstrates her womanhood and is accepted by the womenfolk. The ostracism appears, therefore, to be the only solution to the anomaly of having a 'statusless' person in the community (Sarpong, 1977, pp. 76-7).

In Morocco we find that authority is vested in males at a particularly early age, indeed at one when clearly they are still unable to exercise it. Mernissi writes:

> His penis, *htewta* ('little pen'), is the object of a real cult on the part of the women rearing him. Little sisters, aunts, maids, mothers, often attract the little boy's attention to his *htewta* and try to teach him to pronounce the word, which is quite a task given the guttural initial letter 'h'. One of the commonest games played by adult females with a male child is to make him realize the connection between *sidi* ('master') and the *htewta*. *'Hada sidhum'* ('This is their master'), say the women, pointing to the boy's penis' (p. 96).

Little girls, meanwhile, are told in detail about the vagina and the uterus, and about the penis's 'destructive' effects on these two parts of women's bodies (p. 95).

Among the matrilineal Ashanti peoples of Ghana (who are discussed by James, below), the birth of a girl is greeted with special delight. A boy 'is completely incapable of providing successors for his matrilineage, in the girl the lineage has potential males as well as further potential females'. The Ghanaian anthropologist, Peter Sarpong, goes on to give a 'jural' explanation of the type identified by James below. 'A man without sisters is haunted by a sense of frustration because in the absence of sister's sons he is hard put to it to get heirs to whom he may bequeath his legacy.' There is less jubilation on the birth of a boy, therefore. This is the opposite case to the Muslims of Tunisia, described by Abu Zahra, where the midwife is paid only half the fee she obtains for a boy for delivering a baby girl. Among the Ashanti, girls undergo initiation ceremonies (which do not include clitoridectomy) whereas traditionally boys did not. Only in recent years have some boys become circumcised, following the fashion of others. However, while women are highly prized (Sarpong writes), in a family of children

> the boy begins to assume from the earliest possible moment, a position of authority and exercises a certain influence over at least some of the women with whom he is closely related. His sisters and their children see him as a man, even when he is scarcely adolescent . . . From her mother the Ashanti girl learns how to be serviceable and

submissive to her father, brothers, and any other older person and to respect everyone even (in the old days) a slave. She is not considered to be in a position of inferiority, but she remains a child *vis-à-vis* even her younger brothers until her maturity is attested through marriage.

Sarpong's view (1977, p.10) is that for a boy, 'gradual introduction into manly status therefore begins at a very early age. This seems to indicate [to Sarpong] that there is less need to demonstrate his maturity through the performance of a ceremony than there is to orientate the girl into the society of adults.'

Sarpong quotes Rattray to document the Ashanti belief that children grow up and live in a kind of borderland between the world of men and women and the world of ghosts, the bonds with the latter weakening until they are severed at puberty. Sarpong goes on to say: 'This belief perhaps throws some light on the resemblance between the treatment of a human corpse and the treatment of the [female] neophyte. Both the corpse and the girl are purified with the same objects'; they are groomed and praised in the same way. Sarpong is mystified as to why girls are selected for this treatment and not boys. He does not feel that it is adequate to assume that it is because the dead person is being admitted to the 'other world', while the female is being admitted as a true citizen of this world. He speculates that it may be because the girl menstruates, and this process needs ritual purification (see Sarpong, pp. 72-3). Yet this hardly explains why she is treated like a corpse. One cannot help feeling (from reading of the authority of young boys over women, and knowing they do not have to perform initiation rites at puberty) that among the Ashanti boys become fully human at an earlier age than do girls.

In some ways slots on either side of, or around, a category help to define it. It is often easier to recognise something by saying what it is not, than what it is (cf. Scobey, note 2 below). A hole in the ground is defined by the earth around it, yet it may be the hole and not the ground which is significant. Thus attention may be concentrated upon virginity in order that sexually experienced, or fully adult women may be more clearly defined (see Hastrup). The manner in which the Ashanti use the same symbolism in connection with the two categories which bound that for adult women (initiates and corpses) is not without interest. We may also note that among the Asaba Ibo, virginity had a *post facto* effect, helping to define the category that follows it. Throughout her married life a woman could remind her husband that she was 'a complete woman', for which 'she qualified by her premarital virginity', and thus he had no justification to misbehave towards her (Isichei, 1973, p. 686). Loss of premarital virginity was expected to lead to promiscuity and partial or total sterility. Elsewhere infidelity was thought to have a *post facto* effect, causing physiological difficulties during childbirth (see Callaway below).

Positively and Negatively Marked Categories

To continue our discussion of non-comparable systems of classification: if, following the practice suggested, we take the man/woman pair in a universe of *adults* and superimpose it on a universe of *fecund persons* divided into sexes, we find another 'empty slot', which corresponds to post-menopause adult women (see Hastrup). The slots or categories which are brought to our attention by such mismatching give rise to tensions, which may be expressed in terms of pollution fears, or ridicule, or even idolatry (cf. Douglas, 1966). Persons who fill these categories may become witches or deities.

In a system where the universe is concerned with possession or authority, or one sex is given status by another, 'anomalies' may arise which are so embarrassing that the dominant structure of society attempts to blot them out. This appears almost to be the case in Greece, where women, as daughters and wives, are 'legitimised' by men, as fathers and husbands. The young manless widow is a marked category, or 'anomaly', and until she corrects her position by remarrying, she is swathed in black, she averts her eyes, she closes her mouth and thereby hopes to avoid catching the attention of society (see Hirschon). Structurally she is 'not there'. She becomes a 'black hole' in the Greek universe (cf. E. Ardener, 1975). It is not uncommon, of course, for elderly women to be regarded as 'honorary men', the fact of their being women seeming an embarrassment, because to face this would throw the definition of women into disarray. The old may do things or exhibit characteristics, or lack certain features, which by definition women do not do, or do not have, or should have. In Hastrup's terms they may have lost the 'specificity' of women, and are therefore reclassified by their 'general', man-like characteristics.[19]

The Mongolian case presented by Humphrey is interesting. It seems, from looking at the material given by her, that the only category of woman that fits comfortably into the Mongolian system is the mother of a married son, the mature wife, who is past her childbearing (and sexual?) activity. Unfortunately difficulties arise because to enter this category, a woman must first become a young wife and mother (or daughter-in-law, depending upon the viewpoint of the classifier). To cope with this unfortunate necessity, social conventions, which apparently reflect the interests of the dominant male, the husband's father, ensure that she avoids certain spaces: she must walk only behind his tent, sit in a lowly place, avoid mealtimes and so forth. She is also muted: she should not attract attention to herself, but when she must she has to make herself slightly peculiar by her circumlocutions. Ideally she should not exist.[20] The dominant male does, however, recognise his own wife, and the rest of the society follows suit, so that when a woman's husband becomes old enough to replace his father as head of the household, then she becomes visible again. Interestingly, it seems that there is another boundary to the category of 'mother of an adult male'. When, through the processes of time, a woman passes across this boundary, she is found no longer to be fully present: she has entered into the quasi-supernatural state of holy woman. On her son's recognition of his wife being socially acknowledged, she becomes redundant, anomalous; logically she should no longer exist, again.

In our English society, the young mother and the old (but not senile) grandmother are valued categories, and ones that we find 'comfortable'. But it seems that the intermediate phase has a lower status and, ideally, for us should not exist. When matched to the male pattern, it appears as a 'ruck' in the social fabric which spoils the transformation from one ideal state to another. When it is forced upon our attention, it sometimes gives rise to unease and even ridicule. Hence women try to prolong youth into middle age, and shorten the period until they can become old with dignity. Women experience some problems in society, including in the political field, and in other areas where authority is exercised and where clarity of identity is important. Hilary Callan gives her attention to the particular experience of nurses, below. Perhaps both *young* female politicians and executives like nurses, and the very *senior* of them, are acceptable, while those in the *middle* who in fact often have the most appropriate mix of energy and experience, are resented, are felt to be ambiguous. This may account for some features of women in public life. Queen Elizabeth I prolonged her youth. By insisting that she belonged to that anomalous category 'virgin', she could be what she could not have been were she to have been a 'woman'. She could take advantage of being the 'third sex', and available for deification. Hastrup tellingly cites below the case of the transformation of a young unmarried, *de jure* virgin politician who was the centre of press attraction; when she was transformed into the more reassuring and less controversial category of 'young mother' she became

less noticeable. We know that Queen Victoria was maternally productive, but she was more popular in her youth and old age than in her,
more controversial, mature prime. The middle category seems to fit
better in the dominant structure in Mongolia, however. Perhaps, therefore, societies divide and 'mark' categories of women in different ways.

It might be possible to express the mismatch of the English male and
female life-trajectories lineally, as in Figure 1.2, showing the suggested
positive and negative 'rucks' in the social fabric.

Figure 1.2: The English Case

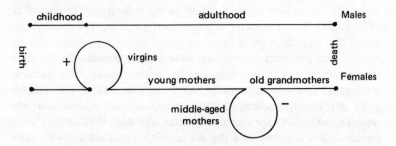

The Mongolian case might be as shown in Figure 1.3.

Figure 1.3: The Mongolian Case

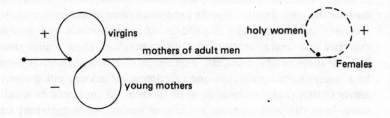

No exact time scale is implied by relative length in these diagrams.

With regard to Mongolian females who remain spinsters all their
lives, it appears that only as children do they conform to the 'unmarked'
norm of their society. It is unclear from Humphrey's material exactly
how they are regarded in their maturity, but it seems that in later life,
they may become positively marked 'nuns', a form of other-worldli-
ness, or they may be regarded negatively, as witches. This could be expressed as shown in Figure 1.4.

Figure 1.4: Mongolian Spinsters (two alternatives)

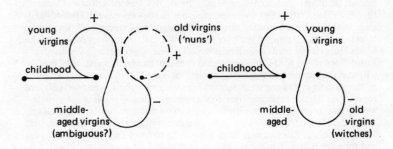

Thus the categories through which a female may pass in her lifetime are not all the same in every society. In England among those available are some which are traversed willy-nilly. A young female becomes a baby girl when she first draws breath. Girlhood, adolescence and womanhood follow inexorably until she becomes an 'old woman'.[21] Our society may recognise certain legal statuses, but these are known to be somewhat arbitrarily selected (they have changed from time to time). In other communities, however, it may be different, and ceremonies must be performed before a female passes into some of the categories available.

When we consider the many overlapping systems of classification in each society, and if we accept that systems can impinge one upon another at different times, in changing contexts, and according to the different structural positions from which they are perceived, then we begin to realise that the content of our 'universal' category *woman* may be a little unstable. All societies seem to recognise a category of persons approximating to that which we label 'woman'. There would be much common agreement, perhaps, should we try to identify persons to which we could apply the term or its variants. Nevertheless, even if, like sheep-dogs turning their lambs into a pen, we could agree on how to sort persons into common categories, problems of definition and meaning would remain. The most admired, the most typical 'woman' may not everywhere be the same. What a Mongolian, a Kikiyu, and say, a German, would each 'see' should they direct their attention towards, say, an Indonesian female, still remains to be fully understood. The chapters which follow should, however, help us to begin to perceive the nature of the question.

Notes

1. Keith Hope's generosity and continuing interest must be specially mentioned. Of others who carried responsibility on the Women's Studies Committee, first Elizabeth Durbin (who was spending her Sabbatical leave in Oxford) and later Jo Garcia have taken the chair, while Marguerite Duprée has been the secretary. Sheila Hazelden has borne part of the task of typing and administration. Linda Murgatroyd made a particular contribution, along with Jo Garcia and Penny Boumelha, to the bibliographical exercise. Sandra Burman and Mary Jacobus will edit the second and third volumes in this series. The Committee is grateful to the authors of the papers presented here for giving their time and skills, and for waiving part of their royalties. I must add my own appreciation for their kindly toleration of various editorial suggestions and comments. Selina Grant typed the MS with her usual expertise and commitment. Edwin Ardener, Drid Williams, Sandra Burman and Keith Hope read some of the MSS of the papers and introduction, and made valuable suggestions. Lastly we should thank the Warden and staff of Queen Elizabeth House for providing and preparing the venue for our seminars, and the University and its officers who administered our finances.

2. Speaking of the social anthropologist returning from fieldwork, David Scobey notes that his task 'is not to show us what we are – which he can do mainly at the cost of being obvious – but to show us what we are not, to show us particular alternatives to ourselves' (review in *Journal of the Anthropological Society of Oxford*, Vol. IV, No. 1 (1978, p. 80).

3. In trying to illuminate our past from studying other people's present, no simple mapping should be made, such as equating modern technologically simple societies directly with our own prehistoric past. On the other hand we should also beware of expressing all of our own fashionable values in our model of our past. The television reconstructions of early society which give the people dirty faces and rough manners, may, for instance, reflect certain English middle-class mores current today, rather than the true conduct of the people of those days!

4. Ardener, 1971, 1977. Williams has worked on the 'dancer's body'. Hilary Callan has pointed out that in hospital there are at least three bodies: the one the patient sees, the one the nurse sees and the one the doctor sees. For a variety of analyses, recently presented, see J. Blacking (ed.), *The Anthropology of the Body*, 1977.

5. Denial of what we see to be the biological facts of the role of the father in procreation is sometimes said to be a result of their presumed irrelevance in contrast to metaphysical considerations (see Hastrup), but it could also derive directly from the 'inconvenient' nature of the biological facts themselves. Physical paternity is difficult to prove, unlike maternity. If fatherhood can be attributed to other, indisuptably visible, 'marked' social or mystical causes, such as the need to be living on the father's land, then fatherhood more closely resembles motherhood, in being easily publicly attestable.

6. The association of food and sex is well known. The erotic meaning which can be given to eating was demonstrated by the film *Tom Jones*, among others, It has been said that this association is known and made use of by advertisers of food products. In African polygamous households the offering and accepting of food is often taken as promise of a sexual assignation later on. Among the Asaba of Nigeria, the condition of food and how it is served is often the subject of household quarrels. Patrick Isichei (1973, pp. 685-6) tells us that 'a dish lost much of its dignity the moment a portion of it – no matter how small – was eaten, and it was considered bad manners to serve it to any other person without disguising the fact . . . left-overs were meant for servants, maids and slaves.'

Married women often compared themselves to cooked food. In referring to their pre-marital chastity, they might say to their husbands 'surely on my arrival at yours, you did not find me the left-over of a yesterday's meal, did you?' Another reference might be to the fact that the husband had eaten 'the whole palm fruit'. Isichei perspicaciously notes that the implication of these two phrases taken together is that the defloration of a wife by a husband indicates that he has symbolically eaten her all up, while premarital loss of virginity by another man merely reduces her 'food value'.

7. The high regard in which some domestic work is held contrasts with the generally low status of domestic labour in the market-place. There are a number of reasons for this, among them the generality of the skills involved. In an interesting paper (written for the seminar on Woman's Work which will be the basis of a forthcoming book in the present series), Maureen Mackintosh shows the need to analyse with more sophistication the division of domestic labour among those who carry it out. We might go on to suggest that the tasks themselves need to be looked at more carefully. Certain of them, like washing dirty linen which has been in contact with the body, may be associated with pollution beliefs, and it is this which lowers their standing. If not performed out of self-sacrificing love, then perhaps some distancing must take place (by the use of machinery, or an administrative buffer which depersonalises the dirt, the wearing of uniforms, and the like) before they can be given status.

8. Thackeray, for instance, admired *Villette,* but thought the subject 'vulgar'. '. . . I don't make my *good* women ready to fall in love with two men at once.' (Gérin, 1971 ed, p. 598). For Charlotte's views on the education of boys and girls see her novel *Shirley* and Gérin (1976 ed., pp. 252-3).
Note: I am partly indebted for my sub-title to Jean Baker-Miller.

9. One of the many useful contributions of the present-day feminist movements has been that of 'consciousness-raising'. The practice draws attention to, by isolating from their contexts, statements which though 'trivial' in themselves carry assumptions with wider significance. It thus employs a technique long known to and attempted by social anthropologists. The perception of 'significant' statements is not without its own skill, and should not be underestimated.

10. When a statement or a discussion is presented it may be only partially 'heard' or 'read' by some, if it offers other than predictable views. It may be misunderstood if it does not fit into the preconceptions of its auditors or readers, or if it is not couched in a preferred mode of language, or in one whose use indicates membership of a group with known opinions which can be read into it. Its words are sometimes paraphrased, or used selectively, while some of its meanings are repressed. These are some effects in the process of muting. Labelling, and other forms of packaging and presentation, also influence the interpretation of statements. The original cool, green cover of *Perceiving Women* displayed a beautiful carving of a woman sitting on the shoulders of a man, selected by me. It was relevant to one of the papers. The inner caption read: 'The figurine is a modern representation (c. 1950), by the Igbo wood carver Agu Chukwu Egu, of the traditional Igbo medicine spirit. The "cooling" female aspect (sometimes referred to as the antidote) is shown "covering" the strong or "hot" (sometimes poisonous) male aspect of Igbo medicine.' When reprinting the book, the publisher substituted a bright magenta cover, ornamented with quotes from the press – kind ones, of course. Included among them is a phrase taken out of its original context (paradoxically a review by a woman supporter of women's studies), saying that the volume is a 'welcome antidote to the swelling literature of the women's lib movement'. The authors now find themselves represented by this *fait accompli* of the publisher, which no persuasion has yet succeeded in affecting. I have discovered that, whereas formerly some assumed the book would be simply a

polemical (feminist) statement, now a few seem to regard it as anti-feminist! Whatever its failings, both views would seem absurd reductions of the contents. Fortunately most of its readers have been generous in their evaluations, and most analyses have avoided such stereotypical positions.

11. Since this introduction to the present volume was written, K. Safa-Isfahani has kindly sent a manuscript giving a very interesting account of certain games performed by women in Iran, in which they are able to express ideas which (it seems probable) they could not present in another mode or forum. Safa-Isfahani writes that he found the theory of mutedness, as given in *Perceiving Women*, helpful in the analysis of his material, and points out that in the particular dramatic mode of expression employed in the games the women are very articulate. No doubt if suddenly projected into this universe, it would be men who would be muted. In conferences 'dominated' by women, it is fascinating to watch how, without any direct action by the women, men sometimes gradually become muted, including those who first display a habitual dominant stance and verbosity.

12. Names can be given or withheld. Thus a man gains power in Ashanti society because the matrilineage depends upon him to perpetuate the famous names of the lineage, which they do not wish to be lost when he names his own children. This is despite the fact that his own children, of course, will not belong to his matrilineage (Sarpong, 1977, p. 9). R. Barnes, in a paper delivered at the Institute of Social Anthropology at Oxford in Hilary Term 1978 reminded us that among certain American Indians, names of living persons can even be given away by third parties. Namegiving may be marked by ritual (and *vice versa*). The role of naming in conferring identity is also reflected in the treatment by Azande of new-born babes, who are not regarded as fully human. They delay giving a child a name for some weeks until it looks as if it will survive, referring to the child as 'it'. When it appears that the baby will survive, it is named; thereby Azande invest it with fuller social status (Evans-Pritchard, 1932; 1962 edition, pp. 120, 130).

13. See, for instance the work of Trudgill (1974) and Labov (1972).

14. In very recent years, many have sought to bring greater recognition to the artistic and other achievements of women, and various explanations have been given for their relative obscurity. The third volume in this present series will no doubt make a valuable contribution to this exercise.

15. See F. Edholm, O. Harris and K. Young, 'Conceptualising Women' (p. 120.) These authors note that, useful though the Marxist approach is, 'The position of women cannot be deduced from a specification of the relations of production for any given case' (p. 102). Our approaches in this present volume attempt to look at some of the underlying social relationships which are expressed in or influence other relationships, including economic ones. On the question of non-violent ways of controlling people: it is interesting to note that certain methods employed in girls' schools in the early nineteenth century, as described by Charlotte Brontë (the punishment by exposure on a stool in Lowood School, the surveillance of pupils in Madame Beck's school), have their counterpart in recent times, as is evidenced by the data in Okely's paper.

16. Ovesen's comment is of interest here. He says that 'every mode of classification is dominant in relation to what is classified by it' (1978, p. 8). We may note here also that the members of a dominant group, which generates the dominant structure, may not all necessarily experience a greater sense of liberty than do members of their counterpart muted groups. The structure may at times appear coercive to them also, just as a promise freely given may be experienced as irksome by, and may even destroy, its generator. Their experience will nevertheless be different from that of those in the counterpart groups, who have not generated the structure.

17. For an interesting account of the Hagen (New Guinea) case see Marilyn

Strathern, 1978.

18. This after-image is the opposite, in its operation, of that retrospective effect which a death has on a life, whereby the manner of its occurrence and the mortuary ceremonies, and the like, enhance or dishonour the pre-existing and already completed life.

19. We may note that, for instance, it is only post-menopausal women who may become nuns in the Orthodox Church (Tamara Dragadze, personal communication). Not only older women but also virgins are sometimes treated as or equated to men. It is interesting to note that in British pantomime, the positive role of hero is filled by a 'virgin' with a romantic style of acting, while the negative role of his mother is filled by a clownish man.

20. Just as veiling and segregation paradoxically enhance, not diminish sexuality, so this kind of 'muting' is counterproductive, in so far that it to some extent 'marks' the daughter-in-law and thereby makes her conspicuous. Here we see again the paradoxical 'power of the under-dog', also. Avoidance between kin of various kinds is not unknown elsewhere, of course, and may include avoidance between men and their mothers-in-law in some societies. Certain matrilineal societies place naming taboos on sons-in-law, as R.H. Barnes has pointed out in another context (see note 12). Seclusion in Iran was sometimes a way of avoiding non-kin, while permitting mingling between kin (Jane Khatib-Chahidi, personal communication, 1978).

21. 'Old Woman' may be a pejorative label – even applied at times to men. The 'grandmother' may be more acceptable because (like the young mother) she is associated with young children, thus meeting in part, at least, the specification for woman (cf. Hastrup). At one time the 'career-girl' was a marked category for women (whether married or not) in some universes. In the corresponding universes today, that category has become the unmarked standard, and it is the category 'housewife' which has become 'marked' (negatively).

Bibliography

Abu-Zahra, N. 'Moslem Women, and Moslem Paradise'. Paper delivered to the Women's Social Anthropology Seminar, Oxford, 1976

Ardener, E. (ed.), *Social Anthropology and Language*. London, Tavistock, 1971
—— 'Belief and the Problem of Women' in La Fontaine (ed.), 1972; reprinted in S. Ardener, 1975
—— 'Problems in the Analysis of Events'. Paper delivered at the ASA Decennial Conference, Oxford, 1973. In E. Schwimmer (ed.), *Yearbook of Symbolic Anthropology* London, Hurst, 1978.
—— 'The Problem Revisited' in S. Ardener, 1975
—— 'The Anthropologist as Translator of Culture'. Paper delivered to the Wenner-Gren Symposium on *Focus on Linguistics*, Burg Wartenstein, Austria, 1977. Publication forthcoming

Ardener, S.G. 'Sexual Insult and Female Militancy', *Man*, 1973, reprinted in S. Ardener, 1975
—— (ed.), *Perceiving Women*. London, Dent/Malaby; New York, Halsted, 1975

Arney-Ebeid, J. 'Egyptian women at home and in the factory'. Paper delivered to the Women's Social Anthropology Seminar. Oxford, spring 1978

Blacking, J. (ed.), *The Anthropology of the Body*. London, Academic Press, 1977

Clarke, I. 'Clitoridectomy in the Sudan'. Paper delivered to the Women's Social Anthropology Seminar. Oxford, 1978

Douglas, M. *Purity and Danger*. London, Routledge and Kegan Paul, 1966

Edholm, F., Harris, O., Young, K. 'Conceptualising Women' in *Critique of*

Anthropology, Vol. 3, Nos. 9 and 10 (1977)

Evans-Pritchard, E.E. 'Heredity and Gestation as the Azande see them', 1932. Reprinted in *Essays in Social Anthropology*. London, Faber, 1962

Gaskell, E. *The Life of Charlotte Brontë*, 1857. Harmondsworth, Penguin, 1975

Gérin, W. *Anne Brontë*, 1959. London, Allen Lane, 1976 edition

—— *Charlotte Brontë, The Evolution of Genius*, 1967. Oxford, Oxford University Press, 1971 edition

Hardy, T. *The Mayor of Casterbridge*. 1886. London, 1974 edition

Humphrey, C. 'Inside a Mongolian Tent', *New Society*, 31 October 1974

Isichei, P. 'Sex in Traditional Asaba'. *Cahiers d'etudes africaines*, No. 52, 1973

Labov, W. *Sociolinguistic Patterns*. 1972. Oxford, Blackwell, 1978

La Fontaine, J. (ed.). *The Interpretation of Ritual*. London, Tavistock, 1972

Lipshitz, S. (ed.). *Tearing the Veil*. London, Routledge and Kegan Paul, 1978

Lock, J. and Dixon, W.T. *Man of Sorrows*. Edinburgh, Nelson, 1965

Lloyd, B., and Archer, J. (ed.). *Exploring Sex Differences*. London, Academic Press, 1976

Mackintosh, M. 'The Political Economy of Domestic Work' in S. Burman (ed.) *Woman's Work*. London, Croom Helm (forthcoming)

Mernissi, F. *Beyond the Veil, Male-Female Dynamics in a Modern Muslim Society*. New York, Halsted, 1975

O'Faolain, J., and Martines, L. *Not in God's Image*. London, Temple Smith, 1973

Ovesen, J. 'Maurice Godelier and the Study of Ideology'. *Journal of the Anthropological Society of Oxford*, IX, 1 (1978)

Roberts, G. ' "Why are you so late?" "Where's my supper?" ' *Sunday Times*, 12 February 1978

Safa-Isfahani, K. 'Concepts of Feminine Sexuality and Female Centered World Views in Iran: Symbolic Representations and Dramatic Games'. Unpublished paper, delivered in New York, November 1977

Sarpong, P. *Girl's Nubility Rites in Ashanti*. Accra-Tema, Ghana Publishing Corporation, 1977

Steiner, G. 'A Note on the Distribution of Discourse', paper delivered to the Wenner-Gren Symposium on *Focus on Linguistics*, Burg Wartenstein, Austria, 1977. Printed in *Semiotica*, 1978

Strathern, M. 'An Anthropological Perspective'. In Lloyd and Archer, 1976

—— 'The Achievement of Sex: Paradoxes in Hagen Gender Thinking'. In Schwimmer (ed.), *The Yearbook of Symbolic Anthropology*, No. 1. London, Hurst, Montreal, McGill-Queen's University Press, 1978

Trudgill, P. *Social Differentiation of English in Norwich*. Cambridge, Cambridge University Press, 1974

Williams, D. 'Brides of Christ' in S. Ardener, 1975

Wolff, M. 'Chinese Women: Old Skills in a New Context' in M. Rosaldo and L. Lamphere (eds.), *Woman, Culture and Society*. California, Stanford University Press, 1974

Wright, S. 'Fieldwork among the Doshman-Ziara people of Mamsani village in Iran'. Paper delivered to the Women's Social Anthropology Seminar. Oxford, spring 1978

2 THE SEMANTICS OF BIOLOGY: VIRGINITY

Kirsten Hastrup

A recurring theme in discussions of the position of women in different societies is the role played by biology. The question is to what extent biology, and notably the difference of sex, can be said to determine sexual behaviour and sexual ideology in any one culture. Often biology has been dismissed altogether, because any universalistic claims for its determining effect have been held to obscure the issue at a point where clarification was badly needed. The aim of this paper is to reinstate biology as an important factor in our comprehension of the position held by women (and men), but as a set of social, rather than 'natural', facts. The 'facts of life' in themselves only operate at the level of biology: as biological facts they tell people how to reproduce the species. But these facts may take on a particular cultural meaning and a specific social significance in different societies. The task of the social anthropologist and anyone else concerned with a total apprehension of the position of women is to analyse how socially significant distinctions are mapped on to basic biological differences, and vice versa. In any social context we must study 'what difference the difference makes', since this will yield information about the social and ideological organisation of the society in question.[1]

In short, I shall enquire into the 'semantics of biology'. My aim is to demonstrate how biological and cultural perspectives on women constantly merge. The method chosen is to present some ideas on the relationship of mutual dependence between nature and culture, and I shall do so with reference to various examples, primary among which is that of virginity.

Basic Categories

'The facts of life' refer basically to the biological facts of sexuality and reproduction. As indicated by the brief introductory remarks, biology here denotes the facts given by nature, and in this sense it is opposed to what is given by culture. When it comes to an analysis of sexuality and reproduction as *social* facts, these concepts are not, however, referring to biology, or nature, alone; they are loaded with a specific meaning, which is by no means given by nature itself. We should be careful to note that this is also true for the medical models

49

of this society, even though we tend to regard medical knowledge as consisting of objective, that is natural, truths.

Medical models are specialists' models, but this fact does not in itself guarantee that they are culture-free, in the sense of being objectively true and universally valid. Like lay models, specialists' models are expressions of particular conceptions of interrelationships between certain elements of a whole. In terms of women's reproductive forces, the case of abortion that has been so vividly discussed during recent years clearly demonstrates how even medical models differ, reflecting the different values attached to a biological problem. The attitudes towards abortion as a social fact cannot be understood without reference to the different (ideological) conceptions of when life starts, and who is responsible towards whom for this new life, and what is the social organisation into which the child may be born and in which the woman becomes a mother. Virginity can be seen as an aspect of female sexuality which is likewise subject to different interpretations; maybe not so much within our own society, but certainly under a cross-cultural perspective. The significance of virginity cannot be understood all by itself. As a biological fact, yes, but not as a social fact, a fact that enters into the lives of young women as a demand or as a virtue. We have to know the meaning of virginity in relation to a larger social whole, and in relation to the evaluations attached to different stages of a woman's life.

This is a general point: we cannot understand the meaning and significance of one single aspect of sexuality and reproduction without knowing its relationship to related concepts within the same semantic domain, as we cannot deduce the significance of this particular domain without reference to the social context in which it leads its meaningful life. Stated in very general terms, it is part of anthropological knowledge that the meaning of specific categories depends on their position within a larger system of cultural categories.[2] Virginity as a category is no exception to this theoretical axiom. The semantic load of this concept is defined by its position within a larger semantic field of 'female sexuality', and this field, again, is defined in relation to society at large.

The importance of relationships in the mapping of the meaning attached to biological facts can hardly be over-estimated. This is already well documented in at least one major field of anthropological investigation, namely that of kinship. Kinship is a way of conceiving of and representing biological facts, but we must stress that kinship by itself is by no means just biology. It is a cultural extension of universal (natural) facts of reproduction. The parts played by men and women in different kinship systems vary greatly from one culture to the next. Even in our own society kinship is an important parameter in the daily lives of most people, if not explicitly, then at least implicitly. Notions of kinship play a role, for example, in many discussions of sexual matters; the discussion of abortion is a case in point (e.g. whether the woman alone has the right to decide). Early anthropologists tended to confuse facts of biology with facts of society, but we now know that the use of biological models, such as notions of kinship, is just a way of marking out culturally significant categories. When Malinowski stated in 1929 that the people of the Trobriand Islands in Melanesia were unaware of the role played by the father in procreation, this was not the same as saying that they collectively believed in virgin birth. But as descent was matrilineal (kin was traced predominantly through women) the actual role played by the father was not important. We shall return to this example later, but here it suffices to note the fact that biological models are used to mark out culturally or socially important categories, and this, again, stresses the general point that apparently biological explanations may be objects for semantic analyses.

Kinship is one way of ordering society into distinct categories. There are other ways of organising oneself, but it is a basic knowledge of social anthropology that all societies use distinctions of some kind in order to operate. No society is completely amorphous, making no difference of the differences between people on grounds of sex, age, access to power or anything else. Everywhere the conceptions of society are in terms of distinct categories. In so-called primitive societies the most important distinction seems to be that of sex and, by extension, that of kinship. This is no great surprise, since biological differences are always at hand when organising society becomes acute.

Distinct categories are established by means of boundaries. Those familiar with the work of Mary Douglas, notably *Purity and Danger* (1966), will immediately recognise the truth of this statement. The boundaries in question are conceptual boundaries rather than, say, physical borders, although the latter may be seen to be an expression of the former. Such boundaries exist around the categories of 'man' and 'woman', to take just one obvious set. A well known example from our personal experience may help to underline the point that the significance to us as social individuals of even this boundary is primarily conceptual, and only secondarily biological. I think that we all know the slight feeling of uneasiness in cases where we cannot immediately establish the sex of a particular person that we encounter. Our enculturation demands that the categories of male and female are discrete, and even though we could theoretically discard the problem as not being our business unless we were going to sleep with the person, we cannot conceptually escape the uneasiness related to the ambiguity, that is the non-distinctiveness of the category. Social intercourse, as well as sexual intercourse, somehow requires that the interacting parties know to which sexual category 'the other' belongs.

This is, then, another basic point: societies operate in terms of discrete categories and established boundaries. The boundary areas, or the ambiguous classifications, are points of danger, in Douglas's terms, because they give rise to ambivalence and marginalisation (Douglas, 1966, and Leach, 1964). I suggest that the ambivalent feelings of most people towards transvestism, and to a lesser extent towards homosexuality, are founded on the fact that the people designated by these terms defy the normal categorisation of male and female. Again, this demonstrates that it is cultural conceptions, rather than biological facts, that matter, because most of the people who can be said to be 'against' transvestism or homosexuality would probably not care if it were a matter of biology only.

If transvestism and homosexuality are concepts of danger, in the sense that they are notions relating to ambiguous areas of classification, then virginity and heterosexuality may be said to be notions of purity, in that they operate with distinct categories of men and women. Together these four notions encircle a semantic field of human sexuality, and to arrive at a full comprehension of the position of any one single theme, we ought to do the analysis full circle.[3]

But to summarise the general points made so far: the meaning of specific categories depends on the relation between categories; social and conceptual order depends on the establishment of discrete categories by means of boundaries between them. The conjunction of these two principles entails that the discreteness of particular categories is a matter of level of speaking, or object of analysis. It is a matter of context: what seems to be a discrete category within one context may be less distinct, less unambiguously 'pure' within another context. And what is 'dangerous (ambiguous) at one level may be seen at another level as an expression of purity.

A final general point is that everywhere *natural* markers of difference are used as models for conceptual (and social) distinctions between categories. This is where biological and cultural perspectives meet.

Man and Woman

It has already been said that the meaning of the category of virginity is in some sense dependent upon its position within the semantic field of human sexuality. Other categories were mentioned and for the moment we shall make a brief enquiry into the notion of heterosexuality, since this was said to be 'pure', as is the category of virginity, and since I think that this procedure will facilitate the apprehension of the semantics of virginity.

Heterosexuality designates a specific sexual relationship between man and woman, conceived of as distinct categories, and made for each other, as it were. The actual sexual relationship is of less interest here; more important is the fact that the notion rests upon a distinct classification of man as opposed to woman. And it is into these categories that we shall now enquire to see whether they are always, both of them, as distinct as one is immediately led to suppose. I contend that they are not, and I will present an ethnographic example as first evidence.

Among the Tewa Indians (Ortiz, 1969), the standard phrase of encouragement to a man who is about to undertake a demanding task is 'Be a woman, be a man,' while the corresponding remark to a woman is simply 'Be a woman.' This usage is repeated in relation to other social events, notably at the naming rite of the young child. On this occasion the spirits are addressed and requested to help bring the boy 'into womanhood and into manhood', while the wish for a female infant is just that she may be brought into 'womanhood'. This and other evidence sustain the conception of men containing both male and female aspects, while women are just women.

The Tewa are not unique in this respect. Actually, we find a similar conception of the interrelationship between man and woman in our own society. Furthermore, this conception is expressed both on the biological and the cultural level. On the biological level it is a matter of genetics. Men possess both x- and y-chromosomes, while women are equipped with x-chromosomes only. This may well be an objective fact, but as soon as we consider 'deviances' from the statistically dominant pattern we are confronted with the cultural and social extensions of these so-called facts. It has been found that some men possess a surplus y-chromosome, and some specialists doing allegedly objective research into genetics have attempted to establish a correlation between this surplus y-chromosome and a tendency for these men to be criminals, sexually more potent and violent than most 'normal' men, or just generally obsessed with he-manship. Conversely, men who possess a surplus x-chromosome are labelled 'cissy' and thought likely to be homosexual.[4] I am not at all in a position to assess medical research of this kind here. Rather I want to demonstrate the inevitable cultural evaluation of natural facts. The notions of 'he-man' and 'cissy', masculinity and femininity are described as if they were facts of biology, and not conceptions of culture. It appears that even when we think we are most neutral, as when we are talking genetics, biology and culture seem to be generically related.

If genetics demonstrates that biologically speaking men are the generalised representatives of mankind, while women are the specified sex, this is culturally underlined by the very notions of man and woman. The relationship between these terms is asymmetric in the sense that *man* includes *women* at a certain level of comprehension. When the category of man is opposed to the category of animal, that is when we are talking of mankind, women are included. At a lower taxonomic level man opposes woman, of course, but the first inclusive relationship remains important. It is important if we want to understand how it is that men again and again talk on behalf of humanity, as it were. Almost everywhere, male heads of households have acted on behalf of the rest of the household members, including their wives. From our own society we even know of wives' functions being considered as part of men's jobs (Callan, 1976).[5]

In social anthropology this asymmetric relation obtains even at a very fundamental level of research. As Edwin Ardener says: 'The fact is that no one could come back from an ethnographic study of "the X", having talked only *to* women and *about* men, without professional comment and some self-doubt. The reverse can and does happen constantly' (1972, p. 138). If field-work dealing with men only has been perfectly conceivable, this can best be understood with reference to the implicit conception of men's world including women, while women's world may not include men.[6] So it appears that even in social anthropology a basic presumption is, or at least has been, that the male world is generalised, while the female world is specified.

By means of a simple diagram we may visualise the relationship as shown in Figure 2.1.

Figure 2.1

inner circle: male, generalised

outer circle: female specified

This concentric dualism gives us a visual expression of the existence of a specific female sphere of reality alongside the male, shared, reality. If we are to understand what this separate reality means to women, this must be done with reference to particular social contexts. But we may also treat it in more general terms, by stating that the notion of *femineity*, as defined by Shirley Ardener (1973, p. 435), may best be understood by reference to the specific female reality. Femineity comprises aspects of self-identification on a deep structural level, as opposed to the less precise and not separate reality of *femininity*, which is loaded with notions of secondary sexual characteristics and with men's appreciation of these (ibid.).

As our conceptual patterns have allowed men to speak on behalf of women over the years, it is little to be wondered at that the specific female reality and women's self-identification have been grossly undercommunicated. The women's movements of recent years have to some extent amended this situation, but still male models dominate, and female models are 'muted' (S. Ardener, 1975; E. Ardener, 1975).

Returning to the question of boundaries, the brief exposition of the content of the categories of man and woman showed that the categories are not always, and in all social contexts, unambiguously defined in respect to sex. It appears that at a certain level of analysis, men are ambiguously both/and, while women are solely women.

Virginity

So far we have only dealt sporadically with virginity. However, the more general discussion of the sexual categories and of the semantics of sex was necessary to the more specific topic.

Virginity is often thought of as female purity *par excellence*. Apart from the fact that this indicates that it is a man who spoils the purity of a woman, and hence puts a (welcomed?) blame on him, it may also be of some personal distress to a woman, whose purity becomes somebody else's concern as well as her own. In some societies the virginity of women is an affair of the entire society; elsewhere it may be the concern of her immediate family, while in yet other cultures it is entirely her own business.

To give an example of the societal concern with the chastity of women, we may mention Indian society, with its strongly endogamous castes. The pollution of women through illegitimate sexual affairs with men is a conceived of as a pollution of the entire caste, and hence a threat to the very constitution of the society (Yalman, 1963). In many places, also outside India, it was the habit to employ a white sheet when a marriage was to be consummated, in order to test the bride's virginity. If she failed to bleed, she might be, or even ought to be, killed by her father or brother, who acted as joint guardians of her honour.

If we stick to the Indian example, this ideal of virginity is recently reported from the Punjab, where, at the same time, the sense of honour of a young man dictates that he cannot consider himself a man until he has had intercourse with a woman (Hershman, 1977, p. 273). This, of course, is a rather paradoxical yet well known situation. The severity with which this ideal rule was traditionally enforced seems to have declined. Nevertheless, even today the purity of the social group, the caste, still depends on the purity of the women, since it is through them that caste membership is transmitted. In other societies it is only particular women who are bound to remain virgins until marriage, while the majority may indulge in sexual relationships as they please. For instance in Samoa it applied to the daughter of the chief only; *her* virginity was a symbol of the integrity of the whole society (Mead, 1928).

Whether chastity is demanded of all the women of a particular society or only of one superior woman, it always acts as a means of establishing distinct social categories. In other words, the sexual state of a woman, or her natural sexual properties, act as symbols of social purity. It is a case of a biological model being used to serve distinct social purposes, and for natural reasons it is the model of women's virginity that is of most use to the society.[7]

Virginity and chastity do not only have a symbolic function in relation to the caste or the society, but certainly also have practical significance for the women involved, and often for the men of the immediate family as well. If virginity is expected at marriage, and if it is the men who exchange women, as is the case in many societies, then the virginity of the women becomes part of the men's deal. If the woman is not a virgin at marriage, it is the men who get a bad deal. This is why the sexual affairs of the woman, or rather her absolute chastity, becomes of direct concern to her family. We know this from the Arab and most of the Mediterranean countries (see, for instance, Hirschon, below, and Peristiany, 1965). Spoiling the men's deal may lead to severe sanctions against the women, even to the point of killing them, as previously mentioned. However dreadful and suppressive this may seem to the women, they nevertheless occupy a key position, because they are, in fact, in a position to destroy the men's game. In other words, women are not only objects, they have to agree to behave as objects, too, and if they don't, the men will lose some objects for exchange (van Baal, 1970). Thus I think that we may conclude that the marginal position of women in most marriage exchanges is rather more powerful than the ideological models would lead us to believe in the first place. Women are not only men's game, they have to play men's game, too. They are both persons and currency, as Mary Douglas says (1966, p. 152), or, in the words of Lévi-Strauss, women have remained both signs and values (1969, p. 496).

Playing the game in some societies requires the women to be very conscious about it. When girls are married off at the moment they reach physical maturity, it may not be all that difficult to stick to the ideal norms. But when there is a considerable delay between puberty and marriage, as is the case among the Zulu of South Africa due to their particular system of age grades, the girls have to invest a good deal of energy in remaining virgins. The bodies of the young girls are often displayed in the community, so that men may admire their purity. A virgin's body is her pride and the exposure of it declares her purity. In contrast to this, the naked body of a married woman is considered to bring defilement (Krige, 1968, p. 174).[8]

What is interesting in respect to the Zulu conception of virginity is the fact that it is seen to be the concern of the age-mates and girl-friends of the young woman. The girls will often examine each other (as they will be examined by their mothers) to see if the hymen is still intact. This is the more pertinent because there exists an institution of 'external intercourse', with a single lover, and one can easily imagine the difficulties inherent in actually keeping the sexual relationship 'external', as it were, when sexual play of a rather intense character goes on for years between more or less permanent partners. If the girl is seduced, that is if she is actually deflowered, her age-mates will soon know and they will take action, since the seduction of the girl is polluting to the entire group of young girls. The girls will take off their clothes and go to the village of the guilty boy to demonstrate their virginity (ibid.). The seduced girl, however, will not uncover herself, since her body no longer expresses the pride of virginity. The girls will demand a goat or ten shillings, which will be given to them by the women of the village,[9] after they have examined the seduced girl to establish the truth of the accusation. They will then kill the goat, tear out the chyme and smear it all over their bodies and go to wash it off in the river. If they are given 10 shillings instead of the goat, they will put them into water and use this water in the same fashion as they use the chyme of the goat (ibid., p. 175). In this way the age-group will be ritually cleansed from the pollution that fell upon them through the seduction of a single girl.

In this case the women themselves are guardians of female purity. It is a matter of keeping a distinct category of virgins within the more embracing category of women. I would like to add at this point that an equivalent purity marks lesbian women in our own society. When lesbianism is an issue of sexual politics, it is a manifestation of the policy involved in keeping the category of women intact. It is a means of not letting men's evaluations interfere with female self-identification. On a more general level this demonstrates that homosexuality is not 'dangerous', ambiguous, from all points of view.

If we are to draw a more general conclusion from the dramatised pride in virginity, it is that sexual states and functions are used as markers of social identity. So once more the natural and the cultural markers coalesce. Furthermore, it appears that the women's bodies and female sexuality at large become a prime symbol of the female identity. We have examples of this from other societies as well, where women jointly have taken action against men, or against male society. Shirley Ardener has described female militancy in West Africa, where reference to biological or sexual particulars of women are used (1973), and from our own society we know that among the first declarations of women's liberationists were forceful demands that we love our own bodies as they are. This does suggest that the prime symbol of female self-identification will for ever be the woman's body. This is not unbearable in itself, as long as it is the women themselves who define the premisses. It must be the women's conception of female biology that sets the frame if biology is to act as a central theme in our self-identification. In short, it should be femineity and not femininity that decides the weight attached to the sexual symbolism.

There is a dimension to virginity other than sexual purity. If we resort once more to the example of the Tewa Indians, we may be able to see that although socially and sexually pure, the virgins may not always be conceptually pure, that is unambiguous. In fact, the Tewa have a third sex category, namely that of virgins, consisting of young maidens that have not yet become specified as women (Ortiz, 1969). What is suggested by this is that a female is not fully specified as a woman until she has been sexually associated with a man. At one level it is the man who spoils the purity of a virgin, but at another level it is only through intercourse with a man that a woman becomes wholly a woman, and thus enters into the pure female category. That virgins defy sexual specificity among the Tewa is suggested also by the names of the mythological founders of the two moieties (the ritual halves of the society). The founder of the female moiety is the White Corn *Woman*, while the founder of the male moiety is the Blue Corn *Maiden*. So, clearly there is a conception of a distinction between the specified woman and the yet unspecified virgin, having aspects of both sexes.

The Tewa example may throw light on similar, yet more implicit, conceptions from other societies. If we recognise that the ambiguous classification may place particular virgins in a powerful, yet vulnerable, position, we may be able better to understand the fate of Joan of Arc, for instance. She is known also as 'the maid of Orleans', and I believe that she would never have succeeded in her campaign in the first place had she not been really or symbolically a virgin. Her real and symbolic power was connected with her ambiguous sexual classification. No men, I think, would have been among her followers, had she been just a woman. Actually, Joan of Arc was a rather ambiguous figure in many ways; that she was finally burnt as a witch does not diminish the ambiguity. (A man in a corresponding situation would doubtless have been executed as a traitor.)

An example closer to our own time is provided by the case of Bernadette Devlin, once a very potent political figure of Ulster. She may still be in some kind of influential position, but it is significant that as a symbol her power has certainly vanished since she has had a child. I shall not push this case any further, as there are of course a whole range of reasons why the fate of this one-time political leader was as it was. I want, however, to note that it is possible that virgins in particular situations or contexts may be classified as sexually ambiguous even within our own society, and that this is best seen by reference to how they are 'used' symbolically.

At the opposite end of the life span of a woman we find the category of old women and widows, who are ideologically devoid of sexuality. In many cases widows (of whatever age) are not allowed to remarry, and in extreme cases we find the desexualisation to be even more marked. In some Brahmin castes of India a widow must shave her head and she is no longer referred to as 'she' but as 'it' (Harper, 1969, p. 90). Even where the defeminisation of widows is not so complete as in this case, I would argue that becoming a widow always entails some kind of despecification of a woman, as does the fact of the menopause.

It seems, then, that the course of life of a woman is basically divided into three stages. The first stage is that of the unspecified, yet creative virgin; the next stage is that of the sexually specified, child-bearing woman, and the course is completed by a final return to unspecificity, this time of widowhood and of old women's impotence. It is a course going from an ambiguous sexual potentiality, through the unambiguous sexual fertility, on to a condition completely lacking in sexuality and devoid of creativity. (I must stress that I am talking of conceptual patterns, mainly.) This course of life is peculiar to women. Only women's bodies can be used to define social states in this way. They can be used as social markers because they are marked by nature in a way that invites the use of these bodies in other than just sexual ways.

Men are just men, all the time. Being the generalised sex, their identification is not tied up with their sexual states to the same extent as is the case for women. The basic asymmetrical relationship is once more conspicuous.[10]

Virgin Birth

The three stages in a woman's life that I defined mainly in terms of creativity are sustained also by notions of miraculous and ordinary childbirths, respectively. At the first stage virgin births are certainly miraculous, and while virginity can be said to be an ambiguous state at a certain conceptual level, the phenomenon of virgin birth is certainly always and from all points of view anomalous. The anomaly of a virgin mother makes her a potent symbol of the relationship between the natural and the supernatural world. The Virgin Mary is the best-known example to us, but throughout the world we find equivalent dogmas of godly children that are conceived by virgins, that is, without inter-ference of mortal fathers. Characteristic of these cases is that both the child and the mother may become immortalised.

Childbirths occurring to women at the second stage are never anoma-lous. On the contrary, barrenness seems to be the sexual anomaly of this stage, since it is very often a legitimate reason for divorce. When a woman is past the menopause or widowed, and hence beyond creati-vity, producing children is, once more, an anomaly. From the Bible we know of a couple of childbirths occurring to old women long past childbearing age, and although they are symbolically 'used' as are virgin births, we should note that the way in which they are used differs from these. Births to old women apparently never result in immortalisation of the mothers, while the children seem to be predestined to become godly heroes (cf. Leach, 1967, p. 43). While virgin mothers are pure, old, long-time married women are not, and I suggest that this is why they are not 'eligible for divinity', as it were.

The Virgin Mary became immortalised, but the interpretation of her actual position and powers varies greatly. A recent book by G. Ashe (1977) is devoted to the many aspects of the myth of the Virgin Mary, and I shall not go into details here. It suffices to note that the differing positions held by her are correlated to differences in the social settings that surround the myth. Phrased generally: the 'natural' miracle is translated into different cultural myths.

Whether or not the virgin motherhood was factually true, it is certainly a generally accepted dogma. As such, it has a specific cultural meaning and a particular social significance. Virgins could be seen to mediate between sexual categories, and a virgin mother, being more anomalous, may mediate between humans and God. This mediating function may be common to all Christian interpretations of the myth, but the social significance of this conception differs. To social anthropologists it is these differences that are of prime importance, rather than the universally accepted 'fact' of Mary's virgin motherhood.

Also of greater importance to the social anthropologist than this single instance of virgin motherhood are those cases reported of a common belief in conception without fathers. It was mentioned at the beginning of this chapter that when Malinowski declared that the Trobrianders seemed to be unaware of physiological paternity, this was not equivalent to saying that they collectively believed in virgin birth. This requires some qualification. It is evident from the statements of Malinowski that the people were fully aware of the fact that virgins could not conceive (1929, p. 180). It was recognised that a man was needed to 'open' a woman, for her to become pregnant. But still, as a cultural dogma, the non-awareness of the role played by the father in conception is comparable to the religious dogma of the Immaculate Conception of the Virgin Mary. Both dogmas are rational in relation to their specific context. Had Mary not been a virgin, her conception by God and not by Joseph could have been subject to some doubt, and so could, consequently, the status of Jesus as the son of God. And, in the matrilineal society of the Trobrianders, maternity was more important to stress than paternity. If we go on to ask about the function of the fathers, we find parallel answers in the two cases: for the children to be legitimate (or socially possible) they had to be born out of legal unions. One would have thought that God might as well have chosen an unbetrothed girl as a mother of his child, thereby saving Joseph from some embarrassment. But this would have stigmatised Jesus in an untimely way, since had he not had an earthly father as well as a divine father, he would have had no legal status in the society. As it happened, it can now be claimed that Jesus was simultaneously the son of God by the

Virgin Mary, and the son of Joseph by his wife Mary. In the first role Jesus is divine and of another world, while in the second role he is a direct descendant of David and of the society. Paradoxical, yes, but rational, nevertheless.

As maternity is indeed more spectacular and dramatic than paternity we shall not expect to find societies, not even strongly patrilineal ones, where the role of the mother is not recognised. On the contrary, even in patrilineal societies we may find cases of non-recognition of biological paternity (Monberg, 1975). But again, even if the details of procreation may not be known (as they are not to many people in our own society), this does not mean that these people are 'ignorant' in any absolute sense. Ignorance is relative (Leach, 1967, p. 41, Monberg, 1975, p. 34), and so is knowledge. Knowledge is relative to world view, and rather than accepting at face value any statement that a people have no knowledge of physiological paternity, we should look for the transcription of the so-called biological facts into different terms. Biology is always to be understood according to a particular cultural rationale.

As Monberg relates from the patrilineal Bellonese:

When a man and a woman moved together in marital alliance they (thus) lived on land belonging to the husband of the family. The Bellonese believed such an alliance to produce progeny, *not* by or because of the man's copulation with the woman, but because the patrilineal ancestors and the deities of the patriline were pleased (*mangaohie*) with the alliance. A woman became pregnant because the deities and ancestors of her husband had sent her offspring. If too much time elapsed before pregnancy occurred, the husband might invoke his ancestors or deities by uttering a short prayer asking them to send a child to his wife. Usually pregnancy occurred after this (Monberg, 1975, p. 36).

What is at stake here, in fact, is not so much the ignorance of a particular people, but the far more fundamental aspect of a general theory of causality. We are used to going for scientific 'causes' and cannot accept that pregnancy is caused by the goodwill of our ancestors. But even we have to accept that sexual intercourse is not a sufficient, although necessary, cause of pregnancy. Inexplicable barrenness occurs again and again, and certainly many prayers are uttered to alter this situation even in our own society. Thus, even if we think that we know all the details of the facts of life, this does not put us in a position to explain when and why conception takes place, or when it does not. If virgin birth is a miracle, so is in fact every childbirth.

Biology and Culture

I stated in my introduction, and I have tried to demonstrate by means of specific examples, that biological facts are always transformed into meaningful categories which are defined by their relationship *to*, and interaction *with*, other categories of society. I have dealt with this matter as being mainly a one-way incidence of objective biological facts being transformed into subjective cultural categories. But, as I am now to conclude the chapter in a more general fashion, I would like to add that the opposite is also true to some unknown and not easily demonstrable extent. In other words, the cultural categories, and of course the social functions of these, may have a certain effect on biological realities. Take the last sentence in the passage on the Bellonese which I have just quoted: 'Usually pregnancy occurred after this.' We have to take this as a statement of fact — when the appropriate rituals had been carried out, biology worked as it should (with exceptions, of course) and pregnancy occurred. Ethnographies are full of incidents like that. I think that we have even become so used to them, that we do not always realise their potency, and their implications on a more general level.

It is part of the job of social anthropologists to eye-witness strange realities, in which 'normal' causal relationships and 'rational' explanations are apparently suspended. But they are nevertheless real enough, as our sometimes painful experiences tell us. I am not going to give any elaborate examples of this, I just wish to state that cultural categories may, indeed, affect natural functions. I think that this is not only part of the professional experience of social anthropologists, it is also part of the ordinary experience of women in this society.

Nature and culture seem to be interwoven with one another, and this is why we have to reinstate biology in our analyses. 'Biology is not destiny, certainly not. But it is a fact of nature which enters into the logic of every social system and every cultural ideology' (Whyte, 1974, p. 7), so we can hardly discard it, not even as *social* anthropologists. What we need, in fact, is a less rigid conception of the relationship between nature and culture. There is no absolute opposition between the two concepts. The distinction is analytical, relative and contextual, to the point where we may even see either concept as context of the other.

I shall not elaborate the argument at this point, since that would be a general discussion that belongs elsewhere. To conclude the paper in terms of its specific topic, I would like to emphasise that the significance of sexuality and reproduction within particular social systems is not understood, either with reference to biology alone, or without reference to the natural facts of sex. Biology and culture are mutually-affecting spheres of reality.

Notes

1. 'The difference that makes the difference' is a notion used by Bateson (1972). That it is this difference that yields information is an axiom of communication theory.

2. This knowledge dates back to the revelations of structural linguistics, notably the work of Saussure (1916). In anthropology it became prominent with Lévi-Strauss (e.g. 1945, 1962a, 1962b). For the most recent position of 'semantic anthropology', see Crick (1976).

3. I have dealt more extensively with all of the four notions elsewhere (Hastrup, 1974, 1975).

4. I draw this information mainly from articles appearing in Danish journals and periodicals over the years.

5. Hilary Callan shows how specific wives' functions are considered part of their diplomat husbands' jobs, but without the wives having any formal position within the diplomatic mission.

6. As Edwin Ardener (1972) convincingly shows, the bias towards men's conceptions of the world is also owed to the apparently 'male' models of social anthropology. Hence, it is a serious analytical problem as well as a general ideological one.

7. In some contexts, sexual abstinence for men as well as for women is a symbol of 'social' purity, but as 'abstinence', it points to something unnatural, as it were. It is a non-fulfilment of the sexual requirements of a particular stage of life – requirements in the sense of being needed to ensure the survival of the species.

8. For a detailed account of the polluting aspects of Zulu women's sexuality, see Sibisi (1975).

9. Actually it is not quite clear that it is the women that pay the fine to the girls. But as it is they who examine the girl, and they who are given the goat to eat after the girls have finished using it, I infer that it is also they who pay.

10. When I delivered this paper orally, some of the men present seemed to react against this idea of men being 'just men', all along. It is true, of course, that men's life is divided into stages, but whether young, mid-aged or old, the stage is not defined by reference to sexual functions. Male 'virginity' exists, in a biological sense, of course, and the transition from 'virginity' to manhood may be extremely important to the individual man, but as it is not biologically conspicuous it is not used as a social symbol to the same extent as female virginity.

The very word 'virginity', when applied to men, is a kind of construction, derived from the use of the term in relation to women. During the seminar, Shirley Ardener suggested the term 'back-formation' for this process of applying terms of female sexuality to 'similar' facts of male sexuality, the latest case of 'back-formation' being the idea of 'male menopause'. In general terms, the process of 'back-formation' suggests that as stages, defined in terms of sexuality, the divisions of men's life are derived from the reality of women.

Bibliography

Ardener, Edwin. 'Belief and the problem of women' in LaFontaine (ed.), *The Interpretation of Ritual*. London, Tavistock, 1972. Reprinted in S. Ardener, 1975
——. 'The problem revisited' in S. Ardener, 1975
Ardener, Shirley. 'Sexual insult and female militancy'. *Man*, n.s., Vol. 8 (1973). Reprinted in S. Ardener (ed.), *Perceiving Women*. London, Malaby/Dent; New York, Halsted, 1975
Ashe, G. *The Virgin*. London, Paladin, 1977
Baal, J. van. 'The part of women in the marriage trade: objects or behaving as objects?' *Bijdragen*, Vol. 126, No. 3 (1970) (Leiden)
Bateson, G. *Steps to an Ecology of Mind*. New York, Ballantine, 1972
Callan, Hilary. 'The premiss of dedication' in S. Ardener, 1975
Crick, Malcolm. *Explorations in Language and Meaning. Towards a Semantic Anthropology*. London, Malaby/Dent; New York, Halsted, 1976
Douglas, Mary. *Purity and Danger*. London, Routledge, 1966
Hastrup, Kirsten. 'The sexual boundary – Purity: Heterosexuality and virginity'. *Journal of the Anthropological Society of Oxford*, Vol. 5, No. 3 (1974)
——. 'The sexual boundary – Danger: Transvestism and Homosexuality. *Journal of the Anthropological Society of Oxford*, Vol. 6, No. 1 (1975)
Hershman, Paul. 'Virgin and Mother' in I. Lewis (ed.), *Symbols and Sentiments. Crosscultural Studies in Symbolism*. London, Academic Press, 1977
Krige, Eileen J. 'Girls' puberty songs and their relation to fertility, health, morals and religion among the Zulu'. *Africa*, Vol. 38 (1968), 173-98
Leach, Edmund. 'Anthropological aspects of language: Animal categories and verbal abuse' in E. Lenneberg (ed.), *New Directions in the Study of Language*. Cambridge, Mass., MIT Press, 1964
——. 'Virgin Birth'. *Proceedings of the Royal Anthropological Institute of Great Britain and Ireland for 1966*, 1967, pp. 39-50
Lévi-Strauss, C. 'Structural analysis in linguistics and in anthropology'. *Structural Anthropology*, 1945. New York, Anchor, 1963
——. *Le Totémisme aujourd'hui*. Paris, 1962 (a)
——. *La Pensée Sauvage*. Paris, 1962 (b)
——. *The Elementary Structures of Kinship*, trans. R. Needham. London, Eyre and Spottiswoode, 1969
Malinowski, B. *The Sexual Life of Savages*. New York, 1929
Mead, Margaret. *Coming of Age in Samoa*. New York, 1928; Harmondsworth, Penguin, 1961
Monberg, Torben. 'Fathers were not Genitors'. *Man*, n.s., Vol. 10 (1975), 34-40
Ortiz, A. *The Tewa World. Times, Space and Being in a Pueblo Society*. Chicago, Chicago University Press, 1969
Peristiany, J.G. *Honour and Shame: The Values of Mediterranean Society*. London, 1965
Saussure, F. de. *Cours de Linguistique Générale*. Paris, 1916
Sibisi, Harriet. 'Some notions of "purity" and "impurity" among the Zulu'. *Journal of the Anthropological Society of Oxford*, Vol. 6, No. 1 (1975)
Whyte, Susan R. 'What difference does the difference make?' Seminar paper, Institute of Social Anthropology, University of Copenhagen
Yalman, Nur. 'On the purity of women in the castes of Ceylon and Malabar'. *Journal of the Royal Anthropological Institute*, Vol. 93 (1963).

3 OPEN BODY/CLOSED SPACE: THE TRANSFOR-MATION OF FEMALE SEXUALITY

Renée Hirschon

Introduction

Most of the material on which this analysis is based was gathered through fieldwork in Piraeus, the main port of Greece.[1] I lived for over a year in a residential locality called Nea Ephesos, about a mile from the harbour, which today has within its administrative boundary a population of over 86,000 (cf. 1971 census). The district is an integral part of the metropolis of Athens and Piraeus, which together form a single urban concentration of some three million inhabitants. Until very recently Nea Ephesos always had the character of a poor district, and it remains a lower-income area although living standards have risen sharply in the past decade. It is indistinguishable from the surrounding built-up area, but its origins were distinctive. It began as a settlement for Greek refugees from Asia Minor and had a population of some 40,000 by 1934, just ten years after its founding.

The people who settled here had been part of an important minority in the Ottoman Empire, with a long history in Asia Minor, and most of them were from large, flourishing cities such as Smyrna, Constantinople. For over fifty years the oldest section of Nea Ephesos has had a remarkably stable population with three or four generations of the original families still present. The Greeks of Asia Minor shared the same culture as those in metropolitan Greece. In language, religion, customs and physical appearance those in Nea Ephesos are still basically similar to their neighbours and any differences which do exist are by and large those of detail only.

The specific focus of this paper is the examination of certain cultural perceptions of the sexual nature of women, showing how this is thought to differ from that of men. We will examine beliefs regarding their physical and biological attributes and their position as these relate to the states of 'open' and 'closed' in the symbolic order. A woman's status and her appropriate conduct can be seen to derive their rationale from the intermeshing of ideas regarding her physical nature and those concerned with her symbolic attributes. These notions are most clearly elaborated with regard to four important areas of a woman's life: her sexuality, her access to the world beyond the home, her use of time, and the control of her speech. The theme which unites these is that of control and restraint, which is exercised both externally — through social convention, and internally — as a moral force.

Sexuality

In this section we will examine beliefs regarding the biology of men and women, and attitudes deriving from them which constitute what might be called part of a 'folk physiology'. We may note that these fundamental perceptions are embedded in a culture with a long literate tradition, and are clearly reflected in life in urban localities such as Nea Ephesos.

The key to attitudes regarding men and women is the belief that the sexual drive in the adult female is subject to her control, while that of the adult male is physiologically imperative and cannot be controlled. A man's sexual needs are incontestable; enforced or prolonged abstinence from sexual intercourse is believed to have serious physical and mental consequences, possibly even leading to insanity. It seems likely that the belief in the absolute nature of a man's sexual drive derives from observation of physiological processes specific to men, such as involuntary erection and nocturnal emissions. Since there are no obvious parallels for women the attitudes to their sexual drive are different.

A second fundamental tenet is that all sexuality should only be expressed heterosexually. There is no acceptable outlet for the sexual drive of a man other than intercourse with a woman. Possible alternatives such as homosexual contact or masturbation are precluded by beliefs regarding the harmful effects of these practices (for example, once again: mental imbalance). The moral stigma and abhorrence of such acts are further deterrents. Indeed, the gravest insults to a man are expressed in these terms — that he is a 'homosexual' (i.e. the passive partner who is called a *poustis*) or a 'masturbator' (*malakas*). Ideas of this kind can be seen to underlie the well known Mediterranean emphasis on the aggressive aspects of masculinity, the *machismo* syndrome.

The need for sexual expression is recognised as being part of the condition of physical maturity in both men and women. The idea of certain mutual conjugal needs and duties regarding sexual intercourse can be elicited in discussions of instances where a wife has gone astray, and where neglect on the part of the husband is given as an extenuating circumstance on her part. A woman's sexual drive is therefore acknowledged. Indeed, the anxiety of parents regarding the early marriage of daughters is derived from this, expressed in the view that during the last years of adolescence 'the blood is hot' (*vrazei to aima*). If a timely marriage is not contracted the girl may fall victim to the natural urges of her youthful condition. The expression of female sexuality is, however, rigidly limited because of concern with the values of family honour, which is preserved by fathers and brothers, by ensuring the chastity of daughters. After marriage fidelity replaces chastity as a focus of attention and becomes the responsibility of the husband.

From the first moments after the wedding ceremony the young couple are made aware of their next immediate obligation: 'With children!' 'To a son!' they are wished (*Me tekna! Me enan yio!*). Brides are already aware of this for it is an often-stated aim of marriage that 'You get married to have children' (*Pantrevesai yia na kanis paidia*). To protect the groom from sorcery which might cause his impotence, various precautions are taken in the preparations surrounding the wedding. The fear of infertility is great, and if conception is delayed or miscarriages occur, the couple go to great expense consulting doctors and undergoing medical treatment. In addition, shrines of particular saints are visited and some of these have become renowned for the miraculous results which such pilgrimages bring (that of St Irene Chrysovalandou being among the most famous). Family size appears to have been larger in the past but younger couples now favour having only two children. The emphasis is not on having many children but on completing the full form of the elementary family through producing offspring. Childless couples have failed to achieve their full status in society and are generally pitied.

It is through its procreative aspect within marriage that sexual relations are redeemed, for, according to Eastern Orthodox ideas, sex is sanctified through the creation of children, and without it man and woman are caught in the web of Original Sin. A long tradition of Church writing elaborates these views (Sherrard, 1971), which are deeply rooted in attitudes to marriage and sex at the popular level. Sexual intercourse, for example, may sometimes be referred to as the 'evil act' (*i kaki praxis*), even by married people. Although the Greek and English words for 'bad' or 'evil' do not correspond exactly, it is worth noting this verbal usage.

Female sexuality has an explicitly procreative end. A woman's destiny (*proorismos*) it is said, is to bear children. Pregnancy is not seen as a shameful condition, as among the Gipsies (Okely, 1975, p. 67), but as the achievement of womanhood and as a reason for pride. Through childbirth, therefore, a woman redeems the fallen state of the male-female relationship and thereby also transcends the limitations of her own nature. The archetypal image of Eve represents unregenerated womanhood, its fallen condition, characterised by inherent weakness, susceptibility to temptation and a propensity for sensuality. A woman must strive to check these flaws which are deeply part of her nature, for if they are allowed free expression, disastrous consequences follow. There is no remedy once they have been manifested; the woman is doomed to lead an immoral and dissolute life and must be relegated to the category of 'one of those' (*ap' aftes*), the unmentionable women who have no accepted place in society. To the observer it is clear that this particular set of ideas constitutes a 'self-fulfilling prophecy': once the woman has erred she is rejected and finds no way open to her but to live beyond the bounds of acceptable morality, thereby providing further evidence for the stated view.

Concern with preventing the unrestrained expression of female sexuality underlines fundamental aspects of Greek social organisation. It is seen as a danger which may undermine a woman's own honour and that of her family, and also as a potentially destructive force which threatens the whole social order. She can unwittingly seduce men from their duties and commitments to their families and thus she is seen as a potential source of catastrophe (*i yinaika einai polles phores katastrophe*). There is a proverb 'Fear only three things – fire, water and woman' (*Tria pramata na phovasai mono – photia, nero kai yinaika*). In many other cultures also there is a noted connection of women with a state of disorder. From another point of view, these ideas constitute a recognition of male vulnerability and susceptibility. Belief in the power of a woman's sexuality is a complement to the belief in the imperative nature of a man's sexual needs.

In contrast to that of Eve is the holy image of Mary, who in Orthodox thought is venerated primarily as the 'Mother of God' or 'God Bearer' (*Theotokos*) (Ware, 1969). Women feel the immediate bond of a shared experience with the *Panayia* (All Holy One), as she is commonly called, and in the everyday difficulties of life they most often appeal to her. The attributes of ideal womanhood, self-sacrifice, love and devotion to the family are patterned on this archetypal figure. The inherent flaws of female nature may be overcome if actual behaviour is based on the precedent of Mary. In Greece this idea is primarily embodied in a positive emphasis on control, restraint and harmony.

Controls are of two kinds: first, those exercised *externally* through prohibitions on movement, gesture, speech and association, and second, those which exist as an *inner* moral force. We shall be dealing fully with external constraints below. Here we can note that in the second case the responsibility is the woman's, and this is the basis underlying the values of 'shame' or 'modesty' (*dropis*) which are seen as essential female qualities.[2] Through the conscious awareness of the redeeming elements in her nature she can counteract her potential for destruction. Since it is believed that, given sufficient moral quality, a woman, unlike a man, can restrain her sexual drives indefinitely with no ill effects, the question of control is simply a moral one. She is not subject to imperative physiological drives, while for men restraint is perceived as undesirable if not impossible, for reasons of his 'physiology'. 'A man cannot control himself, but a woman can last a hundred years' (*O andras then kratietai alla i yinaika – ekaton chronia na paei, borei na kratithi*).

In the conscious knowledge of her responsibilities in maintaining social order she achieves merit. An interesting reflection of these notions is the response of a wife who discovers her husband's infidelity: she will immediately seek the 'other woman' and attack her, quite often physically as well as verbally. The husband is exonerated by the fact of being a man, the erring woman has ignored her responsibility and provoked a situation which it was in her power to avoid. The innate negative characteristics latent in a woman's nature can be counterbalanced through exemplary conduct and devotion to her family's welfare. Both as daughter and later as wife, the woman should be a paragon of the family's honour. She always remains a point of vulnerability, however; if she falters or fails, then the family is ruined.

The Marriage Prescription

For both men and women marriage is an imperative. It is of primary concern to parents that a suitable marriage be contracted at the appropriate age. In Nea Ephesos, as indeed in the metropolis as a whole, there is no accepted stage of independent unmarried adulthood such as exists in Western cities where a young man or woman lives alone and is self-supporting before settling down in marriage. Both young men and women pass straight from their families of origin to their new roles of spouses, and later parents, in the family of marriage. From the point of view of the young, therefore, marriage is seen as the prerequisite to the establishment of full independent adulthood and maturity.

Girls are taught that there is no acceptable alternative to marriage. A woman's destiny (*proorismos*) is to marry and bear children, for in this state alone will she find true satisfaction and her only appropriate aspiration is to become the mistress of her own household. Among the many varieties of wishes which feature in conventional exchange, young girls are frequently urged to 'Get married and open your house' (*Pan-trepsou na anoixis to spiti sou*), while others which they hear from early ages are 'To your joys!' (*Stis chares sou*), 'Here's to a bridegroom!' (*Me enan gambro*) and 'Married next year!' (*Tou chronou pantremeni*).

The vulnerability of females outside the house is a theme in their upbringing. In all contexts marriage is presented as an auspicious state, as the only safe and appropriate condition for adulthood. In essence a girl passes from the protection of her father to that of her husband. In the ideals of this society the less she is exposed to the outside world the better. 'She's straight from her mother's arms' (*ap'tin angalia tis manas tis*), or 'She never goes beyond the front door' (*ap'tin porta tis then vgainei*), are two common ways of expressing approval of such girls. Significantly, it is her husband who will 'take her out into society' (*na tin vgali exo stin koinonia*), and only through her conjunction with him can a woman play a full and acceptable role in adult social life (see below, pp. 77-8).

It is important to note that in this locality of the city, as in a village, the position of a widow if she is under fifty is almost untenable, a fact which emphasises the importance of a husband's presence. Her every action is observed by the surrounding neighbourhood and her be-haviour must be extremely circumspect. Even so, the continual scru-tiny of others will uncover some deviation from the ideals of modesty and purity (cf. du Boulay, 1974, pp. 122-3). A recently widowed woman of forty was advised by her elderly neighbour, 'Get married again. You will never be at peace until you do' (*Pantrepsou allios then tha isichasis pote*). An older woman who had been widowed during the Occupation but remarried five years later corroborated this view, 'Don't I know it? People keep asking, "Where are you going?" "What are you wearing?" "When did you return?" Not even a tom cat came into my yard for five years. It was only when I remarried that they quietened down' (*Then to xero ego . . . Mono otan pantreftika xana isichasane*).

For men marriage is also seen as a necessary state. It is encouraged but the emphasis is slightly different. The informal age limitations for men are less rigid and they can enjoy a longer period of unmarried adulthood. As a man approaches thirty, however, public pressure en-couraging his marriage intensifies, for every man is expected to under-take the duties and responsibilities of family life. An unduly prolonged bachelorhood indicates avoidance of the full status of adulthood and suggests certain deficiencies in character: weakness, frivolity and, ulti-mately, lack of masculinity. For men the emphasis is on becoming the head of a household as well as on the creation of a family. The exhortation commonly directed at unmarried men is 'Get married so that you can have a family' (*Pantrepsou na kanis oikoyeneia*). Their principal concern, however, is to produce sons who will continue the family name. In the different wishes characteristically directed at women and men respectively, a paradigm of their symbolic relation is indicated: a woman must marry to be 'open', a man must marry to ensure continuity of his line (see below, pp. 77-9).

It soon becomes apparent that the sexual dichotomy and the separation of roles which are noted aspects of life in rural Greece have not been shaken in the context of urban life. In action and belief the separation of the sexes pervades all aspects of life in Nea Ephesos. The clearest expression of this division is the *complementarity* and *asymmetry* of male and female roles in marriage and family life, but it also extends to the environment beyond the home. Here, the separate spheres of men and women are clearly defined in economic pursuits and in religious observance respectively. A husband's duty is to provide for the material needs of the family, the wife's is to care for its spiritual welfare. In this capacity women go on pilgrimages to churches, monasteries and shrines all over the country and they make regular visits to the local cemetery to clean and care for the graves of the family's deceased. In these pursuits women do not require male escorts.

To the sexual dichotomy is added a spatial dimension: the locus of the woman is domestic, within the home, having an extension into the world beyond for specifically religious purposes, while the place of the man is primarily in the economic realm, in the outside world. In rural Greek society the opposition between the house and the natural world has been noted (du Boulay, 1974, p. 56). In the urban setting the opposition is translated into that between the 'house' and the 'road'. In the neighbourhood itself the separation of the sexes is further indicated by the areas and facilities frequented by one sex and avoided by members of the other. The men's precincts are the coffee-shop and the barber-shop; the hairdresser and the grocer provide parallel facilities for women. The cemetery is another important focus of female activity, an extension of the domestic realm since concern is for the maintenance of the grave, its cleanliness and attractive appearance. (In Greek villages the fountain was the main gathering-place for women; cf. du Boulay, 1974, p. 209.)

The clear division of the woman's domestic sphere from that of the man means that within the home their relationship is one of mutual dependence. Men are providers of items from the outside world (*o andras phernei pramata sto spiti*) and without this provision the family would have difficulty in surviving. Women play an essential role in transforming these things provided by the men into sources of comfort and nourishment. The complementarity of male and female roles in the family is summarised metaphorically: the house is likened to a bird's nest where 'the male bird brings [things to the nest] and the female builds it. The male brings grass and twigs and the female arranges the nest' (*To serniko pouli phernei, to thyliko ktizei. To serniko phernei chorta kai klaria kai to thyliko phtiagnei tin pholia*). Another metaphor is used to describe the essential presence of both men and women in the family. 'Without the woman there can be no home, it is the woman who warms the house, she is its golden quilt, covering and warming, and so she is essential. The man is the pillar of the house and its base, and he too is essential' (*Choris yinaika spiti then yinetai. I yinaika zestainei to spiti, einai to chryso paploma, to skepazei kai zestainetai. Einai aparaititi sto spiti. O andras einai episis aparaititos. Einai o stylos tou spitiou, einai i vasis*). The role of the male is to provide the necessary items from the outside world while the female's role is the creation of order within the home. This division of activity at the ideal level is a fundamental tenet of family life in the heart of the city as well as in the village. It is a value which has withstood the pressures of economic need and many actual divergences in practice.[3] In fact, the separation is even clearer here, since in village life women are inevitably drawn into the many tasks surrounding agriculture or shepherding.

An interesting feature is the fact that the separation of roles is reinforced by the conviction of incompetence: neither is competent to execute tasks other than those appropriate for his or her sex. It is firmly believed that men are unable to deal with any household chores, including washing plates or clothes, sweeping, tidying or cooking. Not only is it considered inappropriate, it is also considered 'shameful' for men to engage in these activities (*dropis einai na plenei piata o andras*). Parallel beliefs exist regarding a woman's incompetence in dealings beyond the home, especially in any business activity. There is a total correspondence therefore between the idea of what is inappropriate, what is impossible and what is 'shameful'. A woman has no place in the business world nor the man in the domestic realm, and thus, in the Greek view, they are incompetent in these tasks.

The complementary roles of the husband and wife are, however, associated with another feature: the inequality of their status relationship. The superiority of the male sex is an unchallenged notion here, and the husband's position is one of ultimate authority over his wife, as in other Greek communities. The wife is subordinate to the will of her husband and to his decisions. On the other hand, in spite of this clear and unchallenged inequality of status and authority, the influence which a woman exerts over her husband is never denied. Her subtle power is acknowledged by both sexes. 'Women are in command,' people say, 'women decide' (*i yinaika kanei koumando, ekeini orizei*). The notion of a woman's power over men has two aspects; her position in the domestic realm indicates a limited kind of authority in the home, but it is also derived from the belief that her sexual nature is a constant potential threat to a man's integrity. One woman stated it graphically enough: 'She need only wag her tail and the whole world is turned upside down' (*kounaei tin oura tis kai o kosmos paei ano kato*). The common saying, 'Everything depends upon the woman, she can make her husband or she can ruin him' (*ola exartontai apo tin yinaika, ekeini phtiagnei ton andra i ton chalaei*), is a strong but veiled reference to her sexual nature.

For their part, women take pride in their ability to manage their husbands. They must develop special diplomatic skills in dealing with the men of their families, first with fathers and brothers, and later with their husbands and sons. This ability to influence and manipulate people, especially husbands, women refer to as their 'manner'. 'I have my way', a woman says (*echo ton tropo mou*). But in the presence of men women rarely refer to it since the skill itself is that of persuading a man to adopt a point of view or course of action while allowing him to believe that the initiative is his. Even among women this topic is not discussed and any attempt to elicit what constitutes the 'manner' or 'way' fails to gain any clear explanation.[4]

The notion of a woman's power residing in her sexuality presents a paradox when compared with ideas regarding the relative status of the sexes. Women, it is said, belong to the weaker sex (*adynato phylo*) and are seen as 'always inferior' (*panta katoteres*). These cultural axioms are seldom discussed or challenged; women accept these just as men do. This intrinsic inequality in the relation of the sexes is of great importance for, although the complementarity of their roles implies a mutual dependence, the woman is ultimately dependent upon her husband. A woman's position in society depends solely upon her conjunction with a man. As a girl, she is in her father's care and, once adult, she only has access to society through her husband.[5]

It is significant in this respect that women speak of their domestic life in the idiom of 'obligation'; 'I have my obligations,' women usually say when they account for the way in which they spend their time, referring to housework and family duties (*echo tis ypochreoseis mou*). At first sight this may not appear very significant but, when viewed in the context of exchange and the structural dimension of relationships, it highlights the asymmetrical statuses of men and women. A woman's position in society depends upon her husband and family, and so she is in a sense 'indebted' to them for her social existence. The nature of this debt is such that it cannot ever be fully discharged; her commitment is total and absolute for there is no alternative open to her except marriage and, once she attains this state, selfless execution of her duties is demanded. For both sexes marriage is not only desirable but an essential stage in the achievement of full adult status. But for women an added dimension exists in her ultimate dependence upon a man, her husband, for her access to the social world.

With regard to sex itself, married women's attitudes characteristically express indifference and boredom. Women believe that all men have the same sexual capacities and thus extra-marital affairs are doubly incomprehensible and aberrant. 'All men are the same,' women say, 'so why go with another?' (*Ephoson einai oloi oi andres idioi, yiati na pas me allon?*) They conclude that women who err in this way have an inherent moral and constitutional flaw; they are of 'bad constitution' (*kaki pasta echoun*). Even in harmonious marriages and those based on love, only the husband may demonstrate affection or flirtatiousness in front of others and any open sign of coquetry on the wife's part is not acceptable. A wife who shows feelings for her husband in which an erotic element can be discerned is criticised. Katina's excitement, for example, at the news of her husband's impending return from sea after eighteen months' absence and her undisguised longing to meet him was considered vulgar. The couple had been married for fifteen years and had three children. Neighbours and relatives ridiculed her, saying, 'She's waiting like a bride' (*san nyphi perimenei*). As her husband appeared to share her joy, they concluded that the couple were 'both crazy' (lit. 'rabid') (*lyssasmenoi kai oi duo*).

From the middle years of their lives, husband and wife should not be bound by erotic love. The appropriate emotion which they should share is that of *synnenoisis*, a common understanding and ability to come to agreements. Marriage is seen as a co-operative effort and it is a working arrangement essentially, based on the complementary roles of husband and wife and their relationship of mutual (if asymmetrical) dependence. Romantic love is a notion foreign to the accepted basis of marriage. The pragmatic nature of the marriage bond is clearly revealed in the intense and interested nature of dowry negotiations. In old age the spouse is often described as a *syntrophos*, a companion or comrade, who provides company against the state of loneliness (*monaxia*) which is the lot of the widowed or single person. But the term *syntrophos* does not indicate the sharing of mutual interests or personal communication, for the individual compatibility of the spouses is not an important consideration in marriage.

The Open/Closed Opposition in the Symbolic Order

The nature of woman and her role in Greek society is clarified further by examining the perceptions already discussed in the wider context of the symbolic order. Among the conceptual categories of the society is a set of perceptions surrounding two opposed states: that of the 'open' and that of the 'closed'.[6] As ideal conditions these present two antithetical modes of orientation; in the full context of social life, as we shall see, modification and compromise take place.

In its ideal sense 'opening' is an auspicious state; it is propitious and desired. 'Closing' is associated with misfortune, it is unfavourable and, in its ideal sense, should be avoided. 'Opening' is related to sets of positive notions regarding social life and sociability, while 'closing' suggests an abhorred state of isolation and the absence of contact and association. In Greek society, prestige and reputation, which are the measure of the individual's merit and that of his family, depend upon the opinions of others. Hence social life in all its aspects is vital, while withdrawal and isolation are equivalent to social death. Significantly the most effective way of indicating disapproval and of dealing an insult is to 'cut off the "Good morning" greeting' (*na kopso tin kali mera*). To engage in verbal conflict – or even to come to physical blows – is a recognition of the other's existence (cf. Coser, 1956). The strongest sanction is to ignore one's opponent and thereby effectively deny his social existence.

The generally auspicious nature of the state of 'openness' is revealed in many and varied usages and contexts, some of which may be mentioned here. A state of joy, for example, is expressed as 'having one's heart opened' (*anoixe i kardia*), while the opposite, a 'closed heart' indicates sorrow, and response to misfortune. It is used in the connotations of 'luck' (*tychi*), for it is said that important events occur and decisions about the future are made when one's luck is 'open'. If a person has been unsuccessful in contracting a marriage, for example, the conclusion would be that 'his/her luck has not yet opened' (*then anoixe i tychi tou akoma*). In association with the metaphysical and supernatural realm this notion of opening is also present. Communication can take place when there is no barrier and the way is open. Thus prayers and requests to saints are answered when 'the heavens are open' (*anoigei o ouranos*).

In sharp contrast are the many negative connotations associated with the state of being 'closed' and of 'confinement'. Its generally unfavourable quality is revealed in the common word *stenachoria*, inadequately translated as 'depression, worry, vexation'. Its literal meaning is that of lack of space, a narrow or cramped area. A person in this mental state is typically in low spirits, subdued and turned in upon himself. Much can be said about the high value placed on sociability in Greek society. Company with others has an intrinsic value, solitude is abhorred and the personality type most approved is that of the 'open' and 'warm' individual, while someone described as 'closed' is also seen to be 'cold' (cf. Hirschon, 1976, p. 358). In contexts where sorcery is discussed its unpleasant effects are said to 'bind' the victim: someone who is under a spell is 'bound' (*demenos*), many spells are described as 'binding' and they include the action of tying. Notably the action of absolving persons from their sins is expressed, in a Biblical passage, in the same terms – loosening and binding.

The perceptions regarding the 'open' and the 'closed' are most interestingly revealed with regard to the sexual dichotomy, providing another dimension to the complementary opposition of the sexes which has already been explored. In the context of this symbolic ordering, the *asymmetrical* relationship of the sexes is clearly expressed. For women the state of 'openness' is highly auspicious but only in the condition of marriage and domesticity and specifically in conjunction with one man, her husband. The man is the medium through which this propitious state of 'openness' can be attained. We have seen how a compound image is employed for marriage from the woman's point of view – the idiom is that of 'opening a house', not only in the formalised wishes directed at unmarried girls, but also in everyday usage. The 'open' aspect of marriage denotes two related states, the first being the achievement of full adult status through the establishment of a separate household after marriage.[7] Contained in this notion is the synonymity of the 'house' and the 'family' (cf. du Boulay, 1974, pp. 17-20). In essence the opening created by marriage is that by which a new social unit is brought into existence; the creative dimension of 'openness' is a central and fundamental one.

A second aspect of the 'open' state which marriage entails is that of sexual union and of child-bearing, one of its explicit aims. For the woman a fusion of 'quasi-physiological' and metaphorical notions are expressed. People describe the effects of marriage on a woman's body in these terms, 'her body opens' (*anoigei to soma tis*). This is said to account for the change in her figure, which characteristically tends to become fatter. In Greek culture plumpness is taken as a sign of prosperity and happiness, hence the physical as well as the emotional changes are seen reflected in the woman's body. I have heard these ideas summarised in this way: 'After you marry you are at ease and you get fatter – the body opens, that's why' (*Otan pantrevesai isichazeis, pachaineis – anoigei to soma, y'afto*).

In the specific context of child-bearing the notion is appropriate, since it is the woman's body which opens to allow for growth and finally to bring forth the infant. 'Opening' thus has a close association with creation and with new life, and it is significant that the word for the season of spring, the season of growth and resurgence, is *anoixis*. It seems clear therefore, that the idiom of 'opening' is one which conveys both the idea of social existence, and the physical renewal of life itself.

For the woman this auspicious state can only be achieved through conjunction with her husband; the notion of a woman's 'obligations' and her indebtedness to her husband and family stems from this symbolic association (see above, p. 74). His role as a medium of opening for the woman is not only a physical one, but exists too in the context of sociable exchange beyond the family. A woman cannot be 'out' in society alone, and she is always dependent on a man, as a daughter before marriage, and as a wife thereafter. The position of the young or middle-aged widow illustrates the cultural problem of the unprotected woman; she is an anomaly, and even a 'threat to the community' (du Boulay, 1974, p. 123).

For women, marriage holds the promise that she 'will go out into society' (*tha vgi stin koinonia*), and it is one of her husband's obligations that he 'takes her out once in a while' (*na tin vgali exo kammia phora*). Husbands feel this obligation and, at intervals which vary depending upon the family's means and the husband's conscience, he will suggest taking her out for an ice-cream or pastry at one of the neighbourhood confectioners, or to visit relatives or *koumbaroi* (spiritual kinsmen). Women who have been busy in the home look forward to being taken out. They are by no means secluded within the house but they frequently characterise their daily lives in terms of 'confinement' (*kleisoura*).

Just as 'opening' is effected for a woman through the man, so the family itself depends upon the man to preserve its social identity. In the context of death and the family, the essence of the 'closed' as inauspicious is revealed, significantly, through the absence of men. Social access and communication are permitted through the man's presence, and more fundamental, the family's continuity through time is assured through the birth of male children. The concern with male heirs is expressed as the desire for the male name 'to come out' (*na vgi to onoma*).[8] This verbal usage suggests again the importance of the external or open manifestations, in terms of 'coming out'. In contrast, when an only son dies and the parents are too old to have another child it is said that 'the house has closed' (*ekleise to spiti*). At the time of the death of Alexander Onassis, the shipowner's only son and male heir, this idiom was used by people commenting on the tragedy. The death of an only son is perceived as 'closing', since the continued existence of the family, through the survival of its name in forthcoming generations, has ended.

The inauspicious state which results from the absence of the men of the family was also revealed at the time of the Cyprus crisis. The Turkish Army's invasion of the island in July 1974 provoked the general mobilisation of the Greek Army. Women from all over the city gathered at the harbour of Piraeus and at the railway stations to bid their husbands and sons farewell. A commonly heard cry was 'Now we close our houses' (*Tora tha kleisoume ta spitia mas*).

Redemption, or the Construction of Virtue

Up to this point, we have examined these modes of orientation as ideal types, or as pure states, where the propitious condition of being 'open' is counterbalanced by the inauspicious state of being 'closed' and its allied conditions of 'confinement' (*kleisoura*) 'constriction' (*stenachoria*), and 'binding' (*desimo*). In the context of social interaction and everyday life, however, an element of ambiguity enters into these notions. They become qualified in terms of person and of social context. For those who in terms of cultural notions are vulnerable beings, the state of being 'open' must contain an element of danger in certain contexts. This affects the situation of women and children, since they both have the same quality of vulnerability in relation to life beyond the family. For them being 'open' could be an exposure to potentially harmful forces while 'closing' may be a precaution against misfortune. The ambivalence of these states is linked to the sharp opposition between the home and the outside world, which is itself associated with the sexual dichotomy and the allocation of roles appropriate to each.

The woman's role in Greek society is founded, as we have seen, upon perceptions regarding her physical nature. The emphasis on control and restraint is an underlying principle in the definition of her role and in the assessment of her virtue. Through her adherence to precepts regarding her activities she may achieve merit and redeem the in-built flaws of her nature. In this section we examine how these restrictions are elaborated in three areas: her movement and comportment outside the home, her use of time within it, and the control of her speech.

1. Space and Danger

In the urban environment the outside world is presented in the image of the 'road'. It is perceived as an area of dangerous forces holding all the temptations which threaten the vulnerable individual's moral purity, thereby jeopardising the family's honour. Since the road is the most likely place for a woman to meet unscrupulous persons, it is natural that seclusion for women is seen as an appropriate condition. Virtuous girls are described as being 'of the house' (*tou spitiou*) before their marriages, and they are not expected to carry out errands in the neighbourhood on a regular basis. In the road a woman may encounter bad company and other distractions which lead her away from devotion and commitment to her home and family. Here she may be approached by unscrupulous men who are intent upon trapping women, who will lead them astray by false promises of marriage (if they are young) or attempt to press their attentions upon them if they are older and married. However, if a girl does complain of being followed or pestered, she will most likely be admonished for not having observed suitable comportment. Since seclusion is not practicable, there are clearly defined conventions regarding a woman's movements outside the home. Even on short trips to the bakery and while shopping in the neighbourhood a woman's pace should be brisk and her demeanour serious. Loitering, standing alone and gazing around with a pleasant expression are ways of inviting adventure and misfortune. Girls and women who conduct themselves in this way are strongly criticised for their foolishness and lack of sense.

Women who have lost their reputation and who are considered irremediably immoral are called 'of the road' (*tou dromou*), which is also a way of describing wild and undisciplined children. In both cases such conduct sets a bad example which challenges the ideals of family life. It is in the road that a child playing with others will learn bad habits, dirty language and undesirable knowledge, all of which undermine the purity and innocence which are the natural attributes of childhood. A closely related idiom is used for very young children who are allowed to spend long hours out in the neighbourhood, even when accompanied by their mothers: they are 'learning the side streets' (*mathainoun sokkakia*), people comment disapprovingly.

It follows, therefore, that at times when the vulnerability of women is at its peak, when she is most fully 'open', her total seclusion within the house is considered to be essential. The two occasions in a woman's life when this occurs are the auspicious events of marriage and of child-birth, and the traditional ritual practices which marked these transitions serve as paradigms, as we shall see. In Nea Ephesos today the ritual observances associated with the new bride are no longer practised, but seclusion for the newly delivered mother, called the *lechona*, is still widely observed, although to varying degrees. The *lechona* and the new-born infant are kept confined to the house, which is closed to outsiders for a period of forty days. The period is terminated by a short ritual service in church during which the mother and child are blessed by the priest.[9] Nowadays, when women cannot always rely on the presence of close family to help them with their errands, mothers of new babies may have to go out to the neighbourhood shop, but they will always avoid entering it and will stand outside on the doorstep and ask for their purchases to be brought to them.

The older women who recall the customs of their youth when seclusion both for the bride and for the new mother were strictly observed practices, point out the connection between these events: 'How could the new bride go out? She was kept in the house for the first days just like a *lechona*. The bride and the *lechona* are similar — they have to be careful' (*Pou na vgi i nyphi — mes' to spiti itan tis protes meres san tin lechona. I nyphi kai i lechona einai paromoies — prepei na prosechoun*). The connection between the bride and the newly delivered mother is evident in terms of the symbolism of the 'open'; their situation serves to clarify the dual nature of this state. Although there is no doubt about the auspicious nature of 'opening' in marriage and in creating new life, this is perceived in terms of an ideal state. In the total context of life in the social world (which is by nature a fallen world), ideals are refracted and motivations compromised. For women the value of the 'open' is dependent upon context, and its auspicious aspect exists only if contained within the family headed by her husband. The house is the environment where she can experience this state; it is her realm. The woman's use of space is defined and restricted in terms of the domestic imperative.

2. Time and Temptation

The conventions which specify a woman's activity are very clear with regard to her use of time, and again the locus is primarily a domestic one. For Greeks a woman's ability as a housewife is of paramount importance and is an indicator of a married woman's prestige and reputation. The first major criterion by which a wife is judged is her proficiency in maintaining cleanliness and order in and around the house. Diligence and hard work are highly valued, while laziness is abhorred, for it results in the neglect, dirtiness and disorder of the home. The emphasis on the creation and preservation of harmony is a theme which recurs in the ideals associated with womanhood. It is most clearly defined with respect to her housekeeping ability. A somewhat extreme case illustrates the fundamental importance of this criterion: a young man divorced his wife after a year of marriage because 'she was not a good housekeeper, she was dirty' (*then itan kali noikokyra, glitsou itan*). This reason was given by people who had known the couple, and by his close family. They never criticised the girl's character — indeed they all agreed that she had a 'good heart' (*kali psychi*). He remarried, and the second wife proved to be highly competent in the home. She was admired for this, but even while praising her people noted that she was a conceited and envious woman (*phantasmeni, ziliara*).

The second main expression of domestic competence is the provision of nourishment for the family. Much can be said about the association of women with food in Greek society. It is a fundamental notion elaborated in various contexts, from the emphasis on dining-room furniture as part of the dowry provisions to the 'food battle' which characterises the mother-child relationship when discipline has broken down (Hirschon, 1976, pp. 101-2, 141-2). Housing arrangements in Nea Ephesos are also revealing in this respect. The dowry provision in the form of a 'house' is often more accurately only a separate living area of one or two rooms in a shared dwelling. In spite of overcrowding (in several cases three or four elementary families live under one roof) the provision of a separate kitchen area, however small, is a clear priority for each married woman (Hirschon and Thakurdesai, 1970). The separate kitchen area symbolically marks the existence of an independent household, and emphasises too the woman's primary role in providing sustenance for her family.[10] This association undoubtedly derives from the suckling bonds of the woman with her children and she continues to be seen as a source of sustenance throughout her life. The wife is solely responsible for the purchase, preparation and offering of food and drink, a concern which extends beyond the needs of living members of the family to include the preparation of ritual food (*kolliva*) at various occasions during the year for the deceased. It is the medium by which hospitality is offered, even to the most casual visitor, and it is always the woman's duty to offer the drink and sweetmeats (*kerasma*).

Although a woman's activities do not concern general economic matters and she may not take the initiative regarding most kinds of expenditure, the intimate connection between women and sustenance overrides this demarcation. It is a matter of her judgement alone how the household money should be spent for the weekly groceries. In those families where husbands spend Saturday mornings at the central market of Athens doing household shopping the men are always following their wives' instructions, for both spouses acknowledge that this is the realm where the wife 'is in command' (*kanei koumando*).

A woman's domestic duties are extremely time-consuming, then, and this is a feature of great significance. The logic of the dictates regarding a woman's time is clear: she should be fully occupied around the house to prevent the possibility of temptation. The desired reputation for being a 'good housewife' (*kali noikokyra*) depends upon maintaining objectively very high standards so that constant effort and long hours must be devoted to household duties every day. It is interesting that the preparation of food, so important a part of the wife's role, also has this time-consuming characteristic. Most dishes involve a number of steps and require careful attention to detail. Stuffed vine leaves, *dolmades*, and *moussakas* are just two well known examples of this genre of cooking, but many other dishes are similarly intricate. The older women explain that quickly prepared meals indicate laziness or ignorance of proper cooking methods. Far worse, though, they leave the housewife free time in which she might easily get into mischief. Significantly, in time past, any such quickly prepared dishes (*procheira, tis oras*) used to be called 'prostitute's food' (*tis poutanas to fai*) by Greeks in Asia Minor.

The value of 'saving time' is not part of the indigenous system of thought, therefore, and all modern labour-saving devices directly challenge the set of notions regarding a woman's correct and appropriate occupation. The rhythm of the day centres on the house, on the preservation of order within it. After the daily cleaning and making of beds (bed linen is aired daily), the remaining hours of the morning are spent in preparing the day's meals and then in making one of the great variety of preserves or sweetmeats from fruit which is an essential ingredient in offering hospitality to a visitor (the *kerasma*). A quick trip to the bakery or neighbourhood grocer is a permitted interruption in the morning round of household chores. In any free time which may remain, usually following the afternoon siesta, the wife occupies herself with handwork, for a high value is placed on her ability to crochet, embroider or knit. 'A woman needs to have handwork' (*to ergocheiro chreiazetai stin yinaika*), people say, and it is seen as an essential complement to a woman. It is another measure of her competence and a means whereby a woman can improve her reputation by impressing those around her with her skill. A woman's time must be spent in and around the house. The dictates of her domestic role reinforce the limitations on her movement beyond the home. The restrictions which are implicit in the woman's use of space and of time are directed at reducing her exposure to dangers and temptations to which, by nature, she would be susceptible.

3. Speech and Disorder

The third area of cultural concern related to the woman's nature is her verbal capacity, and it is one other criterion employed in the assessment of her virtue. A woman's speech is held to be dangerous, her words may be irresponsible and likely to have disruptive consequences. It is referred to usually as 'tongue' (*glossa*) and sometimes as 'mouth' (*stoma*); one of the most damning criticisms of a woman is that 'she has a tongue' (*echei glossa*).[11]

In essence, having a bad tongue has two main implications: verbal outbursts in anger or irritation reveal a lack of self-control, the importance of which we have already noted, while the content of gossip is likely to damage social relationships. Through the uncontrolled use of words a woman may upset the home environment and jeopardise the unity of the family; through gossip and irresponsible chatter she may provoke ill-feeling, discord and trouble in relationships within the neighbourhood. In both cases the result is that of disruption of what should or would, in the conceptual and ideal sense, be ordered and harmonious.

A woman's capacity to create trouble and disruption through words must be counterbalanced by her controlled and quiet demeanour. While men have the right to resort to outbursts of irritation and anger, it is incumbent upon the women to keep silent. Again the responsibility rests upon the woman. The preservation of harmony and order can be achieved through the conscious exercise of restraint over a dangerous aspect of her nature. A frequent injunction to women is 'Don't say anything at all' (*Min milas katholou*), no matter what the injustice of the husband's words.

The ability to control her tongue is clearly seen to be one of the most important assets of a woman, equivalent even to all the other qualities which characterise ideal womanhood — with the axiomatic exception of sexual purity. To 'have a tongue' is so greatly abhorred that even if the woman is highly regarded in all other respects, her reputation is jeopardised when it becomes known that she suffers from this fault. A typical assessment of such a case was that expressed about an energetic and efficient housewife who was devoted to her children: 'Tasia has everything, she's a good housewife, her house is well kept and her children cared for. But with that tongue of hers she loses everything' (*me tin glossa tis ta chanei ola*). Another case illustrates how severe a fault this is: a man had practically abandoned his wife and family and had taken up with other women. Public opinion did not blame him, however — his wife was known in the neighbourhood for her sharp tongue and quarrelsome ways, and people concluded that 'He leaves the house because of her tongue' (*Phevgei ap'to spiti yia tin glossa tis*). So serious a fault is this that it may even spoil a girl's chances for marriage; it was the reason given for the fact that Koula, aged 36, was not married. Even her mother lamented her daughter's 'bad mouth' (*askimo stoma*), saying that men had heard about this fault and would not consider her as a wife.

We have seen in this section how the definition of the woman's role rests upon the explicit limitation of her movements, her use of time, and her speech, and that these ideas are founded in perceptions of her physical nature. These ideas are revealingly conveyed in a now obsolete *rite de passage*, which provides a pattern of values related to the woman at an auspicious moment of her life. This old Asia Minor Greek custom which marked the first period of the bride's life had been experienced and was recalled by the oldest women. Proof of a bride's virginity was provided by the examination of the sheets used on the wedding bed while severe restrictions were imposed on her movements and her speech. For the first week the bride was not allowed to leave the house, and for the first few days she was supposed to keep total silence. Both restrictions were formally removed. On the eighth day after the marriage, normally a Sunday, her husband took her out for the first time to attend the morning liturgy in church and then to a festive meal at the home of the *koumbaros* (wedding sponsor). Her total silence lasted for only two or three days and was formally broken when one of her husband's family decided to 'get the bride to speak' (*na miliso tin nyphi*). He would present her with a small gift and she would respond, saying 'Thank you', the first words to break her silence. This act is itself significant in the context of the obligations implicit in gift-giving and its implications of relative status (Mauss, 1969). The restrictions which marked the period of the bride's incorporation into her new family present a paradigm of concerns regarding a woman's nature. Her subordinate status was impressed upon her by the imposition of restrictions and symbolically by the receipt of a gift which allowed her to utter her first words. Her movements were restricted and confinement in the house emphasised the priority of her domestic role. It suggests too the vulnerability of her position at this stage, presenting the fundamental dichotomy of the 'home' and the 'outside world' which plays so basic a part in the orientation of the woman's activities.

Conclusion

We have attempted to elucidate in this paper the inner logic underlying the definition of the woman's role in Greek society. It is founded in perceptions regarding her sexual nature and elaborated in terms of more general categories of symbolic space. Both her physiological and social conditions are related to the ideal states of 'open' and 'closed', of 'auspicious' and 'inauspicious'. She is seen to be both dangerous and vulnerable. The problem that this poses is resolved in the belief that her sexual nature, unlike a man's, is conducive to restraint. Moral responsibility devolves upon her. Consequently, in the assessments of a woman's virtue, self-control and restraint are persistent themes. The aspects of her behaviour which provoke especial concern are any expressions of her sexuality, her movement, her use of time and her verbal capacity, all of which are bound in by conventional dictates specifying her acceptable conduct.

The relationship of the sexes is that of complementary opposition. Associated with this is the spatial division between the 'house' and the outside world, or 'road', which defines the appropriate locus for female and male activity. Their relationship is one of mutual dependence but it is also marked by the asymmetry of their statuses. In terms of the ideal states of 'open' and 'closed', women are dependent upon men to attain fully auspicious 'openness' while men are always and ultimately superior in structural and symbolic terms. For women the limitations imposed upon their actions reflect the ambiguity of these symbolic states when translated into social terms. Woman's nature is interpreted by culture, her role is defined by this combination.

Notes

1. This material has been presented fully in my D.Phil thesis (Hirschon, 1976). Besides this period of field-work, personal experience has added much to my data and interpretation, for I have lived in Greece for several years and have now married into the society. I am indebted to my Greek family and friends for their role in socialising me, and to my University colleagues and teachers, particularly Dr J.K. Campbell, for guidance in making sense of my experience.

2. Literature on Mediterranean societies has been much concerned with the values of 'honour' and 'shame'; see, for example, with reference to Greek culture, Peristiany, 1965; Campbell, 1964; and du Boulay, 1974.

3. Employment of women has been a feature of life in Nea Ephesos from the first days of settlement. It is not an accepted activity for women, however, even today, and is justified in various ways, discussion of which lies beyond the scope of the present paper.

4. In this regard, as in all other aspects of life, 'women experience the world differently from men' (S. Ardener, 1975, xviii). The problem posed in that volume regarding alternative models remains unanswered in the Greek context. Models presented in this paper are those to which both men and women subscribe, and which constitute the 'dominant model'.

5. Notably a woman's surname in Greek is always given in the genitive (possessive) case: *o Kyrios Mavros, i Kyria Mavrou*, which can be rendered 'Mr Black, Black's Mrs'. This applies equally to her maiden name, so that she is her father's; i.e. 'Smith's Miss' conveys the Greek form *Despoinis Chalkia*.

6. This can only be a summary description of these symbolic categories and a much fuller analysis is possible. There are indications that these categories may transcend cultural boundaries (see, for example, mentions in Cunningham, 1973, p. 231; Rheubottom, 1976, p. 23).

7. Immediately after marriage the young people set up as an independent social unit, even if residence is on the same plot or in the same dwelling as the bride's parents, as a result of present dowry provisions (cf. Loizos, 1975). The independence of the elementary family is an unshaken principle, however. See Hirschon, 1976, pp. 154-9.

8. Concern is for the continuity of the Christian as well as the surname. Male Christian names are repeated in alternate generations: by custom the paternal grandfather's name is given to all first sons. Thus the eldest males of a group of agnatic first cousins have the same Christian name. They are each distinguished by their second name which is their patronymic.

9. Seclusion following childbirth is undoubtedly also related to a belief in ritual pollution. In this paper the emphasis is on other aspects of female nature.

10. The association of the woman with the hearth has been noted in rural Greece (Campbell, 1964, p. 151; du Boulay, 1974, p. 133) and in other cultures (Yalman, 1967, p. 102). Yalman, for example, describes the Kandyan household and the separate cooking place of each married woman. 'The cooking area is private . . . All else may be shared but granaries and cooking places may never be shared' (1967, p. 102).

11. The connection between the mouth and the vagina is made in psychoanalytic theory, and it has been noted that 'there is a strange unconscious neuromuscular association between the vagina and the mouth. . .' (Kitzinger, 1967, pp. 118-21).

Bibliography

Ardener, Shirley. 'Introduction' in Shirley Ardener (ed.), *Perceiving Women*. London, Malaby/Dent; New York, Halsted, 1975

Campbell, J.K. *Honour, Family and Patronage*. Oxford, Clarendon Press, 1964

Coser, Lewis A. *The Functions of Social Conflict*. London, Routledge and Kegan Paul, 1956

Cunningham, Clark E. 'Order in the Atoni House' in Rodney Needham (ed.), *Right and Left*. London, University of Chicago Press, 1973

du Boulay, Juliet. *Portrait of a Greek Mountain Village*. Oxford, Clarendon Press, 1974

Hirschon, Renée. 'The Social Institutions of an Urban Locality of Refugee Origin in Piraeus'. Unpublished D.Phil. thesis, University of Oxford, Oxford, 1976

—— and Thakurdesai, 'Society, Culture and Spatial Organization: An Athens Community'. *Ekistics*, Vol. 30 (1970), 187-96

Kitzinger, Sheila. *The Experience of Childbirth* (rev. ed.). Harmondsworth, Penguin, 1967

Loizos, Peter. 'Changes in property transfer among Greek Cypriot villagers'. *Man*. n.s., Vol. 10, No. 4 (1975), 503-23

Mauss, Marcel. *The Gift*, trans. Ian Cunnison. London, Cohen and West, 1969

Okely, Judith. 'Gypsy Women: Models in Conflict' in Shirley Ardener, 1975

Peristiany, J.G. 'Honour and Shame in a Cypriot Highland Community' in J.G. Peristiany (ed.), *Honour and Shame: the Values of Mediterranean Society*. London, Weidenfeld and Nicolson, 1965

Rheubottom, D.B. 'The Saint's Feast and Skopska Crna Goran Social Structure'. *Man*, n.s., Vol. 11, No. 1 (March 1976), 18-34.

Sherrard, Philip. 'The Sexual Relationship in Christian Thought'. *Studies in Comparative Religion*. Vol. 5, No. 3 (1971), 151-72.

Ware, Timothy. 'The Communion of Saints' in A.J. Phillipou (ed.), *The Orthodox Ethos: Studies in Orthodoxy*. Oxford, Holywell Press, 1964, pp. 140-9

Yalman, Nur. *Under the Bo Tree*. California, University of California Press, 1967

4 WOMEN, TABOO AND THE SUPPRESSION OF ATTENTION

Caroline Humphrey

Taboo

There are innumerable injunctions as to what constitutes incorrect or improper behaviour for women in Mongolia. Many of these rules have the status of taboos, in other words categorical prohibitions (*tseer*) whose breach would bring extreme shame and fear of supernatural punishment. But this does not mean that women appear socially paralysed in everyday life. To the casual observer it would be difficult to tell that the prohibitions exist, and he might simply note that women seem to have their own way of doing things. This points clearly to the area I wish to investigate in this paper, the fact that taboos, although phrased in the negative, always and necessarily imply some kind of positive action. If one act is forbidden, people do something else. The existence of a taboo means that behaviour in that particular field of action is 'marked' or significant, and therefore the acts which substitute for taboos, or are performed instead of them, should not be seen merely as 'ordinary' behaviour, as opposed to tabooed behaviour. They should be looked at carefully, both in their own right (because this is after all what people actually do), and in their crucial relation to the forbidden act. This relation of prohibited acts to allowed acts within a given sphere of action is present in all cultures. But it is easier to discuss and perhaps, in fact, is more important in cultures such as that of the Mongols, where the minutiae of daily life are greatly formalised, usually by categorisation into named types of acts. We, for example, think of 'sitting' as comprised of numerous unspecifiable variations on one basic idea of body posture, but the Mongols divide 'sitting' into six different types; if one is forbidden to sit in the *xölöö xiizh suux* manner (i.e. with legs stuck out straight in front) one nevertheless has to decide on another way, perhaps *söxörch suux* (i.e. with knees together on the ground and the weight on the ankles) or *tsomtsoix suux* (i.e. with one knee up and the weight on the ankles of the other leg), and so on.

It is important to recognise that relatively few taboos are universally applicable to all categories of people in society. We should remember that straightforward structuralist analyses, of the kind proposed by

Mary Douglas (1966), and Tambiah (1969), have only really been
applied in those few cases. Their concern was with what in a system of
ideas becomes taboo, and the question of to whom the taboos apply is
pushed into the background. Theirs is a static logic of classification,
essentially context-free. My concern on the other hand is with the
implications of usages in respect of taboo, and its obverse, correct
behaviour, for modes of relationship in particular contexts of action as
these change through the life cycle. This is much closer to Leach's
approach in his paper on 'Trobriand Clans and the Kinship Category
Tabu' (1962), as opposed to his work on ambiguous categories and the
mechanism of taboos.

For my theoretical purposes it seems essential to introduce not only
the idea of domains of 'marked' actions, which are indicated by the
existence of taboos, but also to introduce the *subject* or *agent* for
whom acts are prohibited or allowed. To return to the Mongol types of
'sitting', *xölöö xiizh suux* is not taboo in an absolute sense, being
quite appropriate relaxed behaviour for men amongst themselves,
but it is utterly forbidden to young married women; *söxörch suux*,
which is a suitable way of sitting for young married women, would be
considered a shameful posture for an elderly man. In this paper the
subject I take is women. The category of 'women' as subject in this
kind of analysis will have to be subdivided later by the three phases, as
the Mongols see it, of a woman's life, but as a starting-point we shall be
dealing here with the following essentially related elements: (a) women,
for whom certain behaviour is prohibited or allowed; (b) taboos and
prohibitions specific to women; and (c) the positive actions taken by
women.

Mongolian Names Which Must Not Be Pronounced

The material of this paper refers to the period before collectivisation,
that is, before the 1950s (although I shall sometimes use the 'ethnographic present' tense). Awareness of socialist political ideas had eroded
some of the taboos among the more urbanised Mongols long before
this, from the 1920s onwards. But in the countryside the prohibitions
continued in force and many linguistic taboos were retained in the
fifties when other traditional injunctions (e.g. in dress) were falling into
disuse.

This paper will be concerned mainly with linguistic taboos, specifically terms of address, because I have more material on this than on
other fields such as gesture, dress and food, but I should emphasise at
the start that the patterns within all of these domains appear to be
correlated with one another in a consistent way.

The linguistic taboos of the Mongols occur within the sphere of naming, and the prohibitions specific to kinship groups in everyday life should be seen in this more general context. All Mongols avoid casual reference to the names of dead people, predatory animals and certain mountains, rivers and springs, which are considered to be inhabited by spirits, and which in the past have caused various natural catastrophes. It is thought that the casual pronunciation of these names would catch the attention of the spirits with possible disastrous consequences to the speaker. In ordinary speech there are standardised alternatives for such names: almost all tabooed mountains, for example, are called *xairxan* ('dear one'), with the result that maps of Mongolia made by travellers are peppered with this name in a most confusing way. It is possible, however, to use the real name in ritual contexts when the mountain is being addressed and offered sacrifices in order to avert disasters to the community.

The taboos which especially concern us here, however, are those which occur among people who are related to each other through the male line (agnatic kin), specifically within the kin group called *törel*. In general, the names of seniors of either sex, reckoned by relative generation and age, are not used in address by juniors, although they may be used in reference. In the latter case such names are usually slightly disguised (Dugar becomes Düger, Gombo becomes Ombo, etc.). In order to address seniors, a junior person can either use a kinship reference term such as *abaga* ('father's brother') or, if the relationship is a more familiar one, he or she can use one of the honorific kinship address terms. I shall describe these in more detail later. This prohibition on the use of the names of seniors does not, however, amount to a taboo; it is more a matter of respect and decorum, a custom which is followed without the notion of very serious consequences if it were to be broken. Seniors, on the other hand, can use the personal names of juniors freely. This differentiation between seniors and juniors should be seen in the context of the general use of honorific words and expressions in dialogue between people of different status. In Mongol many common words, particularly for parts of the body and physical actions, have honorific variants, and these should be used by juniors while speaking to seniors, although the senior uses ordinary language in return.

In one specific case the prohibition on the use of names has the status of a taboo: the *ber* (the wife of a younger brother, of a son, or of an agnatically related nephew) is absolutely forbidden to use the names, either in address or reference, of her *xadamud* (her husband's older brothers, his father, his father's brothers, grandfather, etc.). The taboo includes the names of the wives of close *xadamund*. The *ber* is also prohibited from mentioning the name of her husband's patriclan. Furthermore, she is strictly enjoined not to use any word in ordinary language which enters any of the forbidden names or sounds like them. This taboo was taken very seriously, and even today when honorific language is considered to be 'un-socialist' and is used only in private by old-fashioned people towards respected lamas and teachers, the prohibitions and taboos on names within kin groups are still largely current.

Mongol Names

To understand what these taboos imply it is necessary to know something about Mongol names. Children are given one personal name shortly after birth, either by their parents or in former times by a lama. Names are chosen according to the particular conditions affecting that child and they always have meaning. Broadly speaking, there are two types of names, one which consists of good qualities or symbols for positive values (e.g. the Mongol, Tibetan, or Sanskrit words for 'Happiness', 'Strength', 'Calm', or symbols such as 'Axe', 'Flower', 'Eagle'), the other type being names which are designed to deceive spirits (e.g. 'Nameless', 'Not-like', 'Who knows', or 'Animal', 'Smelly', 'Goat'). Names are thought to represent something of the essence of the person, and the pronunciation of a name in a sense brings that person into being even if they are physically absent. The names aimed to deceive spirits are called *tseerlesen ner* ('names which have been tabooed'), the idea being that the would-be real name is never mentioned and therefore never comes into being, and the person is meanwhile called by a substitute deceit name. In this case the deceit can also be carried beyond naming into ordinary speech. For example, a mother, whose child has been called 'goat' because the family is afraid that spirits will attack it, will say not 'My child is crying', but 'My goat is baa-ing' (Sodnom, 1964, p. 61).

After a year or two children are frequently given a nickname by their parents. This refers to their appearance or personality (*Aman Zunday* = Big Mouth; *Delden* = Long ears; *Nomxon* = Quiet; *Bülten* = Pop-eyes, etc.). These names generally are no longer used in address after the child enters adolescence. They may be employed to refer to a person, although considered to be insulting. Adults frequently acquire further nicknames (*Noxai Sharav* = Bad-tempered Sharav; *Yamaan Sharav* = Jangling-voiced Sharav; *Ulaan Damba* = Red-cheeked Damba, etc.), which come to be used by people when talking about their juniors and equals.

In Mongolia names class people as individuals, not as members of categories. Thus a name given to a child should not be the same as any other name in the agnatic kin group, although it is true that a father occasionally uses part of his name in forming the names of his children. If it happens that two people in a community have the same name it is forbidden for them to pronounce their common name. They call one another *am'dai* (*amindai*), which is derived from the word *am'* meaning 'life' or 'breath'. They are mutually *xetsüü nert* (i.e. 'having a difficult name'), this being the expression which is used to refer to anyone whose name one is forbidden to say. People say, 'One name is one ear' (*Ner negtiin chix neg*) (Sodnom, p. 34) and therefore even outsiders cannot use the *am'dai* name on its own but have to differentiate the two individuals by adding clan names to each expression of the name.

The idea that each individual should have one name which if possible should be unique has resulted in an immense proliferation of Mongol names which encompass many, though obviously not all, aspects of their culture. Related to this is the internal complexity of Mongol names, the majority of which are built up of several components which are thought to 'go together'; *Ariuntsagaan* (pure + white), *Baatarchuluun* (warrior + stone), or *Tumennasanbayar* (thousand + age + happiness). Names composed of five or six parts are not unknown.

The Daughter-in-Law's Dilemma

Consider the implications of this for the unfortunate daughter-in-law (*ber*). She must memorise the names of all of her senior male affines and cannot use them, or any of their constituent parts, either when referring to the seniors, or to other people with the same name, or when selecting the vocabulary of her everyday conversation. The taboo still applies even when the *xadam* has died, and even when the *ber* goes home to visit her own family. She must find substitute words on every single occasion. It is not surprising that some linguists have described this phenomenon as a 'women's language' among the Mongols (Aalto, 1959, 1971). This claim is unjustified, since the differences affect vocabulary only and do not touch on syntax, and in any case only certain categories of women are involved. But nevertheless it is clear that the speech of the women observing the name taboos is constantly required to be markedly different from that of everyone else.

The exercise is seen as a trial of the daughter-in-law's training and quickness of wit. Young girls are told myths and stories in which the new wife of a prince is given a brain-teaser by her father-in-law as a test of her taboo-avoidance abilities. In one of these stories the father-in-law goes out to herd his sheep and finds a ram hanging from the stump of a lone elm-tree at the head of a brook. He goes home, and knowing that there are people called *Usan* ('water'), *Modon* ('tree'), *Xonin* ('sheep'), *Xuts* ('ram'), *Chono* ('wolf'), *Ilzhig* ('donkey'), and *Numan* ('bow') amongst his agnates, he calls to the daughter-in-law, *'Ber ee!* I have lost a fat white ram from my flock. Go and look for it!' The daughter-in-law goes out and searches in the steppe and at last comes across something glimmering at the foot of an elm tree; it is the head of the ram, and a wolf is trotting off into a gully. She goes home and says,

> I found the thing you were looking for. At the head of the current beside the growing-thing is the sticking-out one who is older brother to the bleater; the howler has come along and eaten it up. Why don't you mount the sticking-out-ears and take your shooter and go and see what is up? (Sodnom, p. 61).

This is one of a well known type of story among the Mongols. According to Roberte Hamayon, who has done long periods of field-work in Mongolia, fathers-in-law do sometimes test their daughters-in-law by trying to catch them out, or by setting up further arbitrary word taboos which are not already included in the forbidden list of names (Hamayon and Bassanoff, 1973, p. 54).

Looking at the phenomenon of name taboos more closely, it is possible to make the following observations. First, in practice not only the proper name is tabooed but also titles and descriptive names. For example, if the father-in-law's name is Nyam, but he is commonly called Aduuch Nyam (horse-herdsman Nyam) the daughter-in-law still has to find another word for 'horse' (*aduu*) as well as a substitute for Nyam. Second, the deliberately polluting or absurd names used to deceive the spirits are treated with just as much circumspection as other names. For example, the female affines (of the daughter-in-law category) of a man called Baast ('with faeces' or 'shitty') were required to use the word *xomool* ('horse-dung') when talking about what was in fact human faeces (Tserenxand, 1972, p. 60). Third, words which merely sound like the name, as well as the components of the name itself, are tabooed, even if the meaning of the homophone is completely different. Thus, a woman whose own mother-in-law was called *Tegsh* (meaning 'level' or 'flat') also tabooed the word *tevsh* ('wooden platter') and substituted for it *ix tavag* ('large bowl'), (Sodnom, 1964, p. 63).

We can conclude from these facts that the taboo is not attached to the proper name *per se* in its capacity of representation of the inner essence of a person. It is attached to words which have the function of names in the crucial respect of having the capacity to attract the attention of the person named. Further proof of this is the fact that while homophones of names can be tabooed synonyms never are (see list below).

As for the words which the *ber* decides (or is required) to substitute for the tabooed words, the first observation we can make is that they are standardised within local communities, but often include dialect words and tend to vary over Monoglia as a whole. In Xovd Aimak the substitute for *gal* ('fire') was *zel* (presumably a dialect word, in the general language 'tethering-rope'; see Tserenxand, 1972, p. 60) while in central Mongolia and among the Khorchin Mongols the substitute was *tsutsal* ('spark'). This pattern indicates that while no overall system exists within the language with regard to tabooed words, an important requirement is that the substitute words should nevertheless be understandable within the community. In other words, the daughter-in-law cannot pay out her father-in-law by talking gibberish, nor can she exercise independence by inventing totally original substitutes.

If we look at the following randomly selected list of tabooed names and words, it is clear that the substitute word is by no means always a synonym for the word it is supposed to replace.

Table 4.1

Name	Tabooed Word	Substitute Word
Ornyn Tseveen ('Tseveen the deputy'; **oron** = job, place: Tseveen – Tib.)	**orox** = to enter	**shurgax** = to penetrate, jump in, insert oneself (Sodnom, 1964, p. 63)
Shar (shar = yellow)	**shar** = yellow	**angir** = a species of diving duck, yellow coloured (ibid., p. 64)
Xazai	**xazaar** = bridle	**nogt** = halter (loc. cit.)
Galzuud (galzuu = rabies, madness)	**gal** = fire	**tsutsal** = spark (ibid., p. 65)
Sandag (Tib.)	**saya** = million	**toot** = 'having number' (Tserenxand, p. 60)
Bayadaa (bayad = West Mongol clan)	**bayan** = rich	**uyen** = ermine (loc. cit.)
Xarzuu (xarax = to look at)	**xar** = black	**bargaan** = darkish, obscure (Kuo-yi Pao, 1964, pp. 287-8)

We can conclude that it must always be obvious that a tabooed word is in question when the *ber* uses one of the substitute words, since she will always be talking somewhat oddly on these occasions. One can imagine her saying, 'Shall I put the cooking-pot on the spark?' In other words, her kinship status as *ber* in a given household is constantly being made obvious by her linguistic choices.

It is clear even from this short list that the substitute words are quite distinct from the tabooed words from the phonemic point of view. Instead of employing the sort of devices used by other kinsmen (i.e. non-*ber*) when referring to people whose names are tabooed in address, regular slight deformations of the name (Ombo for Gombo, Eren for Tseren, etc., and many other similar small additions or subtractions from the name), the *ber* herself must choose a word which sounds quite different, that is, one that is made up of different component morphemes, even at the expense of semantic exactitude. This practice is what we should expect if the aim is not so much to substitute a synonym for a tabooed word but to suppress the *sound* of the tabooed word altogether. This supports my theory that it is the attention-catching function of names which is at issue here. But I should point out that not all similar-sounding words in everyday language are automatically tabooed. For example, while in the case of the name Sandag, the word *saya* ('million') is tabooed, *saya* ('only just') is not. This could perhaps be explained by the fact that *saya* ('million') is a different part of speech from *saya* ('only just') and hence is usually spoken with much less emphasis and a different intonation. But this is probably not the case with many similar-sounding words in Mongolian, some of which may be tabooed when the homophones (like-sounding words) are not. Therefore, it is clear that what we are dealing with is not a complete ban on all sounds homophonous with the set of recognised fathers-in-law's names — which would render the daughters-in-law's lives linguistically impossible — but a formalised and socially determined rule which *stands for* such a complete ban.

Naming and Address — A 'Marked Domain' of Taboo

At this point it is worth saying more clearly how the taboos observed by the *ber* fit into the more general system of naming and address among the Mongols. First of all it should be emphasised that the *ber* is the only kinship category to extend name taboos into general speech. Indeed, the verb from *ber, berlex*, has the meaning 'to observe linguistic taboos'. Incidentally, this verb has other meanings which are relevant to the argument of this paper; the first is 'to be ashamed, shy, or confused', and the second is 'to perform services for a respected person'. There are five regular differentiating features of the Mongolian address system.

(1) There is a distinction between second-person pronouns *ta* 'you' (senior), and *chi* 'you' (junior); this is exactly like the distinction in French or Russian, where the respectful form is the same as the plural.

(2) Kin reference terms are also used as terms of address; this can occur in own and senior generations, and junior generations of the mother's brother's lineage, and is a sign of respect and formality.

(3) Intimate honorific address terms are used. These are very different phonetically from the reference terms and are instantly recognisable by the fact that they commonly consist of two repeated sounds, e.g. *dziadzia, gagaa, nyanya, möömöö*. Many, if not all, of these terms can be applied to several categories of kinsmen. For example, some people told me that they call the paternal uncle *dziadzia* while others said the term is used for the older sister. The very similar term *adziaa* has an even wider spread, being used not only for any senior male of the kin group and respected lamas, but also for the father and mother, and any male or female friend of the family of the parents' generation. It is apparent that families sometimes invent their own variants of these terms, as it were from the baby speech of the children. Probably the use of these terms was more formalised and specific at the beginning of this century, since Aberle (1958) for the Kalmuck Mongols and Kuo-yi Pao (1964, p. 307) for the Khorchin Mongols were both able to give lists of terms with the kin categories they were applied to, and they were both working with early-twentieth-century material. It seems that many of these terms are like our 'granny' or 'grandad', in that they are sometimes used by people in the community who do not stand in a grandchild relation to the person addressed. As a general set, these terms thus combine respect with intimacy and with local knowledge. Outsiders to the community do not use these terms, and it seems clear that they *could not*, since each family has different conventions for their application.

(4) The fourth category of the Mongol address system is the use of nick-names. These are used in the family circle by seniors for children up to the age of about ten. If they are used in address after this age, and particularly for adults, this is an insult.

(5) The final possibility is the use of personal names. Names are not used in any circumstances for the generation above the speaker and can be used for older siblings only in combination with

the reference term, e.g. *Damdin* (name) *axa* (older brother). However, the special honorific address terms are more common for older siblings. Names can be used for younger siblings of the speaker and people of descending generations.

To sum up: there are two ways of addressing kinsmen senior to the speaker, by reference terms and by special honorific terms, the former being more formalised than the latter. The *ta* version of the second person is used with both of these. There are also two ways of addressing junior kinsmen, by names and by nicknames. The *chi* version of the second person is invariably used with both types of name.

The totality of this address system is a domain within which *actual* usages are marked (significant) in relation to *potential* usages, including those which are forbidden. But it is impossible to understand the meaning of actual usages by citing only the rules in the abstract, since such rules are only generalisations after the event. In order to understand the total system it would be necessary to describe the social contexts in which every subject is speaking. In this paper, however, I am looking specifically at Mongol women and shall only sketch in the contexts in which men operate. I shall argue that women's modes of address, although occurring within the total set of social relations which are dominated by the male descent system, should not be seen merely as an epiphenomenon or a reflection of more fundamental social relations: they are *as themselves* an important means by which the system is reproduced.

The Mongol Local Community

Mongols in the central nomadic zones, at the time to which my fieldwork relates, lived in small encampments of two to six tents, each tent being the home of a nuclear family. (Collectivisation, which took place in 1959-60, has subsequently altered the settlement patterns and living arrangements to a great extent, cf. Humphrey, 1974). The core group was the patrilineal extended family, with dependants, friends and servants camped alongside. Sometimes two or three unrelated men joined together, but usually the pattern was of a nomadic grouping of brothers or of a father and sons. In the more settled farming regions on the fringes of China and in parts of Buryatia the extended family included more people and was more stable, since sons could not easily move away. Nevertheless, even in these areas pressure on pastures and fields forced some men into migration. In the greater part of Mongolia, which was nomadic, sons could easily move away. There was thus a constant tension between the desire to keep the agnatic group together for economic and political reasons and the prestige of its headman, and the belief of individual herdsmen that they might be better off economically somewhere else.

Women moved between agnatic groups, being born into one group and becoming wives in another. Those very few exceptions who did not marry and remained with their fathers were considered to be bad omens, and after they reached the age of forty or fifty were called *shavgants*, 'lay-sister' or 'nun'. Kuo-yi Pao reports that they were thought to attack newborn babies and eat their flesh (1964, p. 40).

Some girls, usually only when a man had no sons, made an uxorilocal marriage, and were able to inherit their fathers' property for their own lifetimes. In these cases, the incoming son-in-law was adopted by the girl's father, often at an early age, but the girl remained the head of the family, the property being held in trust for her children. It is interesting that the position of the son-in-law in uxorilocal marriage was in many ways parallel to that of the daughter-in-law in normal virilocal marriage. He had similar low status, and was expected to work for his parents-in-law, but, however, was not required to observe the extension of name taboos into ordinary language. In other words, he avoided his parents-in-law's names in address, just as did all people of junior generation, but he could use the names in reference and did not have to taboo similar-sounding words.

Women in Context

1. The Girl

The first context of a woman's life was her girlhood at her parents' home which lasted until she left to become a wife. A daughter at home was treated with far more indulgence than a son. One man said that fathers did not reprimand their daughters because they realised that they would start having hard lives as soon as they married into their husbands' families. Sons, on the other hand, had to stand straight before their fathers and say *'dzee!'* when replying to questions. This is a word implying absolute obedience and was formerly used by servants when replying to their masters. A daughter could even joke with her father, and she also had a warm relationship with her mother.

Although girls did not have a position in the status hierarchy of their lineage of birth (cf. the Khorchin saying *'oxin xün üye ügei'*, 'a daughter has no generation') (Kuo-yi Pao, p. 290), they were considered to be its property. A girl's reputation and the bride wealth she gained were a matter of common concern. In some Mongol groups this sense of property applied even in a sexual sense. Among the Western Buryats, for example, a special party was held for a bride in her own settlement on the eve of the wedding. She was expected to tour the homes of the young men of her own community in the company of her girl-friends and it was not anticipated that she would remain a virgin.

An unmarried girl thus had a privileged position in the generally formal, reserved, and rule-laden Mongol family environment. To recall the mōdes of address, it is apparent that a girl's prevalent mode in these years was informal: she would use the intimate honorific terms (*dziadzia, mōōmōō,* etc.) for older kin, and nicknames for the few people junior to herself (her younger siblings).

2. The Young Wife

The second context is that of the young wife in her husband's family, this stage lasting until her own children were old enough to marry. A young married couple had their own tent, but the wife was required to do all the housework for her parents-in-law in the *ix ger* (the 'big tent' of the camp). She was required to rise first in the morning and go to bed last at night, to be always occupied and never be seen to rest, and to be always ready to perform any task required of her. She was not allowed to eat together with the men and senior wife of the group, but neither was she allowed to save a bit of food for herself to eat after they had finished; she could have only what was left over. She was subject to an extraordinary number of regulations in dress, comportment, orientation and the like, of which I shall mention only a few. One set of rules was concerned with maintaining a calm, almost blank demeanour. She was not allowed to raise her head, to laugh, to cry, to sing without being asked, to grind her teeth, or make any noise when eating. A second range of prohibitions forbade the slightest hint of her sexuality, especially when in the presence of the father-in-law or other men of the *xadam* category. She always had to wear a hat in his presence, do up all her buttons, pull down her sleeves over her wrists, never show her knees, never be seen undressing, or urinating or defecating, never feed her baby at the breast in front of her father-in-law, never comb her hair in public, and always hide away her own personal clothes in a special box (Hamayon and Bassanoff, 1973).

Childbirth and menstruation were both polluting. According to Petri (1925) the Buryats saw childbirth, particularly the blood of childbirth, as the more dangerously polluting of the two. A pregnant woman, on the other hand, was not impure, and she was not subject to the restrictions imposed on menstruating women or women who had just given birth. Among the shamanist Buryat a pregnant woman could even attend rituals normally reserved for men only. This was because she was able to attend in the capacity of bearer of a yet unborn son of the lineage. A woman herself was always polluting in her reproductive functions.

In all situations where status was measured, such as the distribution of meat, the *ber* could expect the most humble portion. It was expected, in fact it was considered right, that she would appear both tired and hungry.

It follows from this that she could expect little help from any of her affines. The father-in-law had little to do with her, and instructions he issued were usually transmitted as commands through the mother-in-law: 'Tell that girl to do such-and-such!' The relationship with other senior male affines, even the husband's brothers, was almost as formal and distant. With the mother-in-law a woman was expected to behave with great respect and was required to say *'dzee!'* when addressed by her. The mother-in-law ran the households of the camp, and it was the daughter-in-law's duty to follow her instructions. The husband's younger siblings, especially his sisters, were not friendly either, and would tease a young bride unmercifully. Kuo-yi Pao (p. 290) explains that this was because of jealousy at the incoming women taking away their brothers.

The young wife's relationship with her husband was particularly ambiguous. Husband and wife had to maintain an attitude of indifference in public, and a wife had to avoid use of his name in address. In reference she could use the name, but only by disguising it by changing the vowel-harmony (*Dugar* became *Düger,* etc.). A wife addressed her husband as *ta,* while he called her *chi* and could use her name (Aberle, 1958, p. 54). Generally, a wife avoided calling her husband anything and attracted his attention by exclaiming *'xui!'* ('hey!').

It was considered a disgrace for a husband to neglect his parents' or agnates' interests in favour of his wife, and a man had to take special precautions to avoid seeming dominated by his wife in case he be despised and criticised. For example, when a man went away on a journey he did not greet his wife on his return, but first bowed to the family altar and then gave an account of his journey to his father. His wife should make no sign of her happiness that he had returned, otherwise her sister-in-law would tease her; she should remain calmly at work. However badly a young wife was treated, her husband was the last person who could help her. Even an appeal to his own siblings or to his mother might lead others to think he was over-influenced by his wife.

A daughter-in-law had to be careful to avoid saying anything which might affect the relationship between her husband and the rest of the agnatic group. In particular she had to be careful not to act as a wedge between her husband and her mother-in-law, because the mother-in-law was the only person in the family who could legitimately protect her. Brothers often quarrelled over matters of property and prestige, but a young wife was not supposed to intervene even if her husband appealed to her. She should say, '*taden türsen ax-düü xoyolaa xereg namad xamaa ügei*' — 'things between you and your own born brother have nothing to do with me' (Kuo-yi Pao, 1964, p. 285).

A wife's position improved after she had children, particularly sons, but even so, neither she nor her husband could intervene if senior members of the agnatic group punished her children (Vreeland, 1954, p. 55). Among some Mongol groups, if the young wife got on well with the family, the father-in-law would lift the restriction of her sitting north of the fireplace and walking round the back of his tent (two particularly irksome restrictions), and she would be known as *darxan ber* ('freed daughter-in-law') (Badamxatan, 1965). It is interesting that among the western Buryat, where the *ber* was the wife of a politically important man, her more distant *xadam* relatives could 'refuse' the relationship. The *xadam* in this case ritually took off her hat and did some other previously unthinkable act such as urinating in front of her and thereafter the *xadam/ber* prohibitions were at an end between them (Petri, 1925, p. 31). This has not been reported for the Khalkha Mongols, where political position more nearly coincided with genealogical position.

After her marriage a woman's relations with her own family continued to be warm and informal, and she was allowed to visit them annually after the 'new year'. A girl's father gave her an endowment (dower) of cattle soon after the marriage, and these remained her own property. At each visit to her father she was given presents which could include more cattle, and her husband and children were treated with great indulgence. The gifts increased her father's prestige, by demonstrating his wealth and his generosity. However, her own family would not encourage her if she wished to leave her husband. As a last resort, a wife could run away home taking her wealth with her, but she might well be forced by her father to return to her husband's camp.

3. The Mother-in-Law

The third and final context of a woman's life was when she herself became a mother-in-law. By this time, since the Mongolian expectation of life was until recently fairly short, a woman's own parents-in-law were probably either dead or retired into a religious and other-worldly old age. The mother of a grown son was now part of the senior generation. She hastened to find a bride for her son to carry the burden of household chores, and her role thereafter was to direct activities, particularly in acting as a mediator between the senior men of the lineage and the incoming junior wives. Her increasing identification with her husband's lineage was really on behalf of her sons. This in turn altered her relationship with her own natal family. If she had previously been a favourite daughter returning home for a few days of indulgence, she now became, together with her son, more like an interloper, entitled to ask for things, but being given them only with some reluctance. In her husband's household, on the other hand, she was now accorded the privileges of seniority, including eating and sleeping in the place of honour, being served first and greeted first by people entering the tent. Her own name was now almost never uttered, since the senior agnates were no longer around.

Thus we can say that the junior wife's characteristic mode of address was formal: primarily she used the kinship reference terms, since virtually everyone she was in contact with was senior to her, although she could use names for her husband's younger siblings. The senior wife, on the other hand, would use personal names on most occasions, since she was surrounded by her own children and their spouses. For grandchildren she might well use the teasing nicknames.

Kinship and Property

What I have been discussing up to this point has been the developmental process within the family from a woman's-eye-view. Certain essential socio-economic actions which take place between men, such as bride wealth, have been ignored up to now. As a system (i.e. the cognitive realisation of the dominant structure), Mongol kinship is coherent only when seen from the point of view of men, whose interest it appears to reflect. The agnatic group entered into relations with other similar groups to exchange women and bride-wealth. Rules of eligibility of spouses, always in general established by men (who were the guardians of genealogies) prevented the marriages of daughters or sisters to men of the groups from whom mothers or wives had recently been taken. The kinship reference terminology divides agnatic groups into five categories outside a man's own patrilineage (*torelmüüd*): (1) the groups from whom his mother, his father's mother, father's brother's mother, etc., had been taken (*nagatsnar*); (2) the descendants through women of this group (*bölner*); (3) the group from whom his wife has been taken (*xadam*); (4) the groups giving spouses to his children (*xud*); and (5) the descendants through women of his own agnatic group (*zee*).

In the Mongol system non-reciprocal usages of address (i.e. *ta* and reference terms from one side, and *chi* and names from the other) establish the mother-giving groups (*nagats*) as superior to him while the daughter-receiving groups (*zee*) are junior. Moreover, a far greater interest is shown in the differential status of women-givers (that is mothers/wives/daughters-in-law givers), each of which have a separate term. The descendants of the women of a man's patrilineage, on the other hand, are all called *zee*, whatever generation they belong to.

I see this imbalance as closely related to the distribution of property. At marriage a substantial, previously agreed-upon bride-wealth is paid by the husband's entire agnatic kin group to the woman-giving agnatic group before the wedding can take place. The amount is frequently more than the total property of one nuclear unit. The wife brings with her a different kind of property as a dowry, not cattle, but jewels, clothes and utensils, which have been prepared by women and pass between women. After the marriage, however, the bride's family, as already noted, can give her large numbers of cattle as an endowment (*inj*) which belongs to her alone. The amount is determined by her father at his own free will. In rich families it can equal the bride-wealth, and further instalments can be given when the bride visits her home with her husband and children.

If we recall that the aim of the senior men of a patrilineal group is to keep the families together so that they personally can enjoy the management of a large pool of property, it becomes clear that incoming wives are dangerous points of potential defection from the group. In a nomadic society such wives are individual centres of independence, each with their own small accumulation of property. If, on the other hand, they are kept under control, they can be seen as points whereby the sources of wealth of affinal groups can be tapped for the benefit of the agnatic group as a whole.

It should be pointed out here that leadership in the agnatic group is at odds with property inheritance within it. The headship passes collaterally from brother to brother before it descends to the next generation in the person of the eldest son of the senior brother. Property, on the other hand, goes lineally from father to son. There is thus a tendency for brother to split from brother as soon as there has been a division of the father's property, and the leadership pattern can be seen as an attempt to counteract this. The in-coming endowment of each wife from a different source is a constant stimulus to independence for each man, since this property is in theory his wife's alone and not disposable by the agnatic group. It is in this context that I would say that the love of the young couple for one another is a direct challenge to the authority of the patrilineage, since it might inspire the man to promote the interests of his nuclear unit over those of the larger group.

The terms of address and the rules of interpersonal behaviour in the family are ideological and practical means of preventing the defection of younger men. One facet of this is the enforced submission of the sons, so that they do not demand an early division of the father's property. Another is the negation of the influence of young wives on their husbands, which lasts until women begin to act in the interests of their own sons, who still have to inherit from the seniors of the group and be allotted bride-wealth. Just one example, which clearly represents the ideal structure of the extended family, is the sitting pattern at meals of the Korchin Mongols in the 1920s. The senior man and his wife sat at one table in the place of honour together with their unmarried children, and each of the married sons sat at a separate table with his own unmarried sons. The women, apart from the senior wife, cooked and served the meal, and then ate and fed the small babies after everyone else had finished (Kuo-yi Pao, p. 31).

Conclusion

In conclusion, I shall give an answer to what seem to me two crucially and inextricably related questions: first, why is such peculiar cultural weight, or ideological distortion, placed on the relationship between the *xadamuud* (father-in-law, senior male affines) and the *ber* (daughter-in-law, in-marrying junior women)? And second, why does this take the form of taboos on personal names and the homophones in everyday speech?

Take the second question first. Earlier in the paper I made a series of observations on the name taboo. Personal names in Mongol culture class people as individuals, not categories. Titles, descriptive names, deceit-names (and probably even nicknames) are also tabooed. Homophones are tabooed, but synonyms (i.e. words which mean the same as the name but sound different) are not. I conclude that what is at issue here is the suppression of attention. It is clear that the *sound* of the words involved is very important, and my explanation for this is that personal names, and words which are phonetically similar to the name, not only attract but *compel* the attention of the person addressed. If we look at the whole domain of address, it is clear that personal names have this quality to a greater extent than either special intimate address terms or reference terms used in address. The former do not compel attention because each term can be attached to several categories of kinsmen and women. The latter are less compelling for a different reason: their relativity. Unlike a name, a reference term used in address is not absolute but invariably includes the speaker. Thus a woman does not look up when someone calls 'Mother!' unless it is the voice of her own child calling.

Mongols do not name certain people (nor, indeed, dangerous rivers, wild animals, dead ancestors, etc.) directly because to speak the name aloud does not merely make the named-one look up, as it were, but actually focuses attention on the pronouncer of the name. It is to avoid such potentially dangerous focusing on oneself that each person takes care not to say the name. So what the name taboo between the *xadamuud* and the *ber* establishes is that the father-in-law (and other senior males) will not have his attention compelled by the daughter-in-law, and *refuses* to focus his thoughts on her.

Now the first question: why is the emphasis placed on taboos for the daughter-in-law in particular? If we recall the life cycle of Mongol women it will be remembered that in the beginning of their lives, as unmarried girls, they are identified as junior members of their natal lineage, as belonging to that lineage even if they have no political rights in it. At the end of their lives, as mothers-in-law, women are identified with their husbands' lineages by virtue of their status as mothers of sons in those lineages. These two assessments coincide with the real interests of women in these positions in this patrilineal politico-economic system. Identification with the two lineages appears also in the use of address terms by women at both of these stages, since in both cases a woman's predominant mode of address is the informal, inclusive mode of people who belong. As a young girl, she uses the intimate but honorific special terms (*möömöö, adziaa*, etc.) for seniors, and nicknames for juniors. As a mother-in-law she uses names and nicknames for juniors, and is herself addressed as *möömöö* or *adziaa*.

The period of the taboos, on the other hand, coincides with the middle stage of women's lives when they are *in fact* a danger to the father-in-law's group because their own loyalty and interests are divided. While endowment-cattle are still coming through from their own natal group they cannot yet identify totally with their husband's lineage. Sociologically and psychologically, however, the important point is that a young married woman is already an adult. She lives independently from her natal unit and has control of her own property. There is an imbalance here with the position of a young married man, who still lives near his father and is under the authority of the seniors of the local group. This imbalance constitutes the structural aspect of the daughter-in-law's power.

The threat to the father-in-law is constituted not so much by the daughter-in-law's own ambiguousness of feelings as by her emotional power over her husband. Until he reaches a position of authority himself in the agnatic group he may be tempted to place more importance on his own nuclear unit and even escape the power of the senior agnates by physically moving away. Conjugal sentiment must therefore be trodden down. It is consistent with this that taboos related to sex (between father-in-law and daughter-in-law) are so important, because the *xadamuud* must not recognise the power of what they are trying to suppress. All of the daughter-in-law's marked behaviour in many different domains is governed by the prohibition on her exciting or provoking the father-in-law. Her positive behaviour is such that she must *be seen* to be observing the taboos, for example by using peculiar language. She must not focus attention on herself by saying the *xadam's* name, so that *he* should not be betrayed into revealing an interest in someone whom his own agnatic ideology insists on suppressing. The extension of the taboo to words sounding like his name is a paradigm of the relation: attention is involuntarily attracted by the sound, and the father-in-law must not be compelled.

If this theory is correct, then what I have said should apply to other patrilineal societies where the agnatic group is subject to similar pressures and where personal names have the same kind of function. Junod's material on the Ba-Thonga gives at least one example of the same kind of taboos on names and their homophones (Junod, 1912, pp. 236, 357). There may, of course, be cultures where the hearing of a sound pattern similar to a personal name does not compel attention. And there are, perhaps, cultures where compelling attention by using names is not linked to ideas of power as, for example, among egalitarian hunters and gatherers. However, the nexus of relations I have outlined here does seem to have general significance in patrilineal, non-egalitarian societies. This encourages me to repeat my conviction, expressed earlier, that such taboos are not merely incidental phenomena to be separated off under a heading such as 'symbolism'. They are social practices which are integral to the systemic reproduction of kinship groups.

Thus there is a sense in which, in nomadic societies (or other situations such as labour migration) where men may be absent from the

local group, it is *women* who define the agnatic group by practising
name taboos for a certain range of men, whether they are present,
absent, or even dead. In this way the 'negative' observance of a taboo
in fact requires linguistic acts which have positive social consequences.

Note

I would like to acknowledge the helpful advice of Dr Terence Turner and Dr
Esther Goody in preparing this paper.

Bibliography

Aalto, P. 'Uber die Kalmückische Frauensprache'. *Studia Mongolica*, tomus I,
    Ulaanbaatar (1959)
———. 'Frauensprachliche Erscheinungen im Mongolischen'. *Zentralasiatische
    studien*, 5 (1971), 127-38
Aberle, D. 'The Kinship System of the Kalmuk Mongols'. *University of New
    Mexico Publications in Anthropology*, No. 8, Albuquerque (1958), 30-1
Badamxatan, S. 'Xövsögöliyn darxad yastan' ('The Darkhad people of Xövsögöl').
    Studia Ethnographica, tomus III, Fasc. 1, Ulaanbaatar (1965), 171-2, 184
Douglas, M. *Purity and Danger: An Analysis of Concepts of Pollution and Taboo.*
    London, Routledge and Kegan Paul, 1966
Hamayon, R., and Bassanoff, N. 'De la difficulté d'être une belle-fille'. *Etudes
    Mongoles*, cahier 4, Paris (1973), 54
Humphrey, C. 'Inside a Mongolian Tent'. *New Society*, October 1974
———. 'Mongol Herding Collectives and their Role in the National Economy' in
    Development and Change. Sage Publications, 1978 (in press)
Junod, H.A. 'The Life of a South African Tribe'. Neuchatal, 1912, I, pp. 236, 357
Kuo-yi Pao. 'Family and Kinship Structure of Korchin Mongols'. *Central Asiatic
    Journal*, Vol. ix, No. 4 (December 1964), 287-8
Leach, E.R. 'Concerning Trobriand Clans and the Kinship Category Tabu' in Jack
    Goody (ed.), *The Developmental Cycle in Domestic Groups.* Cambridge,
    Cambridge University Press, 1962
Petri, B.E. 'Vnutri-rodovye otnosheniya u severnykh buryat' ('Intra-clan relations
    of the Northern Buryat'). Gublit, Irkutsk, 1925
Sodnom, Ch. 'Mongol xüniy neriyn tuxay' ('On Mongol Proper Names'),
    Mongolyn Sudlalyn Zarim Asuudal. *Studia Mongolica*, tomus IV, Fasc. 15,
    Shinzhlex Uxaany Akademiyn Xevlel, Ulaanbaatar (1964), 61.
Tambiah, S.H. 'Animals are good to think and good to prohibit'. *Ethnology*,
    Vol. VIII, No. 4 (1969), 424-59
Tserenxand, G. 'Xödöö azh axuyn negdelchdiyn örx ger, ger axuy' ('The house-
    hold and the family among members of co-operatives in the rural economy').
    Studia Ethnographica, tomus IV, fasc. i, Shinzhlex Uxaany Akademiyn Xevlel,
    Ulaabaatar (1972), 60
Vreeland III, H.H. *Mongol Community and Kinship Structure.* HRAF Press, New
    Haven, 1954, p. 55

PRIVILEGED, SCHOOLED AND FINISHED:
BOARDING EDUCATION FOR GIRLS

Judith Okely

Theoretical and Methodological Questions

The public school[1] has moulded a large proportion of the dominant
male élite in British society, as well as their wives and mothers. It has
also had a wider influence and has affected, albeit elusively, the alternative state form of schooling. While we find considerable research into
public schools for boys,[2] there is little serious investigation of the girls'
schools, nor indeed of the larger topic of gender differentiation in
education.[3] It is assumed either that girls' boarding-schools are replicas
of those for boys, or that they are of peripheral importance. The male
and female institutions are not analysed as parts of one system. In
addition to the studies of boys' schools, we have a plethora of auto-
biographies by men, while little comparable information exists from
women, since few achieve the status which calls for an account of
themselves.[4]

Statements about the educational achievements of 'the middle class'
have tended to conceal their gender bias. Certainly some middle-class
girls attend schools, boarding or day, of high academic quality, which
encourage independent careers for their pupils. But there are
other middle- or upper-class girls who are denied this, and *precisely
because of their class*. The development of a distinct class consciousness is seen as more important than scholarship and achievement for
them, as are beliefs which maintain the boundaries of their class. The
girls are protected for a future marriage contract within an elite whose
biological and social reproduction they ensure. They have no economic and political power independent of males such as their fathers, and
later their husbands and sons. Born into a privileged and powerful
élite, the women learn to live ambitions only vicariously through men.

The girls' school may be, invisibly, a preparation for dependence,
while the boys' school is more visibly a preparation for independence
and power. Some of the lessons of a girls' boarding-school carry un-
certainties, or are inapplicable in later life. There is greater continuity
for boys who, for example, are not confronted with the marriage-
career dilemma which, for girls, becomes a source of conflict within
their identity as female. In the boys' education, self-confidence, the

experience of leadership and ambitious expectations are what count. Paradoxically, academic qualifications may not be crucial for public-school boys who, even if they do not progress to university, often move into lucrative and prestigious occupations not made available to their sisters with possibly equal potential. The girls' expectations are circumscribed by marriage.

The boys' and girls' educations are not symmetrical but they are ideologically interdependent. That considered female is partly defined by its opposite: that which is considered to be male. The characteristics of one institution are strengthened by their absence in the other. Qualities primarily reserved for one gender will have a different meaning in the institution for the opposing gender. The two educations are also linked in practice since, in adulthood, individuals from the separate institutions will be united in marriage, for the consolidation of their class. As members of the same social class the girls and boys may share similar educational experiences, but as members of different gender categories some of their education may differ. This aspect is also considered below. Little emphasis is placed here on the academic curriculum and the transmission of knowledge associated with it. Instead attention is paid to the kind of instruction received in contexts other than the classroom lesson, but which is nevertheless integral to public-school education.

The ethnographic data for this preliminary enquiry are largely autobiographical, my main informant being myself. Only these resources are explored fully here. In due course they may be synthesised with accounts by other former residents of boarding-schools, including those giving the perspective of the staff, which, of course, will be quite different. Subsequent comparative research will necessarily reveal a diversity of experiences and understanding. Many women will have enjoyed their boarding-schools, especially those who fulfilled the aims of that education. But for some, including myself, it failed to teach its terms. If my sister and I had learnt our lessons correctly, it is unlikely that we should have gone to university. The extent to which my boarding-school is 'typical' of its time, the 1950s, or is similar to any such institution in the 1970s, cannot be examined here.[5] Obviously there will be considerable variations and changes.

I deliberately confront the notion of objectivity in research by starting with the subjective, working from the self outwards. The self — the past self — becomes a thing, an object. Yet this past creates and governs the present and future. Even social anthropologists who usually study other cultures are led back from the other to the self. Indeed

Pocock (1973, 1975) has suggested that there is a need to explore the totality of one's 'personal anthropology' and its consequences in order to be able fully to perceive others.[6] This interest in the subjective is no doubt strengthened by my being female and brought up so. Women's language of experience is often distinctly personal, but the general implications are always there to be found. We must therefore explore the abstractions contained in our anecdotes.

A word on the epistemological status of the autobiographical. It is retrospective – unlike a diary which is the record of the present. There will be a loss of memory. Some forgotten experiences may nevertheless affect the narrator unconsciously. The past will have become distorted. Misunderstandings will be revealed later if accounts of events are cross-checked with others who were present at them. But their information will also be skewed. The accuracy of childhood events may, however, be less important than the child's perception of them. They may have important repercussions in later life, some of which may be contrary to the conscious intentions of instructors and parents. The validity of autobiographical material is no different from many presentations by social anthropologists based on data gathered from informants during their field-work. The former is merely one account of what is believed to have existed, whereas the latter often include several autobiographical accounts which have been collapsed into one version.

I am concerned with what I believed happened. My information is based on nine years as a boarding-school girl in the 1950s and on all the subsequent years of retrospective analysis. Participant observation (methodologically crucial to social anthropologists) is perfectly split. In the study of childhood a temporal split between participation and observation is special, and in some instances unavoidable, because children cannot articulate their experiences in the language of adults. Only after childhood can it be thus expressed. When young we found the school world the reality, the norm, the only rationality. That was its power. My mother has often said since, 'But why didn't you tell me?' We, my sister and I, could not discriminate that which now seems bizarre. Whenever I inwardly questioned aspects of this education, I thought myself mad, and identified with the mad and isolated, for example, Nijinsky, van Gogh and other heroes of Colin Wilson's *The Outsider* (1956).

The Girls' Boarding-School

Boarding academies for ladies existed in the eighteenth century, offering certain 'accomplishments'. But most of the now famous girls' public schools were established at the end of the nineteenth century and later, long after the boys' public schools were founded. Even in the 1920s and 1930s many middle- and upper-class girls, for example Jessica Mitford and her sisters (Mitford, 1977), were kept at home to be taught by governesses, whereas their brothers were sent away to school. My mother had a governess until the age of sixteen. Her five enjoyable terms at the school I later attended were a release from a somewhat claustrophobic home and gave her a chance to meet other girls. Her brothers went to boarding-school at an early age, but her younger sisters never went to school.

The girls' public boarding-schools may have been depicted as a new freedom and advance in women's education, but there were important class interests. Pauline Marks has noted that in 1898 in England, 70 per cent of girls in secondary education were in private boarding-schools 'often in towns where grammar and high schools had empty places'. The advantage of the schools they attended was their social homogeneity: 'eligibility for marriage and not the content of their daughter's education remained the dominant concern of middle-class parents' (Marks, 1976, p. 189). These observations are relevant to at least one girls' boarding-school in the 1950s.

Even though both private and state schools have been affected by various reforms, including sometimes the principle of equality of opportunity for women, they have failed to resolve a persistent dichotomy, the choice for the future for girls between a career and marriage with motherhood. This is reinforced by a sexual division of labour which, both inside and outside the home, perpetuates women's relative economic dependence and insecurity, whatever their social class, and whether married or single. Educational reform alone cannot resolve this. Its confused policies have alternated from an unrealisable attempt at assimilation of female education into the male model, to an emphasis on teaching the qualities supposedly required of women as wives and mothers; other skills being regarded as secondary (cf. Marks, 1976, pp. 185-9).

It is not surprising that the dilemma between a career and marriage scarcely arose in a middle-class and relatively undistinguished boarding-school such as mine. Ideally, marriage was the ultimate vocation. Without records of the stated intentions of my teachers, I reconstruct these from remembered incidents. Some slogans remain: we were 'fortunate to be receiving a good education', and we believed it. Yet if there was academic intent, this was not borne out by the girls' performance, since the majority left after taking a few GCE 'O' levels. Out of a class containing up to 35 girls, six or less remained to take sometimes a single 'A' level — an accomplishment which simultaneously prohibited university ambition. There is no memory of the word equality. The pattern after school tended to be a year at a private domestic science or finishing school, preferably in Switzerland, and progress to an exclusive secretarial college. The ideal was to be a débutante, before making a 'good marriage'. Another respectable vocation was nursing, and then only at select London hospitals. Teachers' training was *déclassé*. Whereas work as a private secretary or nurse offered contact with a man of the right social class, teaching did not. Few, if any, of the girls entered occupations comparable to their brothers'.

Scholarly achievements and higher education were, nevertheless, reserved for a few girls,[7] possibly marked as vocational spinsters. These had also to conform to the school's ideas of good conduct. Academic proficiency did not guarantee encouragement.

> With 13 'O' levels and while studying for four 'A' levels, I was summoned to the senior mistress. She declared I would be 'selfish to go to University, *even* Aberystwyth', thereby depriving a worthier person of a place. She suggested a career which would make use of my 'A' levels in French and Art — by training as a designer of corsets and lingerie for a famous company in Switzerland.

Separations

The British boarding-school is marked by its forms of separation from urban culture, from other social classes, from family and home, and from the opposite sex. Anthropologists have devoted much attention to *rites de passage*, ceremonies associated for example with birth, adulthood, marriage and death. In the transition of persons from one status to another, a frequent element is the separation of the individual (socially, spatially and temporally), from 'normal life' and from the community at large. In some initiation rites marking the transition from childhood to adulthood, the neophytes are grouped together, separated from the village, perhaps in the forest, and subjected to painful physical experiences, such as circumcision. They are instructed by selected adults in the sacred mysteries of their culture, by the use of special songs and sacred masks. Their pain is mingled with drama and beauty. They return with new knowledge and are reintegrated. A lasting bond is created between the neophytes who shared the same terror. The boarding-school can also be seen as a *rite de passage* from childhood to adulthood.[8] The separation from 'normal' life lasts many years. Although separations exist for both boys and girls, the differing consequences for each sex will become apparent.

1. Geographical and Cultural

British public schools nowadays are almost invariably set in rural areas, distant from urban concentrations, the threatening proletariat and metropolitan culture. Originally the boys' public schools were not so organised. But from 1850 they were increasingly concentrated in large buildings, and some were moved out of London, and 'set in large houses, cut off by great oceans of land from the outside world' (Gathorne-Hardy, 1977, pp. 103-5). The girls' schools followed suit. Apart from the efficacy of isolation and its greater control, the choice of the countryside was consistent with the current British belief that open spaces and fresh air improve moral, as well as bodily, health.

Our instructors never initiated us into nature's beauties, but only marched us through the landscape, two by two. Yet nature in the form of wild scenery was a fortuitous compensation. This was the only sacred knowledge acquired — from the downs, pine trees, woods and the uncontrollable south coast sea. Nature with its lack of discipline confounded their rules. It nurtured our souls.

Compared to boarding-school boys, it seems that girls are permitted even less contact with the world outside the school grounds.[9] For us, the nearby town was banned, taboo, except for perhaps a termly shopping trip under strict surveillance and with our few shillings handed out on Saturdays. We retained our coppers for Sunday chapel collection. Money found on us on any other days brought the severest punishment. Thus we were withdrawn from commerce, from earning and purchase.

We left the grounds about twice a week in 'crocodile' on set rural routes, skirting the town. Over-fifteens could go out for 'walks in threes' on certain days. Parents came and 'took us out', perhaps once a term. Written contact from and to the outer world was overseen. Outgoing letters not to parents were placed in unsealed envelopes for checking, incoming mail was examined, steamed open, even confiscated in some cases.

My sister was crazy about Elvis Presley. Her friends paid for her subscription to the Presley fan club. Nothing arrived. Weeks later, the senior mistress summoned her and showed her the pile of Presley literature. My sister was told, 'You are fit only to dance at Hammersmith Palais!' The papers and pictures were destroyed.

Presley, sexually insinuating, was part of that proletarian culture from which we were to be protected. Yet even tamer forces threatened. Except for the *Illustrated London News* and *Punch* in the library, comics and magazines were banned, even *Woman's Own*, which we read secretly in the lavatory, where its torn pages were hung by matron for wrapping our dirty sanitary towels. All personal books had to be checked and signed by staff. Our storage drawers and our mattresses were searched for any offending literature which might have come from that far, urban world. Like the neophytes, the girls were bound together as partners in pain, or we detached ourselves in shared humour, and laughed at our custodians.

2. Class

Geographical seclusion was matched by our separation from all other social classes in the strange English hierarchy. Parents of middle- or upper-middle-class children demonstrate a desire to protect them from any classes below, and from contamination in what were euphemistically called the 'local' schools. Families may see themselves as randomly scattered and without sufficient contact with others of the same class pretensions, thereby risking inter-class familiarity. The boarding-school solves the technical problem. Offspring are concentrated with their kind and simultaneously separated from others. That is the meaning of 'exclusive' when applied to these institutions. When the children are home for the holidays, their parents can control their friends and contacts.

The children in such schools don't need to be told they are different and superior, since they are able to perceive it, learn it, know it for themselves. The children are isolated from any alternative life and the ways of others become the more alien. Stereotypes take form. We despised the grammar-school children we had to encounter at county music competitions. They were unknown, frightening and inferior, and the males of course were unmarriageable. Henceforth we could never treat anyone from another 'background' as equal. The differentiation was epitomised in the 'accent'. Here we received support from the dominant ideology of the larger society of which we were a necessary ingredient. The children in a boarding-school pool their parents' accents. Differences in a minority of girls in my school, such as the few scholarship girls, were ridiculed and mimicked until repressed. The public-school accent, just as the pronunciation of any language, must be constantly reinforced through childhood. Our inner ears or class tuning forks were sensitised by years of sounds in words. If the school teaches nothing else, it stamps the child with a way of speaking and the awareness of deviation. Style spoke before content. We need only utter a few words — any assortment — to mark ourselves. The consequences of our separation would go for ever with us when reintegrated into British society. The accent is a sign and a weapon.

Along with our accents went a pooling of prejudices and values, and ways of eating and moving — even our handwriting conformed. When I arrived, aged nine, from my Lincolnshire school, my ornate looped writing had to be unlearnt; it was too proletarian. A distinct set of manners was acquired.

Many years after leaving, I met an old school friend who commented on another former inmate who appeared to have slipped down the class ladder: 'She wrote to me on lined paper. I know when a friendship has to stop.'

We were taught that we could give charity but never receive it, thus defining precisely our class position:

A dormitory mate, whose parents were abroad, asked her relatives to forward a parcel of discarded holiday clothes. Several of us shared out the luxurious dresses, skirts and sweaters. The parcel had aroused the curiosity of the authorities. We were summoned, rebuked for 'accepting charity' and bringing shame on our parents, then ordered to repack and send the items to an East London mission. I managed to conceal a skirt and pair of shoes in the recesses of the games corridor until the end of term.

3. Family and Home

Ironically the fifties witnessed the popularity of Bowlby's claims that early separation from mothers would produce unstable children. The arguments were extended to schoolchildren of working mothers. The cry went up of 'latch-key' children. It was really directed at working-class mothers. The upper middle classes continued to despatch their children from home, depriving them of affection though guaranteed twenty-four-hour custodial care. In some cases boarding-school has been justified as the solution after divorce or widowhood. The loss of one parent is thereby compounded by separation from the other.

Unlike prison or Borstal, we were there because our parents loved us. Prisoners and Borstal offenders know they are incarcerated in order to suffer for their own misdeeds. Their relatives and parents may lament and oppose their sentences. Even if the parents of a Borstal offender assisted the authorities, it would be apparent that they had failed as parents or rejected their offspring. The trick for us at boarding-school was that we were not ostensibly there as a punishment. We could not take responsibility for what our unconscious might tell us. Parents were wholly in collaboration with our fate. The school song made us declaim: It is well understood/We are here for our good/So our parents/ And mistresses say/And I fancy that we/Are inclined to agree,/Though we mean it/A different way.

After each verse, the refrain concluded:

> Your lot's not a bad one at all./
> NOT AT ALL!

The last line was shouted — one of the few occasions when the girls were encouraged, and indeed expected, to raise their voices.

The boarding-school can appropriately be defined as a 'total institution' (Goffman, 1968). The holiday intervals with parents are part of a continuous moral universe, since the parents are responsible for boarding their children and demand that they succeed there. Accepting, conforming and surviving can be a duty to the parents whose financial contribution is translated as love and sacrifice for the child's greater good. Whereas Borstal offenders may be able to nurture revenge against the establishment which sentenced them, public-school children dare not think through the ultimate blame upon their parents. The 'double bind' is complete.[10] In contrast to Borstal inmates' attempts to escape, running away from school can only be an emotional appeal to the parents who made the initial decision and may merely send their child back.

We were orphans but did not know it. Ironic that each child was encouraged to have a collection box in the shape of a house — a Dr Barnardo's home. Here we placed our pennies for the 'real orphans'. 'Family Favourites' on the Sunday radio fascinated us. We unconsciously identified with the messages sent between relatives apart. Our separation meant, indeed, the loss of a personal relationship with any adult. The ratio of staff to child within the school made it technically impossible. Moreover, at least from my experience, the demands of the institution overrode even the memory of family relationships. For individuals facing the crisis of the death of a parent or relative few, if any, allowances were made.[11] Misbehaviour arising from these circumstances was punished. We defied the rules to comfort our friends in the dormitory at night.

Denied personal access to adults, we were also constrained in rigid peer groups. Friendships, even prolonged encounters, were not permitted between persons of different forms − since they threatened the rigid hierarchy with its ascending privileges and status. Only love could undermine it. Friendships between different ages were deviant and passionate, though rarely expressed in physical terms. For the authorities such relationships were seen as a dangerous emergence of sexuality, and of course a perversion. There were strict regulations also on intimacy between equals. No two girls were ever allowed to be together alone in the bathroom, lavatory or small music rooms. Thus any loving relationship possible was taboo. Two girls were actually expelled, allegedly for mingling their blood from cut wrists and swearing friendship on the Bible.[12]

There appears to be a difference in the age when boys and girls in England are sent away from home. Boys are more likely to be boarded before eleven or even eight years of age (Lambert, 1975, p. 35), while girls are more likely to be boarded from eleven or later (Ollerenshaw, 1967, pp. 128-9; Wober, 1971, pp. 44-5).[13] A minority of us were younger when we joined our school. This difference between boys and girls may have consequences for each gender's responses and expectations in adult relationships. I suggest tentatively that boys seem to be required to repress 'childish' emotional dependence sooner, and thus more violently, than girls. Boarding for a 'prep' school boy entails an early severance from the mother and her emotional power, and absorption into a future where authority is vested in men. The fearsome school matron is no mother substitute. In other societies, male initiation rites express most dramatically this break with the mother. For the girl who may be at home longer, intimacy and identification with the mother become clearly established. It is at the onset of puberty, when her social and biological virginity must be protected, that she is sent from home and the local school. By contrast, a boy's virginity is of little or no consequence. Thus both boys and girls are separated from home and parents, but not always for the same reasons.

4. Gender

Along with the hierarchy of class, another major division of British society is the segregation of the sexes. For girls, separation from boys and men will have meaning and consequences not symmetrical to that of boys in single-sex schools. Compared to the boys, girls are subjected to greater restrictions and less autonomy.[14] Female adolescence, if not childhood, is socially prolonged in such schools, for this is a dangerous time for girls who are sexually mature, but considered too young for a marriage contract. This is especially true of a girl of a wealthy class, since her prospective spouse must be well established in his occupation, and have property, either transmitted or acquired. So the boarding-school offers safe segregation for girls from males of all social classes. Ollerenshaw hints at this:

> Some parents and headmistresses feel that there is advantage for some girls in their being withdrawn during the schoolday or at boarding schools for the school term from the emotional turmoil of relationships with boys so that they may develop poise and self confidence (1967, p. 29).

Boys, it will be argued, are likewise segregated from females,[15] and are deprived of heterosexuality. Unlike girls, however, they are not separated from the vision of political power. Indeed, separation from women and the domestic sphere consolidates patriarchy. By contrast, girls in a boarding-school are deprived of both heterosexuality and education for power, our glimpse of which would always be vicarious, would always be through males. Like the disease of haemophilia, as Helen Callaway once said, power can be transmitted through females but is only manifest in males. In schools such as mine, we were separated from those destined to monopolise certain political and economic spheres — those who were to acquire lucrative occupations and earn our living for us. Our own exclusive education, unlike theirs, was not for a career.

The school consisted almost entirely of females — the Head, matrons, teaching and domestic staff — most of whom were resident. The males usually seen within the school grounds can be listed:

the school chaplain;
two non-resident gardeners;
the boiler-man;
two elderly retired male teachers, for German and English 'A' levels, who visited perhaps one day a week;
the part-time tennis coach who appeared in my last two summer terms;
the headmistress's male dachsund.[16]

The majority of girls only directly heard the voice of one male, that of the chaplain. On Sundays we occasionally had a visiting preacher. If we were lucky enough to have a wireless we could hear male voices transmitted from the outer world. Yet men lurked somewhere, unseen. The Board of Governors consisted almost entirely of men — for example, a lord, a Tory MP, JPs and bishops.[17]

Men were directly involved in our most important initiation rite, our confirmation within the established Church of England – giving the right to partake of the body and blood of our male God (which had a peculiar British flavour). The day before the laying on of hands by the Bishop (the supremely visible male authority) we neophytes had to retire, not to the school chapel, but to the local church – where we had to write down all our sins in a notebook which had printed questions on each blank page. One question was 'Have I defiled my body?' I didn't know what this meant. I thought it might be squeezing spots. After filling in our books we then read our sins to the chaplain. We were given absolution and returned to the school to give the notebooks to 'Arold the boiler-man, who committed them to the eternal flames of the school boiler. (In earlier years the girls burned their booklets on the hockey pitch.) Thus the man at the lowest end of the social hierarchy dealt with our impurity. The equally inaccessible Bishop at the top, a member of the House of Lords, gave us purity and access to the sacred – the faith of the majority of the governing élite – while we were veiled in white, as if at a dress rehearsal for our future weddings within that élite.

The Bishop's address at my mother's confirmation in 1933, in the chapel where I would also be initiated, included the following:

> You all know Mr. Baldwin. About a year ago he said, 'I did what I believed to be right and I will always stick to what I believe to be right.' That exactly expresses what you and I will be trying to do . . . A year ago I was standing by a grave . . . the inscription was very short: 'Douglas Haig, Field Marshal . . . He trusted in God and tried to do right.' I don't think that you could have anything more splendid said of you. . . . Suppose I go back a long way and quote you a man every Englishman and woman is proud of and it is Francis Drake . . . Drake said to his ship's company, 'Let us show ourselves to be all of a company' (not a bad motto for a school) 'and let us not give the enemy cause to rejoice at our decay or over-throw.'

Parts of the Bishop's address were more religiously inspiring, but hypnotically entangled with lessons about male politicians and British colonial history. Similar examples occurred in the 1950s.

Famous men, not women, were to be our heroic models. The school was divided into four cosmological 'houses', not represented by buildings but as groups of girls competing for cups in sports, conduct, drama and deportment — but not academic performance. The houses were named Shackleton, Scott, Livingstone and Rhodes, after male explorers and chauvinists of the colonial kind whom we, as Penelope to Ulysses, could never imitate. We could only marry and beget these kind of men and the Bishop's heroes. Aspirations were stimulated which were simultaneously shown to be impossible for women to attain. Our impotence was confirmed. Even our classrooms were named after male, not female, writers: Shakespeare, Cowper, Kingsley (not Brontë, nor Eliot, certainly not Wollstonecraft). The choice of famous men indicates how completely an alternative, potentially revolutionary, female ideology was suppressed.[18]

With no heroines with whom to identify, heroism was always located in the mysterious 'other', from which we were to choose just one man as spouse. The male/female category was not learnt and created by observable opposition, as was possible for those in mixed schools or living at home, but by an absence or omission. There was no way either to become as men, or to find an independent female way. Our lives and potential were presented as those of failed men. We knew and learnt that women were beneath men in that hierarchy in which we ourselves believed. Only a male could confirm us, preach to us. Marriage offered the only release from this multiple separation. Without a husband, we knew we could not maintain our financial hold in the class system, however exclusive our accent and manners. Our privileges were at the mercy of men.

We learnt this also from the teachers. An exclusively female community does not necessarily have feminist aspirations, nor do its custodians provide models of ideal independence. The majority of our teachers were unmarried[19] and, apart from a few proud and self-sufficient ones, they presented themselves as victims of misfortune — so many tales of fiancés killed in the war — perhaps to justify self-confessed failure. They did not teach us to emulate themselves. We recognised our teachers as of a lower social class, some by their accents. In so far as the girls upheld beliefs in their exclusive background, they could not easily identify with women who came from the stigmatised state schools. Wober's data on girls' boarding-schools in the 1960s confirms that only a minority of staff had themselves been boarded, the majority, 63.6 per cent, had been to day school (1971, p. 40). Women from boarding-school do not wish to return there as teachers, because the desired destiny of most was a marriage which excluded a career. The same is not the case for men. Lambert's study of boys' public schools notes that: 'Most teachers . . . come from social groups which correspond to their pupils ... Over 70% of staff in public schools were themselves educated at public schools and about 10% of them were educated in their own schools' (1975, p. 54). Thus the boys can more readily identify with their teachers.

Containment and Powerlessness

It is sometimes said that girls' boarding-schools are more 'homely' than boys'. Certainly there were feminine touches for us (the rose garden, the floral curtains and coloured bedspreads) and the main building was more a country house than a utilitarian edifice. Wober notes the visual beauty of the girls' boarding-schools and seems almost to justify them in the name of that beauty (1971, pp. 282-3). But within homely or domestic quarters life may still become oppressive. We longed for love and approval from these substitute parents, our custodians, but they were not mothers with relaxed affection and visible femininity. Nor were they like fathers, for we saw how they deferred to male visitors. Girls, in contrast to boys, were addressed by their first names, a practice which states, among other things, that surnames were merely passing premarital stamps of identity. The use of the personal name may not reflect kindness though it speaks of intimacy, which in the boarding-school is not reciprocated between the child named and the adult namer. Some intimacy facilitated greater control. Privacy could be thus invaded. Further research is required into variations between male and female boarding-schools in the extent of control exercised. From the evidence now available, it seems that girls are more rigidly confined within the precincts of the school and subject to greater control (cf. Gathorne-Hardy, 1977, pp. 241, 246). Ollerenshaw hints at the demands made by the invisible fathers who delegated control of their daughters. The girls' schools 'had to establish the academic capabilities of women . . . with the approval and support of Victorian parents – in particular Victorian fathers. Rules of behaviour and deportment were therefore strict' (1967, p. 20).

The ethnography of the school I describe includes the limitations on the girls' movement in space and time, and on their sounds and speech. Movement *beyond* the school grounds was minimal. Only the five or six prefects could ever go out alone. Control *within* these boundaries was infinitely detailed. The focus on minutiae demanding all our concentration impeded the thought of, reduced the possibility of, bolder action. What counted as crime for girls may seem petty, especially when compared to the misdemeanours of boys. But its very triviality affirmed the pervasiveness of control. For instance, to be 'out of bounds' was almost unimaginable. It rarely occurred, and carried the risk of being expelled. Our triumphs were less dramatic, although meaningful to us — when on a 'walk in three', for example, taking the lift instead of the many steps from the beach, and having the pennies to pay for it. (I still have that lift ticket in my album.)

At any time of the day and night, any day of the week, our exact location was ordained. Summer alone gave free range of the garden in the limited play periods. Otherwise we traversed the grounds on set paths to outhouse and games field. Within the buildings, we moved along the corridors to specified rooms. Rules established that each location, such as dormitory, dining-room and common room were out of bounds when the timetable demanded our presence elsewhere. As we moved according to the lines of the timetable, we could neither hurry nor linger:

No running in the passage
No talking in the passage

were cardinal rules.

Just as space, so was time subjected to a changeless grid. An electric bell rang at half-hour intervals, or more often. There was no unorganised time for doing what we wanted or going where we wanted, even at weekends. No way to decide for ourselves the next move. After lessons our prep was supervised: often seventy silent girls sat in one long room. We had no private studies. One of the very few times when the girls were not within sight of an adult was 'after lights out' in the dormitory. The punishment for talking or being found out of bed was therefore the severest. We defied the invasions of our privacy which surveillance implied by hiding in the lavatory or bathroom. I would climb on to the roof at night. A former inmate confessed that she even went for moonlit walks in the grounds. The constraints on space and time were further compounded by the rules imposing silence during the ten or so hours between lights out and the morning bell, also when lining up and entering the dining-room, moving from chapel to 'roll call', indeed in all passages and inevitably in lessons. Not only were our words limited, but at all times sound was abated.[20]

Not being expected to choose, to decide and to make statements, the girls had to exercise extreme self-discipline, especially when they complied with orders which seemed either small-minded or incomprehensible. The notion of 'character' was contrasted favourably by our instructors with 'personality' — a negative trait because it carried the notion of individuality. Leadership of sorts was expected from seniors, not charisma, but the ability to lead others into a conformity to maintain a *status quo* predetermined by adults.

In contrast, in boys' public schools, seniors and prefects assume dictatorial powers, including the right to inflict corporal punishment, to have 'fags' (junior boys as servants) and to establish rules. They thus acquire near-adult authority before they leave school. Cyril Connolly has compared the position of senior boys at Eton to 'feudal overlords' (1961, pp. 194-5). Lambert describes how, in the 1960s, the boarding pupils at the top of the boy's public-school hierarchies exercised 'more real power over others than sometimes the junior teachers . . . and many other teachers in day schools'. Day pupils did not experience 'this dual training in responsible authority on the one hand and obedience on the other' (1975, p. 241). For girls, obedience rather than authority is emphasised. Present evidence suggests that girls' prefect power is weak compared to that of their male counterparts. Certainly the fagging system is non-existent. Wober found that girls gave low priority to being a prefect (1971, p. 78), and that houses in girls' schools were rarely residential entities 'with separate authority and privilege systems' (1971, p. 116). The vertical social grouping found in boys' schools coincides with the extensive supervision of juniors by seniors. The horizontal social grouping of girls coincides with the reduced authority of seniors over juniors.[21]

In girls' schools, authority is placed beyond both the pupils and teaching staff in a single individual: the headmistress.[22] This is described by Gathorne-Hardy as 'the dictator headmistress tradition' (1977, pp. 241-4). The position of the headmistress in my school appeared extremely powerful. Even the school magazine was edited by her. The staff had some authority, but the girls always had to defer to both staff and head. The seniors had no powers to initiate rules, they could not even give out 'bad marks' in the punishment system. The responsibilities of the 'junior sergeants', 'sergeants', 'sub-prefects' and 'prefects' consisted mainly of keeping the other girls silent in the passages and when lining up for meals, serving out the food at each long table, and reporting misdemeanours to staff. The head girl — the most coveted station for a pupil — performed mainly symbolic functions. When the entire school filed in silently to the dining room, she stood in the passage in a focal position raised four inches in a doorway. She announced the 'notices' after lunch (usually timetable changes). At the end of 'roll call' she marched out first to the military music. She helped the headmistress put on her MA gown in the vestry before daily prayers.

At Sunday evensong she held the cross, processing before the chaplain. She sat on the headmistress's right at lunch on high table — her confidante, a ritual handmaid, but no innovatory leader. She had 'character', usually also an ability at games, and academic mediocrity. The closest description of this ideal type is provided in Angela Brazil's *The Nicest Girl in the School* (1909, pp. 20-1).[23]

Punishment by Exposure

In boys' schools, punishment includes the cane — often wielded by other boys. Paradoxically the girls abdicate more freedoms without the terror of corporal punishment. How are they controlled when there is this apparently greater leniency? Foucault (1977) has demonstrated how direct and spectacular attacks on the body by public torture and execution before the eighteenth century were replaced by the more 'humane' methods of imprisonment. These controls were more effective because they entailed intervention in every aspect of the criminal's existence. Girls too are controlled not by material and metonymic weapons upon the flesh, but through intangible and metaphorical routes to the soul.

The system of punishment plays on the behaviour expected of girls, among whom self-control and self-negation take special forms. From infancy they are made modest, passive and withdrawn compared to boys. The pattern is already set before school, but there it is exploited, reinforced and elaborated. I use again the ethnographic example of my boarding-school. The required behaviour, and that which brought the precious reward of non-interference, included modesty, deference and submission. After a misdeed, part of the punishment was a 'row' from a member of staff and later the house captain. Humility, an apologetic stance, downcast eyes — possibly tears of defeat — were the correct forms. Any appearance of pride or dignity provoked further rebukes. Self-defence was rebuked with 'Don't answer back.' The 'right attitude' was rewarded, in that the girl was permitted to merge into the group. Our 'total institution' had all the elements which Goffman has described as 'stripping' (1968, p. 29), by which he means loss of personal identity. Here we see a closed circuit. The more a girl successfully complied with and internalised modesty, humility and the invisibility of the self, the more devastating the threat of their opposites.

We were given a number, useless, but printed on name tapes and stamped in nails on the soles of our shoes. But there was a worse kind of 'stripping' than that described by Goffman for us: being exposed before others as deviant, and regaining individuality as wrongdoer. Both

formal and informal methods of punishment had this common ingredient – public exposure, or individual visibility. To be picked out and
stared at, was to be stripped as naked, with feminine reticence denied.
This threat seems recurrent in girls' upbringing.[24] Control in our
school was maintained not by the ultimate threat of cane marks but
by disembodied conduct marks engraved on the collective mind. Whereas there was only one reward for good conduct, a 'good housemark',
our crimes were minutely subdivided (cf. Foucault, 1977, p. 98).
Running or talking at the inappropriate place or time and other vaguer
acts of 'insolence' earned a 'disobedience' mark (or 'disso'). The slightest delay brought a 'late' mark. 'Order' marks were given for the mis-
placement or loss of items like uniform or books, and for offences so
trivial I cannot remember. Untidiness, even poor darning, brought a
'bad housemark'. We were bound in spiders' webs of fine rules and
constraints until spontaneity seemed to be a crime. On the last morning
of each holidays I would lie in bed wishing that I could foresee and
avoid all my future misdeeds, for their consequences were frightful.

The stage was set at daily 'roll-call' where, in the presence of the
entire school and staff, a girl with a 'disobedience', 'order' or 'late'
had to announce the mark instead of saying 'present'. Hearts thumped
as names came nearer. After a disobedience the headmistress would
always ask, 'What's that for?' and the girl would have to detail her
crime. While the rest of the school was sitting cross-legged on the floor,
she might be asked to stand up and repeat her crime loud and clear.
This public confession was also a symbolic variant of the public execution, with its necessary witnesses among whom fear of a similar fate
would be generated. At 'fortnightly marks' the headmistress would read
out the percentages of each girl's academic performance in the prece-
ding weeks. We learnt that obedience and good conduct were inseparable from and superior to the intellect and academic knowledge.
From our total percentage received for classwork, two points were
deducted for a disobedience and one point for a late or order. The
term culminated in 'Marks and Remarks' where every girl received a
conduct comment, again read aloud by the headmistress to staff and
school. Ideally it was 'good', but terrifying if different and among
the few like 'a poor term', 'Jane resents criticism', or worse. After
this ordeal a girl might weep as I did, in the lavatory.

Conduct marks were given textual form, emblazoned in a public
record of crime or obedience. In the main passage at the chapel en-
trance, for all to see, were four boards, one for each house (Rhodes,
Livingstone, Scott and Shackleton). A large sheet of paper bore the

name of each house member at one edge, with columns marking each day and week of the term. A 'disso' earned a black cross, as did a bad housemark. A 'late' or 'order' brought a nought, a good housemark a vertical stroke. Every week ended with an additional column and an individual square, for painting according to individual conduct. The house colour (red for Rhodes, yellow for Livingstone, blue for Shackleton or green for Scott) was painted in for 'good' or 'normal'. There were different intermediate gradings for bad conduct, the squares being half-white and half coloured, or all white, or half white and half black, in order of severity. The worst was a completely black square with the word 'disgrace' printed alongside. Thus the performance of each girl for each week of the term was mapped and open to scrutiny by everyone. The black squares generated the most curiosity and excitement and the recipient would be picked out wherever she went. At the end of term, the house with the best score in conduct would be awarded the school 'house cup', so each deviant knew the multiple consequences of her misbehaviour. A miniature cup was awarded by each captain to the 'best' girl in the house.

Informal methods of exposure were also used by staff and senior girls. A girl who talked and who failed to respond to the sergeant or prefect while lining up for the dining-room was made to stand in the main passage, her back turned, not seeing those who filed past, but conspicuous to all. A miscreant might be ordered to stand in the aisle of the dining-room, or made to stand up at her table throughout a meal while the entire school sat eating. The final humiliation was standing on high-table, again with back turned, but abjectly visible. One matron would punish a girl by making her sit under the table in the surgery, while she had afternoon tea above.

Thus we were punished by the very terms they demanded of us. If modesty were not pre-existent or not enforced, exposure would be no terror, but instead would call for the bravado so often found among boys. The girls who rejected modesty, submission and shame were impervious to exposure. Only deprivation (such as detention on Saturday after tea and no weekend sweets) might work for them. For one, it was whispered, the slipper was used; the corporal punishment was resorted to because she behaved as a boy. Such girls were eventually expelled. For the rest of us, the more successful our conversion, the more we eliminated individuality, the more terrifying the punishment for any deviation. We were both rewarded and punished for our complicity.

In some contexts public exposure occurred without opprobrium and in pride. Like the duties of the head girl, they were mainly in ritual, in chapel. Girls would be chosen as servers at Holy Communion and for the daily Bible reading from the chapel lectern. They could speak with authority while reading the Holy Word, God's word, not mouthing their own. Here we could expose ourselves, for we were clothed in righteousness, especially on Sundays when our heads were covered by a blue veil, and we were muffled and purified. Prize-giving demanded a brief public walk, before disappearance back into the crowd, protected by the mass applause. Such exposure was different. First, because there were many prize-winners and second, because prizes were rewards for conformity. Some rewards in the form of privileges such as promotion to sergeant, sub-prefect or prefect, came with age, combined with the 'right attitude', and were welcomed. Indeed, not to be promoted with your age group meant further exposure (for instance, having to line up and sit with younger girls in the dining-room). Your state of promotion, or lack of it, was doubly visible, since felt embroidered badges of authority were sewn on the uniform, together with games team membership. There were no badges for academic achievement or intelligence — that which celebrates individual and original thought, and which can subvert.

The Body: Subjugated and Unsexed

The concern with demeanour and carriage is one aspect of a total view of the body which reflects the extent of the institution's invasion and the ambivalences of its intentions. Mauss (1936) has discussed the ways different societies, groups and forms of education make use of the body. These may change over time and there are individual variations. Mauss isolates three factors: social, psychological and biological.

> In all the elements of the art of using the human body, the facts of education are dominant . . . The child, the adult, imitates actions which have succeeded and which he has seen to succeed among persons in whom he has confidence and who have authority over him (1936, p. 369).

In the girls' boarding-school, the pupils must acquire such movements. They may give the longed-for anonymity, as well as conspicuous selection as a team member. Within our school there could be no 'natural' movement which might contradict what the authorities considered correct. 'Bad' ways we had learnt elsewhere had to be changed. We did not merely unconsciously imitate movements and gestures, we were consciously made to sit, stand and move in uniform ways. We were drilled and schooled, not by those in whom we had confidence, but by those who had power over us. Our flesh unscarred, yet our gestures bore their marks.[25] Even when outside the classroom or off the games field, we were to sit, stand and walk erect, chin up, back straight, shoulders well back. At table when not eating, our hands were to rest in our laps. During the afternoon rest period matrons ordered us not to lie on our backs with knees bent. The games mistresses watched girls at meals, at roll-call and in chapel, and would award good and bad 'deportment marks', recorded on a chart, and with house cups. If you were consistently upright you won a red felt badge, embroidered with the word 'Deportment'. This, sewn on your tunic, was a sign of both achievement and defeat. Our minds and understanding of the world were to reflect our custodians. With no private space, we could not even hide in our bodies which also had to move in unison with their thoughts.

The authorities observed accurately the language of the body. However much a girl might say the right things, do and act within the rules, and however in order her uniform may be, her general carriage, her minutest gesture could betray a lack of conviction, a failure in conversion. I remember (after yet another term's anxious waiting for promotion) being called to the headmistress who said that I needed to improve my 'attitude' before I could be made a sergeant. I was baffled because I thought I had successfully concealed my unorthodoxy. I had said and done what appeared to me to be in order. But they must have seen through me, just by the way my body spoke. It also had to be tempered. I eventually won my deportment badge, and then soared from sergeant, to sub-prefect, to prefect. But my conformity overreached itself; the games mistress took me aside and said I was now sitting and walking too stiffly, too rigidly. I was becoming conspicuous again.

Eventually the imitating child becomes the part. To survive in a place which beats down diversity, the victim has to believe in the rightness of his or her controller. Children and adolescents are most vulnerable, their minds and growing bodies may be permanently shaped. Apparently insignificant details such as bearing and posture are emphasised because, to use Bourdieu's words, the body is treated 'as a memory'. The principles of a whole cosmology or ethic are, 'placed beyond the grasp of consciousness, and hence cannot be touched by voluntary, deliberate transformation' (1977, p. 94). At an Old Girls' meeting, I talked with an old form-mate who had tried to train as an opera singer, but who could never breathe deeply enough. She spontaneously laid the blame on her schooling – her chest had, as it were, been too rigidly encased, and later she couldn't free herself, couldn't project her voice. In our bodies, we carried their minds into the future.

The presence of corporal punishment in boys' schools and its absence in girls' schools indicate differing attitudes to bodily display and contact, and possibly a differing consciousness of sexuality. Connections have been made between the childhood beatings of English males and their adult predilections for flagellation in brothels.[26] Although our deportment was continually viewed, our corporal modesty nevertheless stayed intact. In punishment, the girls were fully clothed and untouchable. In this sense, our bodies were invisible, anaesthetised and protected for one man's intrusion later.

As skeletons, we were corrected and straightened, ordered to sit and stand in upright lines. As female flesh and curves, we were concealed by the uniform. Take the traditional gym slip – a barrel shape with deep pleats designed to hide breasts, waist, hips and buttocks, giving freedom of movement without contour. My mother wore such a tunic. Previously women wore clothes which revealed the 'hour-glass' shape, but one made rigid and immobile by 'stays' or corsets. From the gym slip of the 1930s, we had graduated to the tunic of thick serge ('hopsack' we called it), without pleats, but again skilfully flattening the breasts and widening the waist. While my mother's legs had been hidden and desexualised by thick black stockings, we wore thick brown ones, 'regulation shade', and called them 'bullet-proofs'.

In those days before tights, our movements were further constrained lest we expose our suspenders beneath our short tunics. There was no risk of any greater exposure. We had to wear two pairs of knickers – white 'linings' and thick navy blue baggy knickers complete with pocket.[27] For gym we removed our tunics and any girl in linings only was shamed and punished. In summer the navy knickers were replaced by pale blue ones.

> A friend still recalls being given a 'disobedience' for doing handstands and, unknown to her, exposing her knickers to a nearby gardener. She was told only to say, 'for handstands' at roll call.

Thus her unmentionable exposure was effectively treated by psychological exposure. For games, our shorts concealed the existence of a split between the thighs. Two deep pleats in front and back made them like a skirt, but one which did not lift and reveal the thighs or buttocks as we ran or jumped. The lower abdomen retained its mystery.

This was the fifties when the dominant female fashion meant long full skirts. Yet our tunics had to be 'three inches above the knee when kneeling' (note the supplicant pose), even for girls aged 17 years. I have been informed by a girl at another boarding school in the 1960s, when the mini-skirt symbolised fashionable femininity, that her tunic had to be '*touching* the floor when kneeling'. Thus the girls' schools demand the opposite to the notion of sexuality in the world outside. Our appearance was neutered. Our hair could not touch the backs of our shirt collars; in effect we were given the male 'short back and sides'. The crucial inspection time was the daily march-past at roll call. The dilemma was whether to bend forward and be rebuked for 'poking' the head (and not marching in the male military fashion) or whether to straighten up and risk being summoned for mutilation by the hairdresser. We were caught between conformity to the school, and saving our female sexuality as symbolised by longer hair.

The girls' uniform also had strange male traits: lace-up shoes, striped shirts, blazers, ties and tie pins. Unlike some of the boys' uniforms, ours was discontinuous with the clothes we would wear in adulthood. To us the school tie had no significance for membership of an 'old boy network'. We were caught between a male and female image long after puberty, and denied an identity which asserted the dangerous consciousness of sexuality. Immediately we left school, we had to drop all masculine traits, since a very different appearance was required for marriageability. Sexual ripeness, if only expressed in clothes, burst out. The hated tunics and lace-ups were torn, cut, burnt or flung into the sea. Old girls would return on parade, keen to demonstrate their transformation from androgeny to womanhood. To be wearing the diamond engagement ring was the ultimate achievement. There was no link between our past and future. In such uncertainty our confidence was surely broken.

Exercise: Games and Marching

Bodily exercise of a distinct kind competed with and usually triumphed over academic study. For 220 girls there were two hockey pitches, six netball courts converted for tennis in the summer, along with two grass courts, a gymnasium and a swimming pool. The library, an old glass conservatory, half the size of a netball court, with three entrances linked to the main buildings, was little more than a draughty passageway. The games mistresses enjoyed at least equal and, in some cases, higher status than the academic staff. Boys could admire and model themselves on athletes. The games mistresses, however, even more than the academic staff, presented a model we were not willing to emulate either at the time, or after leaving school – the boyish hair style, shorts, aertex shirt, muscular unstockinged legs and sandals on all occasions. Games were compulsory every weekday. On Saturdays those girls selected for teams played in matches, while the rest of us took our compulsory exercise in walks. The timetable also demanded gym lessons twice a week, and those whom the games mistresses decided had flat feet or round shoulders devoted evenings to 'remedials' (stretching, balancing on tip-toe, or hanging on rib stools).

Pressure of exams meant no release from the daily obligation to play hockey or netball in winter and spring, and tennis, swimming and rounders in summer. Sometimes I would bandage my ankle and dare to put my name on the 'non-players' list, hoping no one would confer with my matron – the final authority on my bodily health.[28] Then I would lie on the cold lino under my bed, secretly reading. Before 'walks in threes', we would stuff books in our knickers so as to study in the fields. After 'lights out' we would revise for 'A' levels in the lavatories or in lit passages off the matron's beat. Knowledge and academic success were acquired by stealth.

It can be argued that physical exercise is essential, that youthful energy must be unleashed and directed. This does not explain the special form our exercises had to take. They were not merely to satisfy physiological needs, but another route to the mind. Those traditional 'female' accomplishments, dance, ballet and riding, at which we could excel as women, and which some of us preferred, were 'extras' to be paid for above the basic fees and then only available one hour a week. Games, on the other hand, were compulsory and free. We marched as soldiers out of roll-call but alternative movement to music was absent from the official curriculum. Our gymnastics were not of the modern kind, feminine and flowing, but instead freakish masculine jerks. Hockey and netball captured mind and body, because they concentrated group mentality, required whistle-blown attention, and imprinted rules on the imagination.

In many cultures, the right and left sides of the body, like the hands, are used to represent symbolic and social oppositions (Hertz, 1960). The right is given pre-eminence and may be associated with order, legitimacy and the male, while the left can be associated with disorder, disruptive forces and the female. In our school, the games and deportment badges were sewn on the left, while the badges of authority, including those with a male military idiom, e.g. 'sergeant' and house 'captain', were sewn on the right side of the tunic. Aptitude in the gym was indicated on the left by a miniature shield bearing the word 'Drill'. The red fire-fighter's ribbon hung from the left shoulder while the 'fire captain', the authority holder, sewed her badge on the right. Swimming abilities, usually demonstrated by proficiency in life-saving exercises, were marked on the left. There were no badges for music and dance. In this way, the potentially destructive forces of fire, water, the female body and movement were clamped with maximum control and minimum expression.

Popular images of the girls' boarding-school sometimes give important hints of the ambivalence and contradictions in these institutions. Ollerenshaw refers to the image of St Trinian's, with its 'whisky-swigging, hockey-stick-hacking, little horrors', and that of 'seminaries for nice girls where daughters can be safely locked up for the greater part of their troublesome teenage years' (1967, pp. 21-2). She concludes that no girls' school fits either image. I suggest that elements of both may be found together in the institution. On the games field we were expected to show a certain aggressive muscularity which in no way undermined the simultaneous demand that we be chaste and feminine.

There are indeed certain male and female sports. Those exclusively for boys include rugby, football and boxing. Those mainly for girls include netball, hockey, lacross, and rounders. Tennis, swimming and sometimes cricket are found in both. The association of hockey-stick-hacking' with girls sometimes elicits laughter. Apparently incongruous for females, hockey is yet considered insufficiently masculine to count as a major sport for British boys,[29] and is absent or marginal to the basic curriculum.

What differences exist between male and female sports? First, rugby permits the use of the arms as weapons to hold or push opponents. Boxing depends on an even more forceful drive and punch of arms and fist. In the rugger 'scrum' the players are obliged to cling to each other. There are 'running tackles'; and the players throw themselves at each other. Netball, rounders, hockey and lacrosse do not permit holds and pushes with the arms, fists or body. If you knock or hold an opponent this is a 'foul'. As in the punishment system, there is no bodily contact. The only institutionalised body contact in exercise at our school took place in ballroom dancing lessons (paid for as an 'extra'), or during the Saturday evening dances. In those quicksteps and waltzes, the partners were surrogate man and woman, permitted the one tactile premonition of adulthood.

Other differences between the male and female sports concern the use of the legs, feet and hands. The aggressive use of the legs (kicking, and thus opening or raising the legs forward to expose, metaphorically, the genitals) is not permitted for girls. They must not touch the ball with the foot, must not kick any male ball. Modesty is retained.[30] Thus the 'weaker sex' are made weaker, being forbidden aggressive and defensive use of the arms, legs and feet. All the female sports demand manual dexterity in throwing, catching, hitting, 'dribbling' (hockey), or 'cradling' (lacrosse) the ball. This inhibits speed in running. Rounders is freer in some ways in that players can hit and swing with the full force of their bodies, with both arms raised. Sports, like cricket and tennis, played by men also, demand some manual dexterity, but these, tennis more especially, are permitted for women because they have none of the characteristics of the exclusively male sports discussed above.

Although rugger, football, lacrosse and hockey pitches are of comparable size, movement for girls in that space is at all times encumbered by holding a stick. The rugger and football players can at times run free and fast, hurtling through space. Even the rugger player's flight is not greatly impeded by embracing the ball. For girls, only in netball is movement permitted free of stick, but restricted within the smaller space, and the player holding the ball is rendered immobile. The proximity of lines and many players require delicate avoidance within what amounts to a cage. I understand more clearly now why I would gaze out through the wire mesh of the netball court, repeating Shelley's words:

> Oh, lift me as a wave, a leaf, a cloud!
> . . .
> A heavy weight of hours has chained and bowed
> One too like thee: tameless, and swift, and proud.

Despite the rationale for games as being for exercise and development, netball was experienced by me as an endeavour to domesticate, slow down and humiliate us. In the girls' games speed is reduced, the body peculiarly controlled or burdened. When playing hockey or lacrosse, an intermediary was required between our feet and the ball, between our arms and the ball, between our bodies and the opponent. Off the games field the limited, aggressive skill we had acquired was useless without our tools. We were rendered powerless, impotent without our substitute phallus.

Gathorne-Hardy notes that a girls' game 'however well done, looks unconvincing' (1977, p. 251). He suggests that girls are more sensitive than boys to purposeless activities, and that games reinforce the contradiction whereby girls are educated to be like boys and then expected to be subservient to them later. He examines neither the gender differentiation in games nor their form, whereas I suggest that the contradiction is embedded in the rules of the games and enacted and reaffirmed in each performance. The girls' bodies are extended and constrained in this choreography of their future which they learn unconsciously in legs, arms, hands, feet and torso. The girls' games when contrasted with those for boys affirmed our impotence in speed, attack and defence, leaving us with feminine dexterity and an eye for detail. While our school song acknowledged the greater restrictions on noise from girls, it strove to assert an equality which we couldn't achieve, which couldn't exist:

> So we jog day by day
> On our life's pleasant way
> And although we don't
>   make such a noise,
> There are things I can name
> Such as playing the game,
> We can do them
>   as well as the boys.

Success was circumscribed, for to be truly female, we were not to develop masculine muscles. In any case, we knew that hockey, lacrosse and netball, unlike football, rugger or boxing rarely penetrated the adult sports pages and radio. Tennis, being a mixed game, and one we could continue most easily after schooldays, was not systematically coached unless, like dance lessons, we paid for it above the main fees. Generally we were trained in games we could neither continue, nor identify with, when grown.

We also marched: daily at roll-call and as the major event of Sports Day. For weeks of the summer term we practised on the hockey pitch, while the games mistress gave orders through a megaphone. On the final day we were decked in tunic and clean striped shirts, with white ankle socks and tennis shoes. A hired van blared out recordings of military bands, playing especially the compositions of J.P. Sousa. A shape resembling the Union Jack was chalked on the pitch and we travelled along its lines, dividing, redividing, crossing and regrouping. The parents, staff and honoured guests (the prize-giver was usually the headmaster of a boys' prep school) and the rejects from the marching watched from a raised bank. This was all very exhilarating, but again we were being exercised in an unfeminine accomplishment to be abandoned after leaving school. Only men did national service and marched in the forces.[31] That straight-shouldered gait with swinging arms and regular footwork would have to be discarded, indeed unlearnt, as feminine step took over. We would only need it for country walks and following the hounds. Just as hockey hinted at impotence, so did the mode of marching. Instead of thumping our heels first on the ground, we had to point our toes; the feminised fall of the foot. Our attack was gently broken. Moreover we landed on the sound-dead turf of the hockey pitch; no noisy thrill of tarmac. Beneath the military music we heard only the rustle of our skirts and starched sleeves.

Conclusion

There are similarities between the girls' boarding-school and that for boys: the separation from urban life, from economic production and members of other social classes, from parents and home, and the separation by gender. In this preliminary analysis I have concentrated on some of the differences for girls concerning the choice of heroic models, the degree of control over pupils, the distribution of authority between adults and pupils, forms of punishment, the approach to the body and the types of movement permitted in the games curriculum and the like. For girls, important discontinuities may be found between school and what is realisable in later life. The presentation to girls of models of achievement generally associated with men undervalues any which might be associated with women, and conveys male dominance as inevitable. The girls' school, without corporal punishment, may paradoxically be stricter than that for boys, and allow its pupils less self-determination. Indeed, power may be exercised more completely over girls precisely because it is not visible as physical force. I suggest that in so far as alternatives are not emphasised, the girls are prepared mainly for economic and political dependence within marriage,[32] whether or not this is the intention of the authorities. The differences between the education of boys and girls are important indicators as to how within the same social class each gender is socially defined and culturally reproduced. In this paper, I have taken as an example a type of education usually regarded as privileged, but the analysis may be relevant to other girls' schools without such pretensions.

Notes

1. The terms 'public' and 'independent' refer to private fee-paying schools in the UK, in contrast to wholly state-maintained schools. In 1965 only 2 per cent of girls in the 13-year age group in the United Kingdom were in independent public schools (cited in Ollerenshaw, 1967, p. 13).

2. See Lambert, 1975, Honey, 1977, and Gathorne-Hardy, 1977.

3. See Blackstone, 1976, p. 199.

4. Wober's *The English Girls' Boarding School* (1971) is a pioneering study but limited in scope. The data are based on only 20 weeks of field-work in 23 schools, using questionnaires. It is significant that the terms of the original grant for the larger research project by Lambert on boys' schools specifically excluded girls' schools (1975, p. 5). Gathorne-Hardy's research is largely devoted to boys' schools (1977). His two chapters on girls' schools offer some imaginative, although sometimes erratic observations. Recently there has been a revival of interest in the fantasy literature on girls' boarding-schools (Cadogan and Craig, 1976; Freeman, 1976). Angela Brazil, the major pedlar of illusion, never attended such an institution as a participant member. Inevitably crucial aspects of boarding-school experience do not surface.

5. When I delivered the first draft of this paper at the Oxford Women's Seminar, reactions were mixed. Those who had attended day schools were incredulous, while former boarders found many parallels or echoes of their own experience.

6. See also Okely, 1975.

7. A girl's academic ambitions will also depend on the extent to which she is encouraged by her parents off-stage. Wober notes in his questionnaires among the girls that 'Careers and professions seemed less common as a central focus; instead the emphasis was on "good jobs" . . . that would finance the gay pre-marital years, and thereafter serve for part-time or temporary occupation' (1971, p. 88).

8. Gathorne-Hardy has also found the concept of the *rite de passage* illuminating (1977).

9. Further research is necessary to explore the extent of permitted free movement by individuals beyond the school grounds. Certainly, some of the girls' schools are elaborately bounded by high walls, barricades or 'battlements' to prevent both intrusion by outsiders (Gathorne-Hardy, 1977, pp. 240, 258) and to reaffirm the enclosure of the inmates.

10. See Bateson 1973.

11. The evening after a nine-year-old girl learnt of her father's death, she was told by the matron not to cry lest she keep the other girls in the dormitory awake.

12. Further research might confirm the impression from the literature and other sources that homosexuality is more explicit in boys' schools (see Gathorne-Hardy, 1977, p. 171). As in other areas, the differences would relate also to early socialisation, not merely the effects of schooling.

13. Public-school boys are literally prepared in 'prep' schools. Lambert notes that over 80 per cent of all boys in public schools had been to preparatory schools and that 85 per cent of his own sample had boarded in such institutions (1975, p. 126). Wober found that only 25 per cent of his sample of girls (the majority of whom arrived at boarding-school at 11 or 13) had previously boarded in a prep school (1971, p. 44). Many had attended coeducational schools.

14. See later section, Containment and Powerlessness.

15. There are, by contrast, more persons of the opposite sex in boys' schools, namely the domestic staff, matrons and masters' wives. But 'boys and staff have learned to relegate women to marginal organizational and largely decorative roles' (Lambert, 1975, p. 116).

16. This dog was named after a day of the week, just like *Man* Friday. A colleague from another girls' boarding-school has noted a similar collection of males. Her headmistress had two male dachshunds.

17. Wober records that among his sample of girls' schools 'About one-third of the governors were women' (1971, p. 48).

18. In many schools, girls had to sing 'Forty Years On' which was written specifically for boys and included the inappropriate football chorus (Haddon, 1977, pp. 21-2).

19. Even in the late 1960s Wober found that the majority of teachers in the girls' boarding-schools were unmarried (1971, p. 38) and that only a minority had boarded (1971, p. 40). By contrast Lambert records that the majority of staff in boys' public schools were themselves educated in such institutions (1975, p. 54).

20. Wober notes, 'In most cases, no matter at what time one arrived, the schools appeared quiet; girls, if seen, were scurrying about . . . whispering' (1971, p. 293). Gathorne-Hardy, during his visit to Cheltenham Ladies, noted 'a dead silence . . . a silence more awesome and more indicative of discipline than any bell, 800 girls swished in swift lines down the long, dim, tiled corridors towards the next classroom' (1977, p. 244).

21. I am grateful to Dr Peter Rivière for drawing my attention to this difference in social structure.

22. It is possible that the extent of authority allotted to girls in boarding-schools containing adolescents is similar to that for younger boys in their prep schools.

23. 'No one could really call Patty pretty . . . she was neither dull nor particularly clever, only possessed of average abilities, able to remember lessons when she tried hard, and gifted with a certain capacity for plodding, but not in the least brilliant over anything she undertook. She was never likely to win fame, or set the Thames on fire, but she was one of those cosy, thoughtful, cheery, lovable home girls, who are often a great deal more pleasant to live with than some who have greater talents' (Brazil, 1909, pp. 20-1).

24. See also women's reluctance to speak or speak audibly at seminars where egoistic panache is demanded.

25. See also Foucault (1977, pp. 135-69) for his discussion of 'Docile Bodies'.

26. Stephen Spender has said of his prep school: 'They might as well have had me educated at a brothel for flagellants' (cited by Gathorne-Hardy 1977, p. 111).

27. The navy knickers and linings were a feature of many girls' schools (Haddon, 1977, pp. 75-6).

28. The matron's dominion over the girl's bodily health and sickness cannot be fully explored in this paper.

29. The various forms of these male sports depend also on the public school. Eton has also its own, like the Wall Game. There are also preferences according to social class and nationality within the UK. But the broad gender differentiation occurs in both public and state schools.

30. In the privacy of the gymnasium, the legs are opened when jumping over the 'horse' or when hanging on bars, but not raised in an aggressive kick. Some kicking motions are permitted when helplessly lying on the floor, with no target.

31. The single annual visit to London by the whole school was to the Royal Tournament; an all-male military display.

32. Since the 1950s the girl's biological virginity may be less important although her social virginity must still be protected. Moreover, greater sexual freedom may not alter a woman's economic and political dependence.

Bibliography

Bateson, G. 'Double Bind' in his *Steps to an Ecology of Mind*. Farnham, Paladin, 1973
Blackstone, T. 'The Education of Girls Today' in J. Mitchell and A. Oakley, *The Rights and Wrongs of Women*. Harmondsworth, Penguin, 1976
Bourdieu, P. *Outline of a Theory of Practice*. Cambridge, Cambridge University Press, 1977
Brazil, A. *The Nicest Girl in the School*. London, Blackie, 1909
Cadogan, M., and Craig, P. *You're a Brick Angela!* London, Gollancz, 1976
Connolly, C. *Enemies of Promise*. Harmondsworth, Penguin, 1961
Foucault, M. *Discipline and Punish*. London, Allen Lane, 1977
Freeman, G. *The Schoolgirl Ethic: The Life and Work of Angela Brazil*. London, Allen Lane, 1976
Gathorne-Hardy, J. *The Public School Phenomenon*. London, Hodder and Stoughton, 1977
Goffman, E. *Asylums*. Harmondsworth, Penguin, 1968
Haddon, C. *Great Days and Jolly Days*. London, Hodder and Stoughton, 1977
Hertz, R. 'The Pre-eminence of the Right Hand' in *Death and the Right Hand*, trans. R. and C. Needham. London, Cohen and West, 1960
Honey, J.R. de S. *Tom Brown's Universe*. London, Millington, 1977
Lambert, R. *The Chance of a Lifetime?* London, Weidenfeld and Nicolson, 1975
Marks, P. 'Femininity in the Classroom: An Account of Changing Attitudes' in J. Mitchell and A. Oakley, *The Rights and Wrongs of Women*. Harmondsworth, Penguin, 1976
Mauss, M. 'Les Techniques du Corps', 1936, in his *Anthropologie et Sociologie*. Paris, Presses Universitaires de France, 1938
Mitford, J. *A Fine Old Conflict*. London, Michael Joseph, 1977
Okely, J. 'The Self and Scientism'. *Journal of the Oxford Anthropology Society*, Michaelmas, Oxford, 1975
Ollerenshaw, K. *The Girls' Schools*. London, Faber and Faber, 1967
Pocock, D. 'The Idea of a Personal Anthropology'. Paper given at the ASA Conference, 1973 (unpublished)
———. *Understanding Social Anthropology*. London, Teach Yourself Books, Hodder and Stoughton, 1975
Shelley, P.B. *Selections*. A.H. Thompson (ed.). Cambridge, Cambridge University Press, 1956
Wilson, C. *The Outsider*. London, Gollancz, 1956
Wober, M. *English Girls' Boarding Schools*. London, Allen Lane, 1971

6

MATRIFOCUS ON AFRICAN WOMEN

Wendy James

The Question

Is it possible to make major criticisms of academic categories and models on the basis of intuition and generalised personal feeling? My felt generalisation is this: that in Africa, south of the Sahara, in both traditional and modern conditions and even in Muslim areas, the 'position of women' has a good deal to be said in its favour, by comparison with other major cultural regions such as the Mediterranean, the Arab Middle East, India or China. Of course there are contrasts between one part of Africa and another, even between closely neighbouring peoples. But a reading of the literature, together with personal experience gained from travel, leaves one with a striking series of impressions of the relative economic, political and sexual freedom of most African women. We remember the proud and colourful market women of West Africa; the royal queens, queen mothers and princesses of the traditional kingdoms; the King of Dahomey's female bodyguard; the fighting women of traditional Ethiopia[1] and the rioting women of Iboland in the thirties.[2] There are the organised guilds of prostitutes in rural Niger,[3] and the *femmes libres* of modern city life; and not least the modern women politicians of Africa. Nowhere in traditional Africa, south of the Sahara, were women veiled or wrapped up physically to the extent we see them in the Mediterranean, Middle East or India today. Nowhere were they secluded within the walls of the domestic household and cut off from public life as in some other regions. African forms of architecture and settlement patterns themselves did not permit such seclusion nor such a separation of the domestic from the wider sphere of social life. The very openness of life in the villages makes visible the African woman's daily tasks, whereas her Arab or Indian sister's daily work is hidden where possible from passing strangers. It is true that there is an image of the African woman's lot being one of hard labour and virtual serfdom to her lord and master, even of being 'bought and sold' in marriage, but the payment of bride-wealth is no more 'buying a wife' than European dowry was 'buying a husband'. If I may now add a subjective response gained from living and travelling in Africa, then I can say that as a woman visitor, alone or with unrelated male companions, I often feel personally much more comfortable and unquestioningly accepted in Africa, rather than in say, an Arab environment.

Beside this general feeling about the 'position of women' in Africa, we can place a fact of academic social anthropology. In a global perspective, the African continent is today by far the major home of matriliny, the systematic tracing of 'descent' through women. It is true that the matrilineal principle of organisation was centrally important for a number of traditional societies elsewhere. The Americas, parts of Australia and the Pacific provide examples, but in most cases, in the face of historical change these societies have proved too fragile to be able to preserve their traditional matrilineal forms, or even, sometimes, their population. In parts of Asia, there are scattered groups who practise matriliny, but they seem in many cases to have given up at least its more extreme forms. In Africa, however, there are vast regions of the Congo basin, of east central Africa, and of West Africa, where matriliny was traditionally the dominant form of organisation. And in contrast to other parts of the world, in these African areas matriliny has not only persisted into the present day, but in a few societies seems to have flourished. One reason for this persistence was put forward by Mary Douglas (1969) who has argued that matriliny has certain advantages in an expanding modern economy, as among some of the Ghanaian peoples. Interestingly, in one or two cases there is some evidence that matriliny has actually emerged in recent historical times as a newly dominant principle of organisation. This is what has almost certainly happened, for example, among the Uduk of the Sudan-Ethiopian border, where I have myself carried out field research.

Is it reasonable to ask whether we may connect these two broad generalisations, one based on 'feelings' and one based on 'evidence'? On the basis of an intuitive conviction about the relative personal standing of women in Africa, can we forward an interpretation of the academic facts of the persistence and resilience of matriliny among many of the populations of the continent?

The Nineteenth-Century Answer: Evolution Towards Patriliny

The response to this kind of question has changed over time, and should, I shall suggest, change once more. The standard answer in the last century would have been: yes, the 'position of women' is 'higher' in a matrilineal society. Those who first speculated on the early history of the family, and of marriage, assumed that the tracing of descent through women was a primitive form of social organisation which preceded the development of property and private wealth, and in which paternity of children was therefore clearly of no consequence. The tracing of descent through women was then assumed without question to be connected with the exercise of power and influence by women, variously categorised as the institution of mother-right, or matriarchy, or rule by women. The existence of matriliny today would have been regarded as a survival from the early days of human history, and it would have been taken for granted that this mode of organisation implied a special status and position of authority for women. These assumptions often constituted mythical representations of the past, rather than history.

There are echoes of the Amazon myth of the ancient Greeks in more than a few of the early writings on the evolution of the family. The transition to patriliny and patriarchy meant a real overthrow of female dominance. Engels, for example, after discussing Bachofen's *Das Mutterrecht* and the more down-to-earth surveys of L.H. Morgan, writes forcefully in his *Origin of the Family, Private Property and the State:*

> In proportion as wealth increased, it made the man's position in the family more important than the woman's, and on the other hand created an impulse to exploit this strengthened position in order to overthrow in favour of his children the traditional order of inheritance. This, however, was impossible so long as descent was reckoned according to mother-right. Mother-right, therefore, had to be overthrown, and overthrown it was. This was by no means so difficult as it looks to us today. For this revolution — one of the most decisive ever experienced by humanity — could take place without disturbing a single one of the living members of a gens. All could remain as they were. A simple decree sufficed that in future the offspring of the male members should remain within the gens, but that of the female should be excluded by being transferred to the gens of the father. The reckoning of descent in the female line and the matriarchal law of inheritance were thereby overthrown, and the male line of descent and the paternal law of inheritance were substituted for them. As to how and when this revolution took place among civilised peoples, we have no knowledge. It falls entirely within prehistoric times . . . The overthrow of mother-right was the *world-historical defeat of the female sex*. The man took command in the home also; the woman was degraded and reduced to servitude, she became the slave of his lust and a mere instrument for the reproduction of children. This degraded position of the woman, especially conspicuous among the Greeks of the heroic and still more of the

classical age, has gradually been palliated and glozed over, and sometimes clothed in a milder form; in no sense has it been abolished (1891, pp. 58-9, original italics).

But, as Engels admits, we have no evidence of this early revolution in our affairs. We must therefore agree today that this passage belongs to the realm of myth and fantasy rather than history.

A comparable element of fantasy, of emotional reasoning, still enters into the work of some sober historians today. The idea of the inherent supremacy of patrilineal descent, and the ease with which it may dominate matriliny as a system, as men may wield physical power over women, appears, for example, in accounts of the spread of the Arab peoples into the Nile Basin. The indigenous peoples of the central Nile valley, the Beja, Nubians and so forth, have often been assumed to have all followed a system of matrilineal reckoning. The opinion of the medieval Arab geographers that an incoming Arab sheikh needed merely therefore to marry the daughter or sister of a king for the whole kingdom to fall into his lap, is uncritically accepted by some modern historians. The assumption is that the son of such a union would succeed by the matrilineal rule, and then by changing the system to patrilineal reckoning, he could keep the throne in the male line of Arab descent thereafter (see, for example, Hasan, 1967). Matriliny is still assumed in such analyses to be less stable politically than patriliny, and to give way in the course of history to the more powerful organisation.

Unfortunately, some of the new 'women's lib' literature, in attempting to re-analyse the role of women in early society, accepts these unscientific theories in their entirety, merely reversing the moral. Reed's book on *Woman's Evolution* (1975), for example, falls headlong for the simple idea of a former golden age of female rule, wickedly overthrown by greedy property-seeking men. In considering both the earlier evolutionary writers, and their modern topsy-turvy counterparts, we must bear in mind several points. In the first place, the association between the existence of a line of descent and the relative authority or power of the sexes is by no means a clear or simple one. In fact it would not even be agreed by modern anthropologists that such a correlation can be found. Moreover, the presence of a system of reckoning by one mode of lineal descent in a given society does not exclude the use of other principles. Indeed there are virtually always other modes of reckoning relationships which coexist with lineal descent, and the two apparently alternative modes of unilineal descent may even be present together. And further, it must be understood that although there are known cases of matrilineal reckoning being replaced for jural purposes of inheritance and succession by patrilineal or non-unilineal reckoning, this is not a historic universal. Matriliny still persists, even among some communities which have a highly sophisticated political, economic and military organisation. History may occasionally show how even a latent principle of matrilineal linking may become a dominant mode of reckoning for jural purposes. We must not forget that, beyond the question of jural purposes, 'matriliny' may be understood in terms alternative to those of the holding and transmission of rights and powers. As a principle of biological and moral connection between the generations it may exist in many societies without finding legal expression as a channel for the handing on of power and rights, and yet nevertheless be of profound consequence for the lives of the people.

Engels' picture, then, which parallels the thought of many authors of his time and which has attracted the reforming wrath of some of our embattled sisters, is easily faulted for representing matriliny and female rule as the same thing, for assuming that modes of lineal descent are mutually exclusive, and for claiming that the history of all societies has shown a one-way revolution from one mode of jural descent to the other.

The Twentieth-Century Answer: Jural Models of Male Control

Some of these faults in early evolutionary anthropology were corrected with the establishment of professional field reporting in social anthropology, and the systematic empirical search for comparative principles of social organisation. During the middle part of the present century, constitutional principles of a quasi-legal kind articulating the main forms of social organisation were sought, almost to the neglect in some cases of more humane considerations as to what the complexities of personal and moral life might be like for people actually living in various forms of social structure. Matriliny, for example, quite correctly detached from the crude idea of rule by women, was unfortunately separated from any question concerning its more subtle consequences for the character of women's lives, or relations between the sexes and within the family. It was seen merely as a neutral organising principle, diagrammatically connecting men between the generations. The idea of rule by women was happily relegated to the realm of myth, for the empirical evidence appeared to show that everywhere societies were 'ruled by' men. In matrilineal societies no less than elsewhere, women were seen to be 'under the authority' of their menfolk. The dominant model of society remained one of the system of *rule*, of the arrangement and transmission of rights and duties and powers. In matrilineal systems, it seemed, these powers were transmitted from males to males as in patrilineal systems, the only difference being that an intermediate female link existed. This 'jural model' of society, being founded in Radcliffe-Brown's writings, for example those dealing with the structuring of men's rights over things and rights over persons (including women), tends to leave women out of the picture even in matrilineal systems.[4] The idea of descent itself came to be equated with the transmission of power and authority, though the ethnographic evidence surely shows that there may be many other components in the idea.

The primacy given to jural authority and power by many anthropologists in defining the essential form of society led to the famous 'matrilineal puzzle'. Audrey Richards formulated this puzzle in relation to a series of Central African peoples. A woman marries a man outside her own group, but her children inherit within it from her brothers. A father exercises some control over his own children, and they may be brought up at least for part of their childhood in his village, but they are part of their mother's brothers' lineage living elsewhere. There is thus a conflict, over the children, between the authority and interest of the father and that of the mother's brothers, who are by definition of a different lineage and living elsewhere (Richards, 1950). Schneider and Gough's major survey of matriliny (1961) also sees it as a problematic power game for men. Robin Fox, one of whose main principles of human kinship is that 'the men usually exercise control' (1967, p. 31), again formulates the problem clearly from the viewpoint of the men of a matrilineage: how are they to keep control and exercise authority over the lineage when the succeeding generation of young men are likely to be brought up in dispersed places as a result of their mothers' marriages? There are various solutions. For example, domestic marriage as we might recognise it may not exist, and the women of a matrilineage may be kept together under the eye of their brothers, while their husbands come and go on a visiting basis. But this, it seems, is a 'problem for men' too, since their lives are divided residentially. If they spend time at their wife's home they cannot exercise control over their own lineages. Fox represents the essence of the matrilineal problem (for men) as being 'how to combine continuity and recruitment through females with control by the *men* of the lineage' (ibid., p. 113, author's italics). He admits that if his principle about male control did not hold, the problem would not arise,

and an Amazonian solution would serve. In this the women hold the property and the power, men would be of no account and would be used for breeding purposes only. Such a sinister practice exists only in the imagination . . . Women don't ever seem to have got quite such a grip on things (ibid., p. 113).

Patrilineages do not face the same kind of problem as matrilineages, since they combine continuity of residence, the line of authority and descent without any difficulty – from the men's point of view. The fact that women in such a system have to move geographically and socially from their own to their husband's place on marriage does not constitute a structural problem in this kind of analysis, for they are not the main holders and transmitters of control and authority.

Lévi-Strauss sees the special character and problematic interest of matrilineal societies in much the same way.

The husband is a stranger, a 'man from outside', sometimes an enemy, and yet the woman goes away to live with him in his village to bear children who will never be his . . . Matrilineal descent is the authority of the woman's father or brother extended to the brother-in-law's village (1969, p. 116).

Lévi-Strauss too sees a conflict between the principle of matriliny and the universal asymmetry of the sexes in terms of political control, which he too considers cannot survive in politically developed societies:

It is true that in societies where political power takes precedence over other forms of organization, the duality which would result from the masculinity of political authority and the matrilineal character of descent could not subsist. Consequently, societies attaining this level of political organization tend to generalize the paternal right. But it is because political authority, or simply social authority, always belongs to men, and because this masculine priority appears constant, that it adapts itself to a bilineal or matrilineal form of descent in most primitive societies . . . (1969, pp. 116-17).

He writes of the 'basic asymmetrical relationship between the sexes which is characteristic of human society' (ibid., p. 117). For the anthropologist, because of the various ways in which matrilineal societies try to get around these difficulties the study of a matrilineal society represents the promise of a complicated social organization, rich in strange institutions, imbued with an atmosphere of the dramatic . . . it is no coincidence that almost all monographs which have had wide repercussions have been about matrilineal societies (ibid., p. 117).

Evans-Pritchard puts the matter in a comparable way in his essay on the position of women in primitive society:

In primitive societies men invariably hold the authority, though in some societies and in certain circumstances old women may exercise authority as well. As you well know, there are societies in which inheritance and succession pass in the female line, but in such societies the ordinary woman, in so far as she does not come under the authority of her father or husband is under the authority of her mother's brother or her own brother.

In the commoner primitive societies, 'a woman passes at marriage from under the authority of her father to that of her husband . . . The husband's authority as such is not challenged' (1965, pp. 50-1).

Repeating metaphors of hierarchical spatial arrangement, of asymmetry and of some people being *under* the authority of others run through these discussions and are perhaps inseparable from what has become an orthodox view of society as constituted by rules governing the exercise of power and control. Although the concept of authority itself has been treated much more sensitively in some of the other writings of the authors I have mentioned, and indeed itself is often *contrasted* with the notion of dominant power, in discussions of kinship in general and matriliny in particular, the principle of authority is usually represented in terms of crude power. The jural model based on these assumptions is still with us. Lewis, in a recent textbook, states:

Where descent is traced matrilineally, through women, the men nevertheless monopolize all the positions of power; a man's closest relative is his sister and his most immediate heir and successor (after his brother) is her son. In such circumstances men must seek control of their sisters, and their sisters' children (Lewis, 1976, p. 269).

The jural model of society is indeed difficult to dissociate from the idea of brute male power. Later, we read:

The difficulties in matrilineal systems stem directly from the conflict between male domination and citizenship traced through women. If women were to seize political control, making matriliny matriarchy, or to employ artificial insemination, things would be very different (ibid., p. 273).

Thus the mid-twentieth century answer to my opening question, of whether there can be any connection between my intuitive feeling on the one hand that women are under less constraint in Africa than in some other regions, and on the other the relatively common occurrence of matriliny there, would be 'No. You are under a sentimental misapprehension, for male domination is a universal social fact; in matrilineal systems men may not have organised their collective power very efficiently, but with increased economic and political development they will correct this.'

An Alternative View of Matriliny

But must we look at societies as power structures? Certainly this way of looking at things reveals contradictions and conflicts in matriliny. But do the people who practise matriliny see it foundering on contradictory principles? Do they see it as a structural power game more puzzling for men than other modes of organisation? Or is it possible that they may see the system in a different perspective? Perhaps their ideas of citizenship and identity, and of authority, their definitions of status and ties of loyalty are far more complex and subtle than those of the average structural anthropologist. Perhaps the intellectual, moral and even political view of matriliny taken by those who live with it may yield a more integrated picture than we suspect. And perhaps the notion of 'domination' is far too crude to enable us to understand the relative authority of the sexes in any society.

There is a clue to alternative ways of approaching the whole matter in the concluding paragraphs of Evans-Pritchard's essay. He implies here that the position of women in relation to men cannot be stated solely in terms of higher or lower status, or of differential wealth or rights, for it is a moral question of much wider implication.

Ultimately the status of women, and particularly her status in the home, goes beyond the scope of sociological analysis. It is fundamentally a moral question, and whilst it is true that the findings of sociological inquiry must be taken into full consideration in making a judgement, the judgement itself must derive from some code of ethics (1965, p. 56)

We may take this as a starting point for building a more constructive approach to the question of women and matriliny; and also to the problem with which I opened. To understand matriliny, we may find that we have to put aside the jural model of power distribution altogether. Having done that we may remind ourselves of what matriliny means, minimally, when we use this term, and what therefore it should minimally indicate in the thinking of the people of whom we use it. We do mean by 'matriliny' a principle whereby, in the thinking of the people under discussion, a connection between one generation and the next is made, for whatever purpose, systematically through females. This can be represented diagrammatically (and interestingly, in contrast to diagrams of patriliny, the females cannot be left out of the diagram!). Even in the sketchiest of matrilineal diagrams, the females are clearly more than unmarked links between men; they are nodal points. Even on the diagram, the 'position' of every individual, men no less than women, is definable only with reference to females, and the continuity of the society as a whole, through the generations, must be represented through them. Now society is more than a diagram; and where the matrilineal principle is enshrined, for whatever practical or symbolic purpose, the nodal position held by women must be more than a diagrammatic matter. There must surely be evaluative connotations, even a theory of the central focus provided by women in the definition of social relations stemming from the matrilineal principle. The granting of a key position to women in the logical, formal ordering of wider relations surely invites us to look further, not necessarily for 'female rule' in a crude power sense, but for equally strong affirmations of the central qualities, even the primacy, of women's position.

Our search is easily rewarded. We may not find Amazons, but typically in the matrilineal societies of Africa we do find characteristically positive evaluation of the centrally creative role of women in contributing to the founding of a family and building of a household, through both their productive and reproductive capacities. The role of motherhood in particular is typically respected and honoured, and represented as a central social category, from which other relationships take their bearing – particularly connections with the next generation.

The Ashanti Case

The Akan peoples of Ghana, and particularly the Ashanti, are the best known and among the most flourishing of the matrilineal peoples of modern Africa. There are many sources on the Ashanti and the ethnography is widely familiar. We need few reminders of the central significance of the mother, in conceptual and practical terms, for Ashanti life. She is far more than a neutral link in the transmission of rights between her brothers and her sons. Rattray, the major early ethnographer of the Ashanti, was astonished at the importance of women in general and the Queen Mother in particular, and based his accounts in the 1920s very much on this discovery. He accepted from the start, in his description and analysis of Ashanti society, their own evaluations of the centrality of the mother's position, and accounted for the wider patterns of matrilineal descent groups, succession and so forth in terms of it.[5] In terms of both moral and biological relations, Ashanti ideas focus on the primacy of motherhood, and other relationships are seen to follow from this central fact. The mother's importance as a personal focus of kinship relations is explained by the Ashanti partly as deriving from their views of the physiology of reproduction: the child's closest physical bond is with his mother, for his body is formed from her blood. The bond with the father is of a less substantial nature, indeed it is seen rather as a complementary spiritual link. I would like to sum up the cluster of ideas surrounding the centrality of motherhood in a kinship system, as found in a very clear form among the Ashanti, under the term *matrifocality*. The term has been used variously, to cover a range of practices and institutions which seem to outsiders to indicate a strong pragmatic importance of the mother in family organisation. But as against this, primarily 'observer's', usage, I shall employ the term to mean essentially *an indigenous view of the moral primacy of biological motherhood in the definition of social relations*. A matrifocal mode of thinking about kinship may or may not find expression in the practical activities and organisation of social affairs 'on the ground'. In the case of the Ashanti, however, it certainly does. Their strongly matrifocal thinking about kinship is the foundation for a relatively prosperous and independent position of women in socio-economic terms, as well as for an overall jural framework of matrilineal descent groups. The 'premiss of matrifocality' among the Akan people as a whole underlies even the non-matrilineal aspects of the jural, political and economic system. The matrilineal descent group is the property-holding and transmitting group, and although patrilateral links are of great symbolic, political and religious importance, they are represented in terms secondary to the central principle of matriliny. The 'position of men' is defined primarily with reference to their mothers; not, I would say, with reference primarily to their mother's brothers, to whose rights they may well succeed within the lineage, but to whom they do not have the same essential link of personal identity and defining connection, nor of primary social obligation.

The basic premiss of matrifocal orientation is accepted as a starting-point for the Ashanti by Rattray, and as having explanatory status in his early ethnographic accounts of their society. But in this respect there is an interesting contrast to be found in the modern ethnography of Meyer Fortes. It is true that Fortes also recognises the important bond between mother and child, which is 'the key-stone of all social relations' and fixes the lineage affiliation and citizenship of the child, in which the role of the maternal grandmother is crucial in the upbringing of the child. The mother-child bond is

> an absolutely binding moral relationship. . . There are very many sayings and proverbs that express the attachment of Ashanti to their mothers and indicate the importance of the mother in social life. . . As Ashanti often point out, a person's status, rank and fundamental rights stem from his mother and that is why she is the most important person in his life (1950, pp. 263-4).

But Fortes is less concerned to base his interpretation on Ashanti premisses than on the general principles of structural-functional anthropology, which, as I have already suggested, provide a stereotype of matriliny and its in-built contradictions which stem from a very different set of premisses. In his various accounts of Ashanti, Fortes sees the society as founded on a conflict of principle, and he seems repeatedly amazed that its matrilineal organisation has survived at all, and certainly up to the present, when one might have thought that pragmatic change would have undermined it. He wrote in 1950, for example:

> The dominant principle of Ashanti kinship is the rule of matrilineal descent. In spite of nearly forty years of rapid social change. . . the Ashanti have tenaciously upheld this rule. The chief problem of kinship relations among them is to adjust the jural and moral claims and bonds arising out of marriage and fatherhood to those imposed by matrilineal kinship. Conflict between these rival claims and bonds is inherent in their kinship system. This problem is most acute for men (1950, p. 283).

If Fortes started from the premiss of matrifocality, as the Ashanti certainly do, these conflicts might not appear so disruptive; but Fortes' unspoken premiss is different. Could we even label it, along with the aggressively explicit reasoning of such writers as Fox, as the 'patrifocal syndrome'?

The Uduk Case

As a second example, may I offer a few brief remarks about the Uduk of the Sudan-Ethiopian border?[6] They are not a powerful people, politically or economically, as the Ashanti are, and matriliny is historically not as entrenched or of such major practical consequence as among the Ashanti. The Uduk are comparable in many ways to those poorer matrilineal peoples stretching in a wide belt right across Central Africa, including, for example, the Lele, the Ndembu, the Bemba and the Tonga.[7] Among the Uduk, as among most of these Central African peoples, however, the premiss of matrifocality is just as crucial to an understanding of both the 'position of women' and the 'social structure', as it is among the Ashanti. Again, in personal and moral terms the mother is the key figure in the kinship world of the Uduk. In biological thinking her blood is the physical source of children, and the father in collaboration with the power of *arum*, spirit, plays the part of moulding, or creating, the child from her substance, as a potter does clay. In these terms, the primary tie and working obligations of a person to his mother's people generally, and to her in particular, are explained. From these assumptions about the central importance of women, other matters are justified. Socio-economically, for example, the freedom of action of Uduk women is notorious in the region, particularly because of the ease with which they make and break their own marriages, and even defend their rights in a man, and their women's honour, through formal stick-duelling or jousting, with rivals. If you ask the Uduk why they live with their mother's people, rather than with those of their father, they will answer that it is because they do not pay bride-wealth, as most neighbouring peoples do; and because they do not exchange sisters in marriage, as a few of their neighbours do. The idea of the direct exchange of sisters by two men in a double marriage is more or less acceptable to them in theory, though they say they would never actually practise it since it leads to too much fighting. On the other hand, the idea of bride-wealth marriage is abhorrent to the Uduk, who say that they will not let their sister go for a few goats, as though she were an animal herself. They regard the payment of bride-wealth as akin to the buying and selling of people in slavery, something of which they have direct experience and understandably hate. Given the primary cluster of matrifocal ideas which form the starting-point of their thinking about biology and morality, and given their refusal to 'trade' in women through bride-wealth transactions, we can better understand the strength of the jural structure of matrilineal descent groups which governs the Uduk system of residence, inheritance, corporate rights in land, labour and so forth. What we may best call 'matrilineal birth-groups' trace their connection through the matriline, and regard themselves as sharing common blood. They are today the core of settlement units. Marriage is virilocal, but a boy leaves his father's home when he is old enough to herd the goats, and goes to join his own people, where he will eventually build a house for his wife. Animal wealth, rights in land and the obligation to work it are all transmitted through the birth-group.

In both symbolic and practical terms, the patrilateral link is, nevertheless, very important among the Uduk. The obligation of a birth-group to the man who fathers a new child for them is felt to be very great. Most of the obligation falls upon the child himself, or herself. In the case of a boy, the ultimate expression of this obligation takes the form of a political duty: if his father is in danger, the boy should fight at his side, if necessary laying down his life for his father. This rule holds even in the extreme situation when a boy's father's people are fighting his own. The implications of this rule reach very deeply into the 'social structure' of the Uduk. In time of danger and of frequent hostilities, a time such as the middle of the last century, boys would not go to live with their own people but would remain with their fathers. Moreover, marriage in those days would take place within a territorially close cluster of allied birth-groups. The pattern of organisation on the ground at such a time, and the logic behind it, might look very 'patrilineal' or patrifocal. But I suggest this would be deceptive. The terms in which Uduk consistently explain the logic of the obligations which lie behind their social organisation, whether in modern times or in the past when settlements and political alignments looked more patrifocal, remain the terms of matriliny, or matrifocality. You live with and support your father in the time of his need because he created you in your mother's womb, nourished you and brought you up for your own people. This obligation can scarcely be repaid, but you should do your best to acknowledge it. In times of peace, the political tie of father and son is of less practical significance and may even be missed by an ethnographer intent on describing actual patterns of residence and daily co-operation. This is because settlements are based on a core of matrilineal kin, and may be widely separated from each other on the ground. They may appear socially self-contained

to the point where the position of the father, and patrilateral relationships, fade into the background.

We as outsiders might at first be disposed to see structural conflicts
built into Uduk society, of the sort which have been identified by
recent writers in so many matrilineal societies. But I suggest that if we
take for granted Uduk assumptions of matrifocality as our starting-
point and do not lose sight of them, we will come to understand that
there is no real conflict. The fundamental axiom of the primacy of the
connection between mother and child, and its extension to the concept of a birth-line, or a birth-group, resolves the conceptual difficulties in seeing the system as a connected whole, even at a time when
other social ties may appear dominant on the ground. The matrifocal
premiss appears in many other areas of Uduk thought and reasoning,
where it provides a theoretical account of matters which otherwise
might appear in a different light to the observer from a society with
different assumptions. For example, when a double rainbow shines in
the sky, the Uduk say that the stronger, brighter bow is the female, and
the pale secondary reflection the male. In the more tricky field of the
idiom of kinship, the Uduk try to explain the logic of their own kin
terminology in matrilineal, or matrifocal, terms, even though it would
not necessarily look 'matrilineal' to the outsider. Visitors learning the
language of kinship would find, for example, that *akam*, in a general
sense 'brother', is used not only of siblings, but also of parallel cousins
on both sides (mother's sister's sons, and father's brother's sons). They
will later hear that 'brothers' are of one blood. They may then ask why
you call your father's brother's son *akam*, for he is surely not of one
blood with you, as your mother's sister's son is? The answer will nevertheless probably utilise, by analogy, the matrilineal principle of blood
connection: 'Ah, yes! But your father, and the father of that fellow,
were themselves brothers of one birth-group, and of one blood; because
of this, you call that fellow *akam*, "brother".'

The separate pieces of data collected by the anthropologist, such as
kinship terminology, residence statistics, rules of inheritance and
political loyalty, may present a haphazard picture, riddled with contradictions and a lack of fit between one piece of evidence and another.
But matrifocal premisses of thought, which one has to grasp as a matter
of fundamental orientation and intuition rather than explicit instruction, help to make sense of the Uduk system, even though theirs is not
as established a matrilineal society as that of the Ashanti; and such
premisses may help to make sense perhaps even of other, and apparently
very different, societies in Africa.

A Comparative African Perspective

Matrifocal assumptions, which grant a logically central and qualitatively positive role to women in the founding of a new family and in ensuring the continuity of the local group in biological and moral terms, are, not surprisingly, found very widely among the jurally matrilineal societies of Africa. Moreover, there is a comparable character in this cluster of ideas not only between the adjoining peoples of the great matrilineal regions of Africa (centred on southern Ghana and the broad belt of Central Africa especially). Striking parallels may be found among a number of relatively scattered and isolated matrilineal peoples on the map — for example, the Kunama and Uduk of the Sudan-Ethiopian border, some Nuba groups of the central Sudan, the Ohaffia Ibo and some isolated groups of central Nigeria and the Cameroons. These widely separated parallel cases might at first seem surprising. But we should now remember that to classify a society by the single criterion of its dominant jural principle, and then mark it off from others on the map, may not be the best way of making comparisons. If we look at fundamental thinking about the biology and morality of the relation between the sexes and the generations, on the other hand, regardless of the jural or power structure of a community at any given time, we may find that the isolated patches of jural matriliny on the map are not so sharply problematic. Contrasts of legal and politico-economic organisation may at any given time obscure more enduring values of a fundamental kind.

This leads into the second major point of my argument about the interpretation of African ethnography: that matrifocal assumptions of the centrality of women are not limited to the jurally matrilineal societies. Comparable ways of thinking may be found in African societies which for the purposes of the transmission of rights and property may be patrilineal, double unilineal or not even lineal at all. The idea of the continuity of a line of birth from a mother to her children, and daughters' children, and the biological and moral intimacy of those born to the same womb over a few generations, is by no means unique to those societies organised matrilineally for public socio-economic and political purposes. Where a matrilineal minority group appears on the map, adjoining culturally similar patrilineal neighbours, we need not assume there is no continuity of fundamental attitudes. Indeed the ethnography suggests otherwise (examples would include some of the Bamenda groups described by Phyllis Kaberry (1952), the Ohaffia Ibo described by Philip Nsugbe (1974), and the Uduk among the other Koman peoples).

It is surprising to what extent, even in the strongly and notoriously patrilineal societies of Africa, we may also find clues to the presence of underlying matrifocal ideas. Almost at random, we could mention for example the widespread matrifocality, identified under this name, among the Ibo as described in an essay by Nancy Tanner (1974); the centrality of women's position among the patrilineal Mende in a contribution to the same volume by Carol Hoffer (1974); and the long-discussed question of the maternal side of family and kinship among the patrilineal Tallensi (see Fortes, 1949). Among the patrilineal Tiv, the centrality of the principle of female fertility is maintained: traditionally a sister given away in marriage was properly replaced by a wife marrying in, sometimes even to become known by the sister's name, whose children were the offspring of the 'stem' of the patrilineage – a notion seeming to mean the fertility of its women, not of its men (see, for example, East, 1939). On the other side of Africa we have the example of the very interesting presence of matrilineal blood-feuding groups among the Murle, who are organised for purposes of inheritance, succession and territorial military companies on the patrilineal principle. The obligation for life itself, and its defence, nevertheless devolves upon the matrilineal kin (Lewis, 1972). For the culturally related Didinga, Kronenberg (1972) has demonstrated beyond doubt that patrilineages themselves are thought of as cumulatively built up by bride-wealth transactions from the child-bearing capacity of out-marrying women, who otherwise would be contributing to the growth of their own lineages. He describes the Didinga patrilineage suggestively as 'the sum of its uterinities'. What is given first place, in Didinga thought, seems to be the fertility of women and their primary contribution to the next generation. Thus patrilineages are artificial constructs built up from the fragments of many natural matrilines.

Even among the northern Nilotes, when we turn from a consideration of the wider patterning of lineage connections between political communities to the closer fabric of lineage structure among communities on the ground, we find that an initial primacy is given to maternal connection. Among the Nuer and the Dinka, for example, it is clear that the position of a child within his father's agnatic lineage is not automatic upon his birth; it is consequent upon the nature of the marriage tie, or lack of it, established with his mother. The child traces his connection with his agnatic lineage through his mother in the sense that he is a member of it by virtue of its acquired rights over his mother. This theme is constant through the very varied particular circumstances in which women may be associated with a lineage by marriage, concubinage, etc. But a child's primary relationship with his mother herself, and through her to her lineage and kin is not dependent on contractual arrangements or the transfer of rights. The relationship derives its character from the fact of birth, and is a personal tie of the closest kind. Those 'of the same womb' retain a close friendship throughout life, often providing each other with refuge and protection when necessary from agnatic kin. Special respect, and the avoidance of bloodshed, obtains between a person and his or her mother's brothers – an attitude of no small political consequence. A mass of detailed evidence from which this brief account could be much expanded may easily be found in the ethnography.[8]

In these examples we find indications of a latent network of matrifocal ties, amounting in some cases to a formula of continuing matrilineal connection, which is not the basis of jural organisation but nevertheless is of vital personal, affective and moral significance. The peoples mentioned appear to accord positive evaluation to the idea of natural descent, traced essentially through women in what we might envisage as a birth-line from mother to daughter, a line which is repeatedly broken and divided by transactions over the fertility of women and rights over their children, transactions made typically at marriage and consisting of bride-wealth payments. Through transactions of the bride-wealth type (and various other modes, for example of the exchange of sisters, which may achieve the same result), the rights of the father and their transmission to his children are secured. Agnatic lineages in the examples we have discussed are not thought of, nor do they act as, naturally given biological descent groups, with all that that might mean for social relations; they are socio-economic and jural corporations built up through the acquisition of wives and responsibility for their children in contractual exchanges which cut across the naturally given line of descent through women. Characteristically, where bride-wealth has not been handed over to secure a legal marriage, a woman's children remain the responsibility of her own lineage.

In a varied range of African societies therefore, both matrilineal and patrilineal, we can discern a common cluster of ideas about the wider importance of women's child-bearing capacity, their creative role in bringing up a new generation, and even a recurring notion about the natural line of birth being handed on through women. We find at the same time that given this positive moral evaluation of the nodal place of women in the definition of the wider society, the 'position of women' in the sense of personal freedom and responsibility is not necessarily very different in those societies which are dominantly matrilineal from those which may be dominantly patrilineal.

From Matrifocus to Matriliny

Changing historical circumstances may affect the socio-economic features of a people's existence. Animal property may come and go; political power may be built up and then wane. Settlements may migrate, some peoples may flee the expansion of others, and in recent decades, governmental decree may change the practical circumstances of life overnight. The modern cash economy may also have profound effects on traditional practices. But it is not so easy for the fundamental elements of a people's moral culture to disappear or to be turned upside down. I would like to suggest that there is some evidence that the cluster of ideas about women and motherhood that I have outlined may survive great socio-economic change, and may even be the basis for the development of matriliny as a jural principle. Where transactions over what is seen as the natural birth-line of descent from mother to daughter (typically marriage transactions) are suspended, or are made impossible for some historical reason, this line may itself emerge as the dominant principle of public jural organisation. 'Matriliny' may thus suddenly appear on the map.

I believe this is what has happened among the Uduk. Among the Komo, one of the closest of the neighbouring peoples within the Koman language group, people belong to patrilineal clans. These named clans stretch back in traditional history to early times, and ideally each clan has been built up through marriage with women from other clans, on the basis of the direct exchange of a sister or other clanswoman for each in-marrying wife.[9] Each marriage was traditionally balanced in this way with another, a woman for a woman, and no bride-wealth was paid. On a local level, there is another concept, of the close community of kin who actually live and work together. This is the *is*, literally 'body'. When a wife has been acquired by a proper exchange, her children live with her husband's local group and belong to his *is*. But if an exchange has not been carried out, or has fallen through, the children may return to their mother's local group, and revert to the natural community of their mother's *is*. Now the forefathers of the Uduk almost certainly used to practise a similar system, perhaps two centuries ago when they still lived in proximity to the Komo and other Koman peoples. But they have been obliged to move repeatedly to the north, as a result of Nilotic and Galla expansion, and in the course of these movements their communities were very severely disrupted. The rather brittle system of direct exchange marriage on the Koman one-to-one basis appears to have been abandoned, and the circumstantial evidence suggests strongly that there has been a general shift of ties to what is seen as the natural community of the mother's people. This pragmatic change appears to have been followed by the elaboration of a thorough-going matrilineal system, of which I have given a few notes above.

Matriliny as an overall jural structure may on the other hand be eroded or given up. Of the peoples I have mentioned, for example, there appears to be evidence of its erosion among the Tonga (Colson, 1958) and among the Bemba (Richards, 1950). But in these cases, as in most, matrifocal values appear to persist even in changed practical circumstances.

Conclusion

The evidence suggests that matriliny as a formal jural structure may come and go. It may be present in patches on the ethnographic map even in otherwise culturally uniform regions. Switches of lineal organis-ation may make it appear a superficial and fragile institution. But there seem to be more enduring levels at which common matrifocal values do give coherence to a patchy map of descent systems, and to historically changing customary legal structures. These values appear widely in Africa; but to suggest they were universal would be going too far. There are limits to the potential occurrence of jural matriliny, which we might tentatively associate with the limits of the matrifocal way of thinking about biology and morality.

It would be very difficult to represent some of the other ethno-graphic regions mentioned earlier as matrifocal in the same way: that is, the Arab Middle East, the Mediterranean, or the major culture regions of Asia. Some of the other papers in the present collection demonstrate the very different way in which men and women are regarded in these areas − for example, Renée Hirschon on Greece, and Caroline Humphrey on Mongolia. Now in practice, the economic con-tribution of women in these communities may be vital; as women they may be entitled to personal respect and affection; and they may exer-cise a good deal of independent action, even occasionally in the public sphere. But the basic theoretical view of women defines them in a dep-endent relation to their menfolk, and circumscribes the contribution they may properly make, because of the nature of womenfolk, to the life of the community. Basic definitions of this kind, which give the cen-tral biological and moral role to men in the founding and maintenance of families and the definition of wider social groupings through to the next generation, can scarcely be a possible foundation for matriliny.

I have suggested in this paper that we can make a tentative generali-sation about African societies (which may well prove easier to criticise

than to defend!). Characteristically, in a range of these societies, including all of those with a formal jural principle of matriliny and not a
few with a formal jural rule of patriliny, there is a deeper and historically more enduring level at which the nature and capacities of women
are given primacy in the definition of the human condition itself.
Although this 'matrifocal' way of thinking may allow all kinds of
economic, personal and sexual freedoms to women, this is not necessarily always the case. We can, however, certainly say that a matrifocal
orientation is a basic prerequisite for the development of jural matriliny.

Where the basic definition of human circumstances is 'patrifocal',
even though women may have importance as persons, jural matriliny
could scarcely develop, whatever the historical and material changes
that might take place. I have had the frustrating experience of trying to
teach classes of Arab students about matriliny! 'We' in the West can at
least envisage it; but although there is some evidence of a closer connection with the mother's side of the family even in middle-class communities in this country, this is a scrap of circumstantial fact, and is neither
here nor there in our fundamental theory of the nature of the family
unit, which retains much of its Victorian and definitely 'patrifocal'
character even today. This unspoken theory runs through our comparative discussions of other societies, and, I have suggested, has given us
particular difficulties with matriliny, in the present century as in the
last. And it is this persistent patrifocal thinking of our contemporary
society which is so annoying to the present generation of the women's
movement, rather than any demonstrable injustice in jural or economic
rights. Indeed, generalising for European and North American populations today, whether distinguished on the basis of nationality or class,
one could say that the more equal the legal and economic rights of men
and women, the greater the sense of fury and frustration among women
who realise that it is far more difficult to dislodge and reform a whole
way of thinking about biological sexuality and the moral bases of the
family than it is to change, piecemeal, the political and economic
conventions.

Notes

1. My attention has been drawn to the important part played by women in the
military affairs of traditional Ethiopia by the work of Tsehai Berhane Selassie.
2. The famous Ibo women's riots have been described, for example, by
Caroline Ifeka, 1975.
3. Described, for example, in the work of Mette Bovin (Bovin and Holtedahl,
1975).

4. This is clear from several of the articles in Radcliffe-Brown, 1952.

5. The first major work of Rattray, *The Ashanti* (1923) sets out quite explicitly the matrilineal values of the people before describing their other customs and institutions. This book was followed by other works which took the same starting point (for example, 1927 and 1929).

6. My research in the Sudan-Ethiopian border region, in the Blue Nile province of the Sudan, was carried out in the first instance from the University of Khartoum, which generously supported me with study leave in 1966 and research funds provided by the Ford Foundation for the University. Work among the Uduk took place during various periods between 1965 and 1969. Further research has since been undertaken in western Ethiopia as a Visiting Scholar of the University in Addis Ababa, with a grant from the SSRC in London, 1974 and 1975.

7. See for example Douglas, 1963, on the Lele; Turner, 1957 and 1967, on the Ndembu; Richards, 1950, on the Bemba; and Colson, 1958, on the Tonga.

8. See particularly Evans-Pritchard, 1951, and Lienhardt, 1961.

9. I have described some of these matters in James, 1970 and 1975.

Bibliography

Bachofen, J.J. *Das Mutterrecht*, 1861

Bovin, M., and Holtedahl, L. *Frie Piger i Mangaland*. Copenhagen, National Museum, 1975

Colson, E. *Marriage and the Family among the Plateau Tonga of Northern Rhodesia*. Manchester, Manchester University Press, 1958

Douglas, M. *The Lele of The Kasai*. London, Oxford University Press, 1963
——. 'Is Matriliny Doomed in Africa?' in *Man in Africa*, M. Douglas and P.M. Kaberry (eds.). London, Tavistock, 1969

East, R. (ed.). *Akiga's Story*. London, Oxford University Press, 1939

Engels, F. *Origin of the Family, Private Property and the State*, 4th edition. London, Lawrence and Wishart, 1891

Evans-Pritchard, E.E. *Kinship and Marriage among the Nuer*. Oxford, Clarendon Press, 1951
——. 'The Position of Women in Primitive Society' in *The Position of Women in Primitive Society and Other Essays in Social Anthropology*. London, Faber, 1965

Fortes, M. *The Web of Kinship among the Tallensi*. London, Oxford University Press, 1949
——. 'Kinship and Marriage among the Ashanti' in *African Systems of Kinship and Marriage*, A.R. Radcliffe-Brown and D. Forde (eds.). London, Oxford University Press, 1950

Fox, R. *Kinship and Marriage*. London, Penguin, 1967

Hasan, Y.F. *The Arabs and the Sudan*. Edinburgh, Edinburgh University Press, 1967

Hoffer, C.P. 'Madam Yoko: Ruler of the Kpa Mende Confederacy' in *Woman, Culture and Society*, M.Z. Rosaldo and L. Lamphere (eds.). Stanford, California, Stanford University Press, 1974

Ifeka, C. 'Female Militancy and Colonial Rule' in *Perceiving Women*, S. Ardener (ed.). London, Dent/Malaby; New York, Halsted, 1975

James, W.R. 'Why the Uduk Won't Pay Bridewealth'. *Sudan Notes and Records*, 51 (1970)
——. 'Sister-Exchange Marriage'. *Scientific American*, Vol. 233, No. 6 (December 1975)

Kaberry, P.M. *Women of the Grassfields: A Study of the Economic Position of Women in Bamenda, British Cameroons*. London, HMSO, 1952

Kronenberg, A. 'The Bovine Idiom and Formal Logic' in *Essays in Sudan Ethno-graphy*, I. Cunnison and W. James (eds.). London, Hurst, 1972

Lewis, B.A. *The Murle: Red Chiefs and Black Commoners.* Oxford, Clarendon Press, 1972

Lewis, I.M. *Social Anthropology in Perspective.* London, Penguin, 1976

Lévi-Strauss, C. *The Elementary Structures of Kinship.* London, Eyre and Spottiswoode, 1969

Lienhardt, R.G. *Divinity and Experience: The Religion of the Dinka.* Oxford, Clarendon Press, 1961

Nsugbe, P.O. *Ohaffia: A Matrilineal Ibo People.* Oxford, Clarendon Press, 1974

Radcliffe-Brown, A.R. *Structure and Function in Primitive Society.* London, Cohen and West, 1952

Rattray, R.S. *Ashanti.* Oxford, Clarendon Press, 1923

——. *Religion and Art in Ashanti.* Oxford, Clarendon Press, 1927

——. *Ashanti Law and Constitution.* Oxford, Clarendon Press, 1929

Reed, E. *Woman's Evolution: From Matriarchal Clan to Patriarchal Family.* New York, Pathfinder Press, 1975

Richards, A. 'Some types of family structure amongst the Central Bantu' in *African Systems of Kinship and Marriage*, A.R. Radcliffe-Brown and D. Forde (eds.). London, Oxford University Press, 1950

Schneider, D., and Gough, K. *Matrilineal Kinship.* California, University of California Press, 1961

Tanner, N. 'Matrifocality in Indonesia and Africa and among Black Americans' in *Woman, Culture and Society*, M.Z. Rosaldo and L. Lamphere (eds.). Stanford, California, Stanford University Press, 1974

Turner, V.W. *Schism and Continuity in an African Society: A Study of Ndembu Village Life.* Manchester, Manchester University Press, 1957

——. *The Forest of Symbols: Aspects of Ndembu Ritual.* New York, Cornell University Press, 1967

Postscript

After this paper was written, a letter appeared in *The Times* (11 May 1978) which strikingly confirms the 'patrifocal' orientation of our own culture. From an Italian address, Patricia Rouse expresses her astonishment on discovering that as a single woman, she cannot pass on British nationality to her child:

> Sir, In the days of supposed female equality, I have just suffered what I consider to be a very basic case of discrimination. As an unmarried pregnant British tax-paying citizen living abroad, I rang the British Consul to confirm my baby's rights. To my amazement, I discovered that only men under our 'equal' British law have the right to pass on citizenship. Unless I return to Britain to have my baby, or marry an Englishman before the birth (anyone would do!), my baby cannot have British nationality.
>
> Apart from the sexual discrimination, it seems ridiculous that a woman who can always prove that she is the mother of a particular baby has no right to give it her nationality: whereas a man, who would find it very hard to actually prove his fatherhood, has every right.

British women are less privileged, in this respect, than their sisters in most parts of Africa.

7 'THE MOST ESSENTIALLY FEMALE FUNCTION OF ALL': GIVING BIRTH

Helen Callaway

The Representation of Birth

Evans-Pritchard (1973, p. lx) has stated that for him two of the finest essays ever written in the history of sociological thought are those by Robert Hertz, the one entitled 'The Pre-eminence of the Right Hand' (1909) and the other 'The Representation of Death' (1907). In these essays Hertz selected salient facts of nature and showed how these have been transformed by culture, how various societies have taken these biological facts as focal points in their collective systems of ideas and action which invest their everyday world with meaning. But Hertz went further than merely describing diverse customs and beliefs. Through his probing analyses he revealed underlying symbolic patterns of world-wide significance, such as the use of right and left as the physical basis on which many societies have calqued elaborate orders of dual classification (see Needham, 1973). In these systems of symbolic opposition Hertz noted how the male is most often related to the right or superior side and the female to the left or inferior side. Indeed, he showed remarkably modern insights for an essay written nearly seventy years ago.

> Every social hierarchy claims to be founded on the nature of things, *physei, ou nomō:* it thus accords itself eternity, it escapes change and the attacks of innovators. Aristotle justified slavery by the ethnic superiority of the Greeks over barbarians; and today the man who is annoyed by feminist claims alleges that woman is *naturally* inferior (Hertz, 1973 reprint, p.3).

Hertz went on to make the then radical proposition that what appears to be 'the testimony of nature' may well be the results of social definitions.

Birth is another salient fact of nature. As a biological event it is 'universal' among human groups, yet its practices in different societies show considerable diversity. Our interest in these activities, however, does not lie merely in how they satisfy biological needs, but rather in how such practices form part of larger systems of 'collective representation', the term used in the writings of Durkheim and his colleagues of

163

the *Année sociologique* at the beginning of this century, or part of 'world-structures', a concept from the more recent theory of Edwin Ardener (1973, 1975). While birth might be considered as a focal event of the same order as death and marriage, compared to these widely investigated categories it has been relatively neglected in anthropology. Like these categories, birth is a focus of social rules and strategies which define and reinforce the classifications of male and female, and thus its study holds particular interest today.

Whatever other distinctions there are between male and female, these categories are primarily differentiated by their sexual complementarity in the procreation of the human species. This is so obvious that it would seem to be unworthy of examination, but in anthropology we have come to realise that what is most taken for granted may well be highly problematic. Indeed, in calling this paper by a line from a newspaper, 'the most essentially female function of all', I am placing this very ordinary phrase under scrutiny. What does it mean to be a woman? To be a man? Here a curious lack of symmetry emerges in the everyday, expected definitions. To be female is first to be identified with biological reproduction — 'the most essentially female function of all'. In contrast to a woman, a man is likely to be designated as father of a family only incidentally to the list of public activities and achievements which proclaim his identity. The word 'labour' has an interesting gender split in its popular uses. In connection with women, unlike men, 'labour' is usually first associated with childbirth and the domestic sphere.

Asymmetry in sexual identifications is characteristic of a wide range of societies besides our own. Among the Angas of the Nigerian plateau, for example, the woman is called not by her own name, as a man is, but by her child's name with a prefix 'mother of'. In Kabylia, as shown in the ethnography of Pierre Bourdieu (1973, p.99), the spatial arrangements in the household exemplify the association of women with nature and men with culture. The 'natural' acts — sleep, sexual intercourse, giving birth, dying — take place in the space assigned to women. In her discussion of this theme, 'Is Female to Male as Nature is to Culture', Sherry Ortner (1974) finds the crux of the argument in the classic study by Simone de Beauvoir, who had pointed out that proportionately more of woman's body space, for a longer period of her life, is taken up with the natural processes associated with the reproduction of the species. According to de Beauvoir, the human male 'remodels the face of the earth, he creates new instruments, he invents, he shapes the future' (1972 ed., p. 96). He 'transcends life' through his creative acts. The female, on the other hand, merely repeats life through the procreative powers of her body.

Birth is one of the stages of the individual life cycle which have been called 'life-crises' in anthropological theory. Other stages include initiation, marriage, reproduction and death. For males and females there are, of course, biological differences in the progression of the life cycle. These are often marked by cultural symbols. The rituals of birth might be seen to follow the general pattern of *'rites de passage'*, as set out by Van Gennep in his well known essay of 1908: first there is a 'separation' from the old state or previous social condition, then a 'marginal' or 'liminal' stage occurs (the time of danger), followed by an 'aggregation' to a new condition, or 'reaggregation' to the old. Van Gennep gave us the insight that even where membership of a social class is hereditary, the child is not a 'complete' member by physical birth alone; on the contrary, a child must be incorporated into its group by certain ceremonies. Again, Van Gennep distinguished between the physical and the social return to ordinary life of a mother after childbirth. He also observed that while modern societies (in his view) reduce as much as possible the distinction between male and female, this distinction is emphasised among what he called 'primitive' peoples who rigidly separate men and women in economic, political and religious activities. Here Van Gennep has pointed to the central problem. Clearly there is a puzzle about this apparent necessity for the ritual marking of differences between men and women, to the point of extreme polarity, and for the various elaborate superstructures which cultures have mapped on to the universal sexual complementarity of reproduction. And, we might add, this is a characteristic not only of 'primitive' societies.

Folk Models

Procreation for a man is momentary and external to him, while for a woman it lasts for a long period and is internal. Birth marks the fruition of this process. The foetus which has been growing and kicking within the enclosure of her womb makes its journey of separation to emerge as a new human being. We have all been born, and perhaps we retain a lingering submerged remembrance of this. But as Donnison concludes in her history of inter-professional rivalries between midwives and medical men, 'it is women, and only women, who must carry and give birth to children, ... childbirth still remains, in the last analysis, "women's business" ' (1977, p.201).

Although in our society at present male obstetricians usually supervise the delivery, clearly there is no necessity for men to manage this process. Women midwives or doctors often exclusively attend to the mother and the newborn infant. A woman can even safely deliver her own child. My grandmother, an indomitable pioneer in the settling of the American West, told me that she herself had delivered her sixth child because she was alone at the homestead on that endless expanse of prairie. She had no difficulty. After the baby's first vigorous cry, she tied the umbilical cord and cut it with a paring knife.

A Yoruba woman living in the urban maze of mud-walled compounds in the old city of Ibadan, Nigeria, gave me the details of how she had done much the same. Her reason was different: not that other women were not available in her husband's compound, but that childbirth is a time of danger from witches. She was referring indirectly to the possibility of malevolence by jealous co-wives or wives of her husband's brothers. Having (as she thought) lost two previous babies from these evil, unnamed and invisible influences, she wanted to make sure this child survived. When her time came, she told me, she spread out a rubber sheet on the rough concrete floor of her bedroom, then kneeled down and took the baby in her hands as it emerged. The placenta expelled itself and, in Yoruba custom, was buried by the father of the child.[1] Her daughter, eleven months old at the time of our talk and tied firmly to her back, was proof of her success and of the rationality of her action, given the premisses of her particular cultural system of ideas. Her self-delivery was determined not by an exigency of nature (as my grandmother's had been), but by the dictates of culture.[2] The event thus had a different meaning for each.

During the past few years in Britain and America there has been a profusion of books, magazine articles, newspaper features and television programmes about pregnancy and birth. A 'social fact' of our time, we might call it. Pick up a Sunday paper and there will likely be the diary of an enthusiastic new mother with elaborate details of her breathing exercises during pregnancy and an impressionistic recollection of her feelings during each stage of childbirth. Daily newspapers and women's journals provide accounts of Caesarian sections, delivery by forceps, or perhaps 'birth without violence' with the lights dimmed, according to the method of the French obstetrician Leboyer (1975). Films of birth on television bring what was formerly private and secret into public awareness, even possibly into the field of 'entertainment'. Letters to editors point up the current controversies. There seems no end to this outpouring of autobiography, medical information, reportage. Captain Mark Phillips was present during the birth of his son. This was widely noted and undoubtedly has its significance on the contemporary British scene (a point to be taken up). Here the question arises: at a time when the birth rate is falling, when more couples are deciding to have only one child or none at all, why should there be such a fascination with the event of birth?

The term 'representation' brings us to the discipline of anthropology and the insights it affords on the cultural perspectives on human biology. There may be minor variations among different social and racial groups (in such aspects as the average birth-weight of babies, the incidence of twins, or the prevalence of RH negative blood groups), yet it is generally agreed that the basic physiological process of human reproduction is 'universal' throughout the species. We find on inspection, however, that writings and visual diagrams purporting to set out the 'facts of life' are widely diverse. The history of embryology, for example, delineated so well by Joseph Needham (1959), has its charming and bizarre moments. We learn that the first detailed and clear-cut body of embryological knowledge is associated with the name of Hippocrates (who is assumed to have been born about 460 BC). Concerned with obstetrical and gynaecological problems, he wrote a treatise on the nature of women and on premature birth. His ideas on the growth of the embryo involved an alternation of moistness and drying of the two main constituents of all natural bodies, fire and water (J. Needham, ibid., p. 32). If such an exposition sounds quaint, its grounds were more empirical than the theological preoccupations during the Middle Ages of how and when the soul enters the foetus.

In anthropology 'the denial of physiological paternity' has been a recurring area of discussion since Malinowski asserted in his writings on the Trobriand Islanders that 'knowledge of impregnation, of the man's share in creating the new life in the mother's womb, is a fact of which the natives have not even the slightest glimpse'. Citing this example, Edmund Leach (1969, p.90) took up the problem which became known as the 'Virgin Birth' controversy. He considered that ethnographers who accepted Trobriand and other such statements as ignorance of the facts of life did so because it corresponded with their own private assumptions of the childish beliefs of savages. He argued that anthropologists had taken as literal what were essentially symbolic statements about the relations of men and gods. To Leach's argument, feminists today would add that these symbolic statements are not only about the relations of men and gods, but also about the classifications of men and women.

If 'the denial of physiological paternity' has been the basis for vigorous discussions in anthropological journals, 'the denial of physiological maternity' has received little notice. Joseph Needham calls our attention to ideas held in Greece before the time of Aristotle, ideas which may have had their origin in Egypt, that the father alone was the 'author of generation' while the mother provided only the 'nidus and nourishment for the foetus' (J. Needham, 1959, p. 43). He cites a passage from the *Eumenides* of Aeschylus when Apollo, defending Orestes during the trial from the charge of matricide, brings forward a physiological argument. 'The mother of what is called her child', Apollo makes his case, 'is no parent of it, but nurse only of the young life that is sown in her. The parent is the male, and she but a stranger, a friend, who, if fate spares his plant, preserves it till it puts forth.'

Needham notes that the idea of the female sex as a field in which grain was sown was widespread in antiquity, examples having been collected from Vedic, Egyptian and Talmudic sources. This is also found in ethnographic studies, for example among the Zulu where it expresses their views on patriliny, the child belonging to the man (Sibisi, 1975, p. 19).[3]. Joseph Needham considers such an idea in antiquity would have been a natural concomitant of the practice, widely prevalent at the time, of putting captured males to death and keeping the females as concubines. The conquerors thus had no fear of corrupting their own ethnic group with alien blood. Needham's conclusions have wider application than he perhaps intended: 'The whole matter affords an excellent illustration of the way in which an apparently academic theory may have the most intimate connections with social and political behaviour' (ibid., p. 44).

Indeed, both anthropological evidence and the history of midwifery and medical care (as, for example, by Donnison, 1977) show a close meshing of popular theory about human biology with the social and political structures of time and place. We find it easy enough to think of Zulu views on patriliny, or the Yoruba mother's statements of the danger of witches at childbirth, as 'collective representations' of birth from different cultural frames. The ideas in the ancient Greek treatises on embryology, or those in, say, *The Byrth of Mankind* (translated from German and published in 1540 as the first work on midwifery in English[4]), can be attributed to the pre-scientific era. What we find more difficult is to distance ourselves from our own cultural products and practices, to submit to analysis our own biographical experience, the popular newspaper articles on our breakfast table, and the academic theories in our medical textbooks.

Gynaecological Models

The progress of science through the centuries, and particularly in recent years, has been so spectacular that it carries with it the implied assumption of an ultimate presentation of knowledge that can be free of cultural meanings and the vested interests of dominant power structures. The contemporary gynaecology textbooks in our medical schools, we might assume, are 'scientific' and 'objective' in their delineation of female biology. Yet in their review of 27 gynaecology texts written from 1943 to 1973 in the United States, Scully and Bart found a pervasive male viewpoint (1973, p. 1045). The authors note that 93.4 per cent of gynaecologists in the US in 1972 were male.

It is perhaps not so surprising that in the earlier pre-Kinsey period, in the *Essentials of Gynecology*, Cooke stated, 'The fundamental biologic factor in women is the urge of motherhood balanced by the fact that sexual pleasure is entirely secondary or even absent' (1943, pp. 59-60). Even in recent years, however, after what might be presumed to be the greater awareness of female sexuality with the popular attention given to the writings of Masters and Johnson, Willson could write with 'scientific' authority in a standard work, *Obstetrics and Gynecology*, 'The traits that compose the core of the female personality are feminine narcissism, masochism and passivity' (1971, p. 43). Scully and Bart conclude that in the last two decades at least half of the texts that covered the topics stated that the male sex drive was stronger than the female; women were described as interested in sex for procreation more than recreation.

While no systematic review of British gynaecology textbooks has been made (to my knowledge), it is likely that the following quotation from *British Obstetric and Gynaecological Practice* (Claye and Bourne, 1963) is not unrepresentative:

> Femininity tends to be passive and receptive, masculinity to be more active, restless, anxious for repeated demonstrations of potency, requiring worldy [*sic*] success and its external signs. Childbirth should be the crowning fulfilment of a woman's sexual development; her physical and psychological destiny have been achieved (James, 1963, p. 893).

Here again the familiar classification: woman's destiny encapsulated as biological event. Whatever the basic 'facts' of women's biology, they are presented in terms (however unconscious on the part of the author) which mirror a particular society and the interests of its power groups.

But it is not merely a question of revising the textbooks to present a 'neutral' or even feminist point of view. If much of the feminist debate has been pitched against the strictures of 'biological determinism', the problem gets ever more complex when the 'determining' arrows are seen to be moving in two directions at once.

As an illustration, let us look at pain in childbirth. LeVine (1973, p. 27) tells us that physicians and nurses in a Nigerian hospital reported that Yoruba women cried out and moaned freely during childbirth, while Hausa women hardly ever made any sound even during difficult deliveries. LeVine considers this to be evidence 'that conformity with their respective cultural ideas is achieved even during the pain and stress of this universal biological event'. He goes on to speculate that 'the observed pattern is not merely conformist behaviour but is programmed into personality functioning, determining emotional response to pain.' He is suggesting here that social learning has become 'programmed into' what might be considered as basically biological, the neural system, the perception and expression of pain. If the expression of our feelings during childbirth is 'programmed', what of the array of emotions in our everyday living? What of these traits of passivity and receptivity? Are the sets of emotions considered in our society as essentially 'female' to be attributed to innateness or to social learning? Are the gynaecological texts, and the doctors' advice deriving from them, part of the 'programme'?

The Alleged 'Male Take-over' of Childbirth Management

Both in Britain and America, contemporary feminists argue that childbirth has been appropriated by the male medical profession; for example, Arms (1975), Rich (1975), the Boston Women's Health Book Collective (1976), Oakley (1976), Donnison (1977). Taking the hint from Van Gennep, we might ask: is this a modern way of marking and maintaining the distinction between men and women? Women undergo the physiological process of childbirth, but it is men (in the main) who supervise the delivery, who are dedicated to the advancement of medical practices and the esoteric scientific theories which support these. Is this the way men have transformed an *event of nature*, in which as fathers they are not required to take part, into a *cultural ceremony* in which the woman becomes an anonymous and inferior object and the male doctor the symbolically significant, life-sustaining agent? Seen from this perspective, medical men have become the high priests in the contemporary ritual of childbirth.

Modern advances in obstetrics have become widespread in Britain during this last decade. The use of hormone oxytocin to induce or speed up labour, of pain-reducing procedures such as epidural anaesthesia, of refined technology for monitoring foetal well-being, has brought about 'The Childbirth Revolution', as it was headlined in the *Sunday Times Weekly Review*. The article began:

> Men, it seems, have finally conquered *the most essentially female function of all*: the reproduction of our species. Babies can now be delivered to order on a predetermined day and labour can be virtually pain free. This is the childbirth revolution. But is it the kind of revolution women really want? (L. and O. Gillie, 1974, p. 29; my italics).

The authors make clear that this is *not* what women want. They point out that for the last hundred years men have been telling women how to bring their babies into the world without any first-hand understanding of what it feels like as a physical or an emotional experience, that by degrees normal childbirth has become pathological in what they call 'a process of clinical overkill'. The result of such a technological triumph may mean emotional deprivation for both mother and child, the mother being left frightened and alone during labour and the infant separated from her at birth.

Protests against the extreme practices of 'the childbirth revolution' are coming now from many sides (including some doctors). For over fifteen years Sheila Kitzinger has led a practical movement for the physical and psychological preparation for childbirth which involves the conscious participation of the mother. 'She is no longer a passive, suffering instrument. . . .She retains the power of self-direction, of self-control, of choice, of voluntary decision and active cooperation with doctor and nurse' (1972, p. 23). Although some feminists consider that her writings over-emphasise women's traditional roles of childbearing and the domestic sphere, Kitzinger has been stressing many aspects of childbirth management which have become so familiar in recent feminist demands.

In *Immaculate Deception: A New Look at Women and Childbirth in America*, Suzanne Arms traces the 'deception' that childbirth is inherently dangerous, painful and terrifying to the advent of Christianity and its development of new laws and new morals (1975, p. 14). In her historical sketch, she tells how early Christianity absorbed the Hebrew view that Eve's transgression caused women's travail in childbirth, thus setting the foundation for the negative attitudes towards women's sexuality and child-bearing which have continued in Western civilisation for nearly two thousand years. Arms sets the date for the male take-over of obstetrics at 1588, when the forceps was invented and forbidden to female midwives. King Louis XIV ordered the old birthing stool adapted by midwives to be replaced by a flat horizontal table, while Queen Victoria popularised the use of anaesthesia by accepting chloroform for the birth of her seventh child in 1853. Women thus handed over the autonomy of their reproductive care to the male physicians.

Arms provides detailed and convincing documentation for her sustained criticism of contemporary obstetric practices in American hospitals. As her first chapter, however, she presents an idealised reconstruction of childbirth in the imaginary hunting and gathering society of our distant ancestors. Undoubtedly many women living in such conditions did and do bear children without mishap, yet there is ample evidence that where modern medical facilities are not available both infant and maternal deaths are high.[5] We have only to remind ourselves of Mary Wollstonecraft, whose confinement in 1797 was attended by a licensed midwife, the shivering onset of septicaemia foreshadowing her anguished death twelve days after childbirth (Tomalin, 1974, pp. 217-27).

In an account presented as fiction, but 'true' in general terms, the anthropologist Elenore Smith Bowen (1954, pp. 160-80) relates the story of the prolonged labour and death in childbirth of a young African woman. The anthropologist pleaded to be allowed to send for help to take her friend Amara to hospital, but the offer was refused. All the midwives of the area assembled, concocting herbal medicines, while male ritual specialists performed sacrifices to determine the witch responsible for the case. Accusations and counter-accusations of witchcraft were hurled among members of the dying woman's relatives. As Amara died, her attendants noted the sound of the witch-owl calling ominously in the night. Such a graphic portrayal effectively undermines any sentimental version of childbirth in primitive conditions.

In a recent paper, Ann Oakley (1976) sketches the relations between historical changes in the management of childbirth and the position of women. She argues that the main shift in industrialised societies during the past century has been the transition from control of reproductive care located in a community of experienced but untrained women to a profession of formally trained men. The growth of a medical profession has thus meant the transfer of control from women to men. She states:

Childbirth, contraception and abortion are aspects of women's reproductive life. In most cultures of the world and throughout most of history it is women who have controlled their own reproductive function. That is, the management of reproduction has been restricted to women, and regarded as part of the feminine role. Such knowledge of anatomy, physiology, pharmacology and delivery techniques as exists is vested in women as a group. . . .Women are the experts. Men are not involved, or are only marginally involved.

Europe and America before industrialization, and for some time after this, possessed indigenous female-controlled reproductive care systems. These systems were analogous to those described by anthropologists as existing in small-scale societies today (ibid., p. 19).

Such generalizations have a simplistic ring when stated in such bold terms and removed from the complexity of the data she commands for her argument.

Exceptions immediately come to mind. Lévi-Strauss (1968, pp. 186-205) elucidates a South American magico-religious text, the purpose of the incantation being to facilitate difficult childbirth. When a female midwife finds the case too complex, she calls in a male shaman or ritual specialist to perform the delivery by symbolic means. In Yorubaland of Western Nigeria female midwives often attend women in childbirth, but the traditional medical and scientific knowledge belongs to the male priests of the Ifa oracle. They are not only priests who mediate with the spiritual world but also medical men with as much as ten years of apprentice training in diagnosis and modes of treatment, including sophisticated pharmacology (Callaway, 1975). These native doctors (*babalawo*, translated as 'father of wisdom') are consulted by women for varied problems of reproduction, particularly infertility, and they attend births for ordinary and difficult cases.[6]

Oakley (1976, p. 22) herself notes that there are at present both female doctors and professional midwives in England and Wales (26 per cent of specialist obstetricians and gynaecologists being women, but only 12 per cent of consultants in this field). She argues that they have been incorporated into a male-dominated control structure. It is clear from evidence she presents, and from Donnison's detailed history (1977), that since the early eighteenth century there has been a shift in the management of childbirth in England from female midwives to the male-dominated medical profession. But the question of the 'control structure' of female reproductive care is more problematic, presenting far greater complexity than accounts merely of *who* manages childbirth care. Although in most small-scale societies it would seem that women do deliver babies and take charge of other matters of female reproduction, I will argue that they do so within cultural systems of ideas and practices which reflect the dominant power structures, and which are often detrimental to women. From this different level of analysis, an alternative interpretation emerges: that control structures of human reproduction (including female care) in most societies, not only today but throughout history, have been male-dominated. If this is accepted, then the theme of a *recent* 'male take-over' must be seen as a myth.

The Control of the Ideology of Female Fertility

While references to the practical management and rituals of birth are to be found scattered throughout anthropological literature, few are detailed enough to point up clearly the cultural patterning of human reproduction. J.S. La Fontaine's (1972) study of women's life-crises in Bugisu is particularly valuable in placing childbirth within the more comprehensive Gisu conceptual framework in which the physical stages in the progress from girlhood to full feminine maturity are marked by rituals which invest these biological events with social significance. Many rituals in this patrilineal society overtly express the predominance of men and the descent through male ancestors. It is hardly surprising, then, that the 'rites of passage' for women can be seen to represent male control over female fertility.

Female bodily changes — the onset of menstruation, the loss of virginity, and childbirth — have in common the flow of blood, considered by the Gisu to have powerful qualities both of life-giving and of danger. A girl's first menstruation is the sign for the Gisu that she has become a woman ready for child-bearing. As soon as her first blood-flow has ceased, the rituals begin. They announce her passage to the status of a mature and marriageable young woman. She must now observe not only the set of restrictions identified with the polluting effects of the menstrual period, but taboos against foods, such as chickens and eggs, which are believed to cause women to remain barren.

When she is about to be married, the instruction given to a bride by her own lineage ends with the blessing: 'May you bear many children, many sons' (ibid., p. 169). In Gisu tradition a girl would be a virgin at marriage and the ceremonies coincide with and mark the physical change of the defloration of the bride. The evidence of the loss of blood is exhibited as proof that the bride's parents have guarded her well. A bride who is not a virgin may be rejected and sent back to her parents. She has taken control of her own sexuality and has thereby dishonoured her lineage. La Fontaine points out that while defloration is of the same physical order as menstruation and childbirth, it differs in that it requires a deliberate human act. The time and the circumstances of this physical event can be socially determined. She states:

> It would seem that for the Gisu it represents male control of the female physical powers of creation, a dogma essential to the maintenance both of male dominance and patriliny, and hence it is the central ritual act of marriage (ibid., pp. 172-3).

A Gisu woman does not achieve her full potential as a woman until she bears a child. The ceremonies of the first childbirth are actions taken for the protection of mother and child from mystical dangers and for showing the change in the woman's status. Gisu men and women explicitly compare childbirth with circumcision by emphasising the pain that must be endured and the fact that it makes the immature into full adults.[7] The men claim, and the women apparently agree, at least in public, that childbirth is the lesser agony. La Fontaine shows the parallels in these two rituals; for example, during circumcision the mother of an initiate takes up the posture of a woman in labour inside the hut, while outside her son is being circumcised and hence 'reborn'. The mother's action symbolises his birth as a mature man while identifying the socially imposed pains of circumcision with the natural pains of childbirth. La Fontaine makes clear that Gisu male circumcision rituals can be seen as a symbolic creation in men of the inherent physical reproductive power of women. From this perspective, the Gisu correlation of the pain of childbirth and the pain of circumcision takes on greater meaning: 'in women it is natural uncontrolled bleeding that denotes their (reproductive) power; in men it is social, controlled bleeding that symbolizes and creates superior social power' (ibid., p. 180).

A Gisu woman who is coming near the full term of her pregnancy should take care that childbirth does not take place in the fields or in the bush. Ideally, for the protection of the ritually vulnerable infant, childbirth should occur in the pater's hut. During labour a woman squats, holding on to the centre-pole of the hut, which is said to be the seat of the patrilineal ancestors. To those of us schooled in Freudian observation, the phallic imagery hardly needs stating. As La Fontaine points out in a wider context, the practices and rituals of childbirth cannot be separated into the old divisions of 'instrumental' and 'expressive', since they are likely to be both at the same time. The position of the woman about to give birth, squatting and holding on to the centre-pole of the hut is at once practical in facilitating birth and highly symbolic.

A woman in Gisu tradition is expected to bear her pains in silence. If she cries out, she is accused of cowardice and may be beaten. In this society, as in some others such as the Bemba (Richards, 1956, p. 35), a prolonged labour may be attributed to adultery and the woman is then urged to confess so that appropriate antidotes may be given her. I have wondered whether in such situations of extreme agony a woman might not admit to adultery which may be only in her fantasy, particularly when she is pressed into confession as a way of easing her difficulty. But the literature on this, understandably, is lacking. At any rate, it doesn't require much imagination to consider how girls and young women hearing of the association of adultery with an anguished labour, perhaps even with death in childbirth, would themselves exercise caution when tempted into any extra-marital affair. As a mode of social control for women, this threat would indeed be powerful.

In her interpretation of these rituals, La Fontaine shows how particular emphasis is given to this universal theme: the differences between men and women, their opposition and conjunction in procreation. This is a society glorifying male ancestors, the superiority of living men and sons yet unborn. Its rituals celebrating the bodily changes of Gisu women bring the natural procreative powers of women under the social control of men. The practices of childbirth thus serve to perpetuate the male-dominated 'world-structures' of this society.

Harriet Sibisi (1975) shows how birth forms a significant part of the comprehensive symbolic system of a different patrilineal society, the Zulu of South Africa. Here women are associated with positive mystical forces as diviners and with negative mystical forces as wives and mothers. The Zulu consider states of pollution to occur, with differing degrees of intensity, in marginal states which are believed to exist between life and death. The behaviour pattern required of women during these periods of impurity entails withdrawal from social life, fasting, abstinence from pleasure, speaking in low tones and only when necessary.

As soon as a Zulu woman becomes pregnant, she moves into this marginal state of being both vulnerable and contaminating. When she is newly delivered of a child, she is considered to be highly polluted, a condition that is 'contagious and particularly endangers men's virility, cattle and crops' (ibid., p. 19). At the time of childbirth she therefore withdraws from society into a house of confinement, where only married women may keep her company. For the first ten days, she may go outside the house only by covering herself in a blanket. After that she smears her exposed parts, such as her arms, legs and face, with red ochre to insulate her mystical threat to men, crops and cattle. She is also considered dangerous to the baby. In a sample taken of 161 cases of infant mortality, Sibisi found that 57 of them, or 36 per cent, were attributed to the mother's vulnerability during gestation (ibid., p. 29). Although a mother no longer continues in this state of intense pollution when her post-partum emissions stop, she remains in a lesser state of impurity as long as she is lactating. As a protective measure against unforeseen contamination, pregnant and nursing mothers often smear red ochre on the soles of their feet.

Sibisi points out the paradox of the man who is powerful and demonstrates this by his virility, yet who is nevertheless dependent for the continuity of his descent group on the fertility of a woman. This means that a woman who is ideally submissive towards him and theoretically powerless, neverthless does exercise some power. Women's emissions, a manifestation of her reproductive forces, are considered to be particularly dangerous to men's virility. 'Women are seen to exercise some power that they should not have, and as such they are dangerous to those who are entitled to that power' (ibid., p. 28).

Sibisi asks, 'Why is the society making such demands on women?' (ibid.) She carries out her analysis in terms of power relations and the ambiguities of these networks. Zulu ideas on purity and pollution create ritual boundaries, with women in the role of mediators or bridges between 'our' lineage and 'other' lineages, between 'this world' and the 'other world'. By observing the correct behaviour during their states of impurity, women see themselves as engaged in procreative activity benefiting the society as a whole.

Gipsy society also overtly recognises male dominance and, through its models of purity and pollution, places strong restrictions on the sexuality of women. Judith Okely's study (1975) of Gipsy women shows a group close to us in space and time, yet worlds apart in their cultural views of childbirth. A Gipsy woman in the maternity wing of the John Radcliffe hospital experiences her delivery within a completely different system of ideas from her non-Gipsy neighbour in the next bed.

Okely states that in the stereotyped view of the Gorgio (the name given by Gipsies to all non-Gipsies) the Gipsy woman may be seen as sexually flirtatious and enticing, yet her actual behaviour is circumscribed by strict rules. Menstruation is considered polluting to the male, with a general prohibition during this period on sexual intercourse and, among some groups, on cooking. A female must remain a virgin until marriage (in her field-work, Okely heard of doctors' examinations being carried out as checks for virginity). After marriage, she must remain faithful to her husband. At the risk of pollution to the male, she must observe restrictions in her dress and movements, wash and undress in complete privacy, breast-feed her baby alone. Okely found that most Gipsy women, against the advice of midwives and health visitors, opted for bottle feeding, thus avoiding the polluting risks of breast-feeding.

The greatest potential source of ritual danger for Gipsy men, however, appears to be during and after childbirth. In a separation similar to the Zulu case, childbirth among the Gipsies took place in a special tent, where the mother and child stayed for some days. Later the tent, the bedding and the crockery and utensils used during that time were burnt, a purification by fire which occurs in other symbolic contexts in the society. The newborn baby was considered *mochadi*, ritually polluting, for a time and had to be bathed in a separate bowl, its clothes also washed separately. Today, Okely writes, the mother and child are still regarded as temporarily *mochadi*. Discussion with any man of the experience of childbirth is forbidden, and even the onset of labour pains is told, and then reluctantly, only to the husband. Now, as in the past, Gipsy men must not assist women in labour.

Okely observes that the almost universal Gipsy preference now for childbirth in hospital has been misinterpreted as a conversion to modern medicine and the welfare state. Yet in her field-work she encountered women who appeared to attend pre-natal clinics only to ensure a hospital bed. They threw away such prescriptions as iron supplements. To the consternation of medical authorities, but understandable within their own conceptual context, Gipsy women usually discharged themselves from hospital early. Many Gipsies complained to Okely of rough treatment and poor attention during the birth. Hospitals are considered not a clean place. Okely concludes that Gipsies prefer hospital childbirth not because they consider it safer for women, but because it provides a convenient way for dealing with an event that is still thought to be dangerously polluting. Seen from this perspective, the doctors, nurses and hospital attendants might be compared to the caste of Hindu untouchables dealing with bodily pollution and disposing of the unclean articles. This example again shows how childbirth takes place within a male-dominated cultural system which considers female sexuality to be inherently dangerous and controls it through strong ritual restrictions.

It is often taken for granted that girls in 'primitive' societies learn about childbirth through observation and the experience of home confinements of mothers, aunts and older sisters. But as Lois Paul (1974) shows in her study of women in a Guatemalan village, this knowledge may be deliberately withheld. Victorian-type reticence and embarrassment about sex and reproduction would seem to be carried to an even further stage in the Indian settlement of San Pedro. Here some of the widespread notions of pollution are held: the idea, for instance, that menstrual blood is particularly damaging to men's virility and thus intercourse during menstruation must be avoided. What is different in this society is the degree of evasion of any reference to this condition. A wife excuses herself on grounds of a stomach-ache or headache. What is more unusual is the conspiracy of silence amongst older women which keeps girls ignorant of each stage of their sexual development. 'Menstruation comes as a shock to most girls at thirteen or fourteen' (ibid., p. 291). A girl might go crying to her mother, who supplies her with an old rag and tells her to expect bleeding each month. The mother gives no further explanation except to warn her daughter never to tell the secret of her bleeding to any male and never to let any male see her bloody rag.

On her wedding night a bride finds herself in her husband's home and bed, often in complete ignorance about sexual intercourse, which comes as a shock to her. She might reproach her mother for not having warned her, but she will be told that this is something women must endure. While young men exchange sexual information and associate sexual exploits with masculinity in the Spanish tradition, girls gain no advance preparation or romantic associations about sex. 'The culture of San Pedro assigns pleasure to the male and reproduction to the female' (ibid., p. 293).

This mystification continues through a young woman's first pregnancy. She is prevented from knowing about, or acknowledging any awareness of, her first pregnancy until she is ready to give birth. Until that time the fiction is maintained by herself and those around her that the visits of the midwife are only to cure her illness and restore menstruation. Whatever fears the young wife might have, she cannot speak of them to her husband or to anyone else. Childbirth takes place in private, with only the midwife, the young husband, his parents, and possibly the wife's parents, in attendance. Children of the household are sent away and told later that a baby has been brought by a foreigner. When the young woman feels pains during labour, she is admonished not to cry out lest she is heard by neighbours. Paul reports that the usual apprehension a woman might feel at first childbirth is heightened in San Pedro by the aura of complicity of the older women. This results in the muscles tightening when they should be relaxed, thus increasing the pain and prolonging the delivery.

'What purpose does it serve to mystify menstruation, intercourse, and childbirth?' (ibid., p. 297). Paul suggests that this secrecy can appear to support the ascendancy of men over women, of older women over younger, of parents over children. But in terms of the Pedrano women themselves, the mystification of biological processes brings them to a sense of participation in the mystic powers of the universe. She concludes that although women's lives are more restricted than men's and that they are dominated in sexual relations, women gain a sense of initiation into female mysteries by which they feel themselves in closer touch with the cosmic forces controlling life itself.

Towards a New Division of Labour

The advances of modern medicine in the industrialised countries have changed what might previously have been considered the 'biological imperatives' of women. In those areas of the world where there are no modern health care facilities, the high infant mortality often means that women are expected to bear children throughout their fertile years in order to ensure that at least some children survive. These women have no need to campaign for 'natural' childbirth; in fact, they often ask for maternity and child care clinics as the first amenities in the improvement of their living conditions. Their lifespan is short. In India, for example, the expectation of life during the 1961-71 decade was estimated at 47.1 for males and 45.6 for females.[8] In the industrialised countries, reliable contraceptives have now become widely available, although only in the past few decades. The possibility of choice for the majority of sexually active women of whether or not to have children, and how many, is very recent. And today in Britain, life expectancy is estimated at 68 for men and 74 for women. As has been pointed out so often in recent years, the increased lifespan for women creates the possibility for many years of productive work in public life beyond the years they may spend in bearing and raising children. But if the 'imperatives' of biology have changed, our social institutions have lagged far behind.

In their efforts to change the position of women in society, some feminists have been working on two fronts, those of production and reproduction. They find that the sexual division of labour on the economic scene represents an elaborate construct historically 'determined' by women's reproductive function. The controversy about childbirth can thus be seen more clearly, as women's attempt to gain control over their own creative powers. In Britain, Anne Oakely argues that the male-dominated system of reproductive care operates within a society which discriminates against women in many overt and subtle ways. Women are challenging 'the right of men to determine the level of women's knowledge about, and control over, their bodies' (1976, p. 58). For her, 'A repossession of female control over reproductive care is a basic prerequisite for all other freedoms' (ibid.).

In the United States, Adrienne Rich states that it is extremely difficult and usually illegal for a woman to give birth at home attended by an experienced midwife. The medical establishment claims pregnancy and childbirth within its jurisdiction, as a form of disease. In her view, 'To change the experience of childbirth means to change women's relationship to fear and powerlessness, to our bodies, to our children; it has far-reaching psychic and political implications' (1975, p. 29).

There is an added twist to what so far has been posed as women against the male-dominated medical profession. Today a growing number of men are becoming more sympathetic to the aspirations of women to erase the traditional sexual division of labour and participate more fully in the professional world. They, in turn, are asking to share what previously has been demarcated as women's private scenes.

The concept of 'couvade' has been a classic problem in anthropology, as Rivière (1974) has noted, for over a hundred years, since the beginning of the modern discipline itself. Why should a father limit his diet, restrict his travel, simulate birth pains, and undergo other rituals, thus intimately associating himself with the birth of his child? In his reassessment of the vast literature on this question, Rivière concludes that the ritual actions of the father in simulating the biological parturition of the mother have to do with the creation of the child as a spiritual being.

In Western societies during the past decade or so, increasing attention has been given to the various psychosomatic symptoms men have complained of during their wives' pregnancies. 'The couvade syndrome' as it has been called in the *British Journal of Psychiatry* (Trethowan and Conlon, 1965) may have little to do with the ritual couvade of Latin American societies, other than its adopted label. For a recent study undertaken to ascertain the normal (as opposed to psychiatric) experience of expectant fathers, sociologists interviewed 100 fathers present at the birth and 50 who were present during labour only (Richman, Goldthorp and Simmons, 1975). The fathers who were present at the birth reported being gowned from head to toe, in the role of 'observers only' to the medical attention being given their wives. In their retrospective accounts, 15 per cent said that the main thing they disliked was their helplessness in not being able to aid their wives; 20 per cent disliked seeing their wives in pain. Yet these fathers said they welcomed the opportunity and 93 per cent stated they would be present at the next birth.[9] The three authors of this paper conclude with the provocative statement that fathers will need to become more conscious of their rights in relation to childbirth. At present, they comment, fathers can be said to be alienated from the process of reproduction. 'As women get more involved in "male" activities it is equally a "liberation" that men should experience profoundly female worlds' (ibid., p. 145).

If the rules are changing and the presence of fathers at childbirth is now allowed, and even encouraged in some hospitals, it is too early to tell what meanings this sharing of women's labour portends in our society. Definitions of 'the nature of women' are always, inevitably, social. These classifications are continually being reinterpreted by the institutions of science and religion and, at a more unconscious level, by the submerged social interactions reconstructing the reality of everyday life. What do the new ceremonies of birth tell us about the new possibilities for women?

Notes

1. In Yoruba court cases of paternity, knowledge of where the placenta is buried is often the decisive factor in determining the 'owner' of the child. The symbolic uses of the placenta are instructive. Ammar (1954) writes that in an Egyptian village in the province of Aswan the afterbirth is thrown out at night 'to be eaten by the dogs' with the wish that the woman bear as many children as the bitch bears puppies (dogs being considered particularly fecund). He attributes this idea of the importance of the placenta to the survival of an ancient Egyptian belief.

Among the Birom of northern Nigeria the disposal of the placenta marks the first ritual differentiation between a boy and a girl. Smedley (1974, p. 213) writes: 'The afterbirth of a boy child is placed in a clay pot or calabash and then put high on the branch of a special cottonwood tree in the area of his paternal compound. The afterbirth of girls will be buried in the soil, usually during a special ritual of fertility.'

Describing a birth in the Punjab of India, Gideon (1962, p. 1226) tells how the midwife digs a hole in the mud plaster floor of the hut and buries the placenta. Discussion follows. 'Akki [the midwife] was of the opinion, however, that the placenta should be buried outside for those women who had lost children previously and had buried the placenta inside. In such instances, if death happened to be due to an evil shadow, the burial of the placenta outside usually saved the child.'

2. It should be noted that this interview took place in April 1967 with an illiterate woman in the traditional section of Ibadan. Most women in Yorubaland prefer to go to maternity clinics or hospitals when these facilities are available. This case of self-delivery would be rare rather than typical, although fears of witchcraft are likely still to be prevalent at the time of childbirth among the less educated. Medical care by traditional doctors is being gradually superseded not

only by the availability of modern maternity clinics, but also by the spread of the *aladura* movement, with its healing prayers. A recent childbirth took place in the compound of a church, for example, a midwife assisting, while the church prayed for its success.

3. Sibisi (1975, p. 19) quotes one of her Zulu respondents: 'The woman receives, takes in the seed which grows to be a baby – just like the seed of the maize which because of the warmth of the fertile soil, germinates and takes root. The child belongs to the man because it is he who has sown.'

4. Discussed by Donnison (1977, p. 7).

5. Dr A. Fasan, Professor of Community Medicine at the University of Lagos, Nigeria, estimated on the basis of epidemiological surveys that *maternal* deaths in childbirth in Nigeria are 70 times as high as in the UK (personal communication, August 1974).

6. The signboard of a traditional doctor I visited in Ibadan, Nigeria, in 1967 reads (roughly translated from the Yoruba): 'I, Afiyesi, will heal all kinds of illnesses which are troubling, like a woman who is barren, that is, who cannot get with child, diseases of small children, ears which cannot hear, eyes that cannot see when eyeballs have not yet been broken, soap that will bring good luck, medicine that will make people remember things quickly.'

7. Among the Chaga of Tanzania the association of males with paternity in childbirth was made in their tradition by boys staying in an initiation camp for nine months, corresponding to the length of female pregnancy (Swantz, Henricson and Zalla, 1975, p. 51). This might also symbolise a rebirth, from boy to man.

8. From Government of India Report of the Committee on the Status of Women in India (1974, p. 16).

9. Kitzinger (1971) provides personal accounts of fathers' as well as mothers' experiences of childbirth.

Bibliography

Ammar, H. *Growing up in an Egyptian Village.* London, Routledge and Kegan Paul, 1954

Ardener, E. 'Some Outstanding Problems in the Analysis of Events'. Paper presented at the ASA Decennial Conference, Oxford, July 1973. In the *Yearbook of Symbolic Anthropology,* E. Schwimmer. London, Hurst, 1978

——. 'The Voice of Prophecy: Further Problems in the Analysis of Events'. The Munro Lecture, Edinburgh, 24 April 1975

Arms, S. *Immaculate Deception: A New Look at Women and Childbirth in America.* Boston, Houghton Mifflin, 1975

Boston Women's Health Book Collective. *Our Bodies, Ourselves: A Book by and for Women.* New York, Simon and Schuster, second edition, 1976

Bourdieu, P. 'The Berber House' in *Rules and Meaning. The Anthropology of Everyday Knowledge,* M. Douglas (ed.). Harmondsworth, Penguin, 1973

Bowen, E.S. *Return to Laughter.* London, Gollancz, 1954

Callaway, H. 'Indigenous Education in Yoruba Society' in *Conflict and Harmony in Education in Tropical Africa.* G. Brown and M. Hiskett (eds.). London, George Allen and Unwin, 1975

Claye, A., and Bourne, A. (eds.). *British Obstetric and Gynaecological Practice.* London, William Heinemann, third edition, 1963

Cooke, W.R. *Essentials of Gynecology.* Philadelphia, Lippincott, 1943

de Beauvoir, S. *The Second Sex.* Harmondsworth, Penguin, 1972. Originally published in French, 1949

Donnison, J. *Midwives and Medical Men: A History of Inter-Professional*

Rivalries and Women's Rights. London, Heinemann, 1977

Evans-Pritchard, E.E. 'Foreword' in R. Needham, 1973

Gideon, H. 'A Baby Is Born in the Punjab'. *American Anthropologist*, Vol. 64 No. 6 (1962)

Gillie, L. and O. 'The Childbirth Revolution'. *Sunday Times Weekly Review*, 1974, October 13, p. 29

Government of India, *Towards Equality*. Report of the Committee on the Status of Women in India. Ministry of Education and Social Welfare, New Delhi, 1974

Hertz, R. 'The Pre-eminence of the Right Hand: A Study in Religious Polarity', 1909. Reprinted in R. Needham, 1973

James, G.W.B. 'Psychology and Gynaecology' in Claye and Bourne, 1963

Kitzinger, S. *Giving Birth: Parents' Emotions in Childbirth*. London, Gollancz, 1971

———. *The Experience of Childbirth*. Harmondsworth, Penguin, third edition, 1972

La Fontaine, J.S. 'Ritualization of Women's Life-Crises in Bugisu' in *The Interpretation of Ritual*, J.S. La Fontaine (ed.). London, Tavistock, 1972

Leach, E. 'Virgin Birth' in *Genesis as Myth and Other Essays*. London, Jonathan Cape, 1969

Leboyer, R. *Birth Without Violence*. London, Wildwood, 1975

LeVine, R. *Culture, Behavior, and Personality*. Chicago, Aldine, 1973

Lévi-Strauss, C. 'The Effectiveness of Symbols' in *Structural Anthropology*. London, Allen Lane, The Penguin Press, 1968

Needham, J. *A History of Embryology*. Cambridge, University Press, second edition revised with the assistance of A. Hughes, 1959

Needham, R. (ed.). *Right and Left: Essays on Dual Symbolic Classification*. Chicago and London, University of Chicago Press, 1973

Oakley, A. 'Wisewoman and Medicine Man: Changes in the Management of Childbirth' in *The Rights and Wrongs of Women*, J. Mitchell and A. Oakley (eds). Harmondsworth, Penguin, 1976

Okely, J. 'Gypsy Women: Models in Conflict' in *Perceiving Women*, S. Ardener, (ed.). London, Dent/Malaby 1975

Ortner, S. 'Is Female to Male as Nature Is to Culture?' in *Woman, Culture and Society*, M. Rosaldo and L. Lamphere (eds.). Stanford, California, Stanford University Press, 1974

Paul, L. 'The Mastery of Work and the Mystery of Sex in a Guatemalan Village' in *Woman, Culture and Society*, M. Rosaldo and L. Lamphere (eds.). Stanford, California, Stanford University Press, 1974

Rich, A. 'The Theft of Childbirth', *The New York Review of Books*, 2 October 1975, pp. 25-30

Richman, J., Goldthorp, W.O., and Simmons, C. 'Fathers in Labour', *New Society*, 16 October 1975, 143-5

Rivière, P.G. 'The Couvade: A Problem Reborn', *Man* (n.s.), 9, 423-35

Scully, D., and Bart, P. 'A Funny Thing Happened on the Way to the Orifice: Women in Gynecology Textbooks'. *American Journal of Sociology*, 78 (1973), 1045-50

Smedley, A. 'Women of Udu: Survival in a Harsh Lane' in *Many Sisters: Women in Cross-Cultural Perspective*, C. Matthiasson (ed.). New York, Free Press, 1974

Swantz, M., Henricson, U., and Zalla, M. *Socio-Economic Causes of Malnutrition in Moshi District*. Research Paper No. 38, Bureau of Resource Assessment and Land Use Planning, The University of Dar es Salaam, 1975

Tomalin, C. *The Life and Death of Mary Wollstonecraft*. London, Weidenfeld and Nicolson, 1974

Trethowan, W.H., and Conlon, M.F. 'The Couvade Syndrome'. *British Journal of Psychiatry*, 111 (1965), 57-66
Van Gennep, A. *The Rites of Passage*. Chicago, University of Chicago Press, 1960, originally published in French, 1908
Willson, J.R. *Obstetrics and Gynecology*. Saint Louis, Mosby, 1971

8 THE FEMALE BRAIN: A NEUROPSYCHOLOGICAL VIEWPOINT

Freda Newcombe and Graham Ratcliff

'That's the worst of girls,' said Edmund to Peter and the dwarf. 'They never can carry a map in their heads.'

'That's because our heads have something inside them,' said Lucy.

C.S. Lewis (1951)

Neuropsychology is concerned with the relationship between brain and behaviour, structure and function. Brain structure may be described on the basis of radiological and histological data: function is defined operationally by performance both in daily life and on experimental tests. Inferences about the relationship between areas of brain and their functional role are drawn from studies of healthy subjects and patients with focal brain injury and ensuing disorders of cognition or affect. Bearing in mind what Gray (1971) has called 'the normal processes of sexual differentiation', the question arises as to whether there are differences in the male and female brain and, if so, whether these differences are reflected in cognitive skill, morphology and brain organisation.

Evidence from Physiological Research

Physiological evidence is apposite and uncontentious. In an excellent review, Goldman (1976) cites sex differences in hypothalamic mechanisms regulating taste preferences and differences in aggressive behaviour that have a well established neuro-endocrine basis. There are in fact marked differences in the synaptology of the hypothalamus that may provide the anatomical basis for different patterns of hormonal activity and consequently for these behavioural differences. Goldman suggests that sex differences in structure and function may not be limited to the hypothalamus but may be 'a pervasive characteristic of brain organisation'.

According to Gray (1971), 'sex differences in non-sexual behaviour have rarely been given any systematic attention by psychologists, yet they are constantly being observed.' He gives a succinct review of data on sex differences in aggression and fearfulness in rodents, primates and man, and the dependence of these differences on the endocrine system. From the ontogenetic viewpoint, there are well attested differences in rate of maturation (Gray and Buffery, 1971) which are reflected in the sex-dependent effects of experimental lesions in monkey (Goldman, Crawford, Stokes, Galkin and Rosvold, 1974) and rat (Stein, 1974). The influence of environmental factors in behaviour and the complicated interactions of maturation and experience are not in dispute but, as Goldman (1976, p. 70) has pointed out, these factors have sometimes received more attention than genetic and morphological constraints, particularly in the literature of developmental psychology.

Developmental and Cognitive Studies

The following discussion concerns the evidence for sex differences in man and is limited to *cognitive* performance, specifically — what evidence there is for sex differences in language and spatial ability. There is little point in discussing the question of differences in general intelligence; intelligence tests are often carefully constructed to reduce if not eliminate sex differences. Nevertheless, the 1955 standardisation data for one of the most widely used standard tests of intelligence — the Wechsler Adult Intelligence Scale (Wechsler, 1958) — showed relatively small but consistent sex differences: males obtained significantly higher scores on tests of general information, comprehension, arithmetic, picture completion and block design, whereas females had higher scores on subtests labelled vocabulary, similarities and digit symbol. The designer of the test put forward a plausible suggestion that 'women seemingly call upon different resources or different degrees of like abilities in exercising whatever it is we call intelligence' (Wechsler, 1958, p. 148). Current data are not available on large and representative samples of the population.[1] In contrast, more data are available concerning sex differences in language and spatial skills (see Hutt, 1972). Harris (1977, 1978) has now prepared a comprehensive and illuminating review. The following summary relies heavily on his work.

There is clear-cut developmental and ontogenetic evidence of sex differences. The male matures more slowly and is more susceptible to genetic defect and biological accident (Garai and Scheinfeld, 1968; Ounsted and Taylor, 1972). Regarding language development, more boys than girls suffer from developmental disorders (Lenneberg, 1967; Ingram, 1969, 1975; Critchley, 1964) and/or dyslexia (Shankweiler, 1964; Rutter, Tizard and Whitmore, 1970; Clark, 1970). In contrast, the female achieves the first language landmarks earlier (production of phonemes and of the first word, clear articulation, comprehensible

speech); the female infant vocalises more and girls talk more than boys
(see Harris, 1977). At least one widely used test of language in young
children has separate norms for boys and girls regarding both comprehension and expression (Reynell, 1969). Furthermore, there are reports
of differences in the predictive power of measures of language development in pre-school children: in the female, there is a correlation between scores achieved on language tasks in infancy and measures of IQ
obtained years later but no such correlation has been found in male
samples. Harris (1977) puts forward the interesting suggestion that 'in
girls, linguistic skills may play a larger role in general intellectual ability
– in their thinking and problem solving.' No consistent sex differences
in performance, however, have been found on language tests that demand more than executive skill or fluency, for example – tests of
verbal reasoning.

The clearest sex differences in cognitive ability in adults are in
spatial ability (Sandstrom, 1953; Maccoby and Jacklin, 1975; Harris,
1978) and have been shown in a variety of tasks including the setting
of a rod to the vertical, the detection of geometrical figures embedded
in a complex pattern, and the learning of a maze. Mental rotation tasks,
in which subjects make same/different responses to pairs of two-dimen-
sional drawings of three-dimensional objects (one of which is rotated
with respect to the other), also elicit differences (Tapley and Bryden,
1977).

A widely accepted view has been that these sex differences in spatial
skill do not occur before adolescence, except in children who are under-
privileged (Maccoby and Jacklin, 1975). However, boys tend to surpass
girls at a wide variety of spatial tasks, including aiming at a target in
space and learning a maze. Significant sex differences have been reported at the age of five on rod and frame tasks (Canavan, 1969), up to the
age of seven on maze and other spatial tasks (Mellone, 1944) and from
six to ten years of age on certain spatial visualisation tasks involving
geometric form and perspective (Tuddenham, 1971). Although these
discrete test data inevitably reflect the lack of an accepted taxonomy of
spatial skills, their consistency is not in dispute. As far as we know,
there has been no systematic investigation of spatial skills in infants and
pre-school children (but see Gesell, 1942). Darwin (1877), incidentally,
had some interesting comments to make about his own children:

> When two years and three months old, he became a great adept at
> throwing books or sticks, etc., at anyone who offended him; and so
> it was with some of my other sons. On the other hand, I could never

see a trace of such aptitude in my infant daughters; and this makes me think that a tendency to throw objects is inherited by boys.

In the absence of systematic studies, it is clearly improper to assert that differences in spatial abilities do not occur in infancy. In the meantime, well attested evidence of sex differences in spatial ability in school-children and adults cannot be disregarded.

Functional Organisation of the Brain

The question then arises as to the cerebral basis for this difference. It can be considered in the light of what is known thus far about differences in the functional role of the two cerebral hemispheres. It is known that the processing of language is carried out mainly by the left hemisphere.[2] As far as visual and spatial abilities are concerned, the patterns of hemispheric organisation vary. For certain activities, the right hemisphere appears to have a leading role. These activities include visual perception, particularly when visual cues are reduced by camouflage or brief exposure (cf. Kimura, 1963; Meier and French, 1965; Warrington and James, 1967; Lansdell, 1968; Milner, 1968; Newcombe and Russell, 1969); spatial visualisation and transformation (Ratcliff, 1970; Warrington and Taylor, 1973); and spatial orientation (de Renzi 1967; Ratcliff, 1970; Ratcliff and Newcombe, 1973). For other spatial activities including some tactual tasks (Corkin, 1977) and locomotor route-finding (Semmes, Weinstein, Ghent and Teuber, 1955; Ratcliff and Newcombe, 1973) functional asymmetry is less marked.

Is there any evidence that these patterns of organisation differ in men and women? Relevant data are drawn from experimental studies of both normal subjects and patients with brain lesions. They are by no means definitive and their methodological flaws — the disregard of such factors as culture, age, sex of experimenter, and replicability — have been illustrated with wit and acumen by Fairweather (1976). But they tend to support the notion of sex differences in the functional organisation of the brain, in mode of problem-solving, or in both. Briefly, the data suggest that the functional asymmetry of the female brain is less marked than that of the male brain.

This hypothesis is derived from the performance of healthy young adults on tasks devised to test perceptual asymmetries, that is, differences in efficiency between the left and the right hemisphere in processing verbal as compared with non-verbal, visual spatial stimuli. An enlightening discussion of models of hemispheric asymmetry can be found in Moscovitch (1978).

The experimental investigation of asymmetries of hemispheric function in normal subjects has relied to a considerable extent on tachistoscopic techniques. The tachistoscope is an apparatus that exposes visual stimuli for brief periods of time, well below the speed of an eye movement (i.e. for less than 100 msec). Provided that the subject fixates the centre of the screen, stimuli can be presented in either the left or the right visual field, and so relayed to the right and the left hemisphere respectively. The visual pathways are illustrated schematically in Figure 8.1. Signals in the left visual field (LVF) are captured by the nasal retina of the left eye and the temporal retina of the right eye. They are then transmitted to the visual cortex in the posterior part of the right hemisphere. Some non-verbal information may be processed directly by the right hemisphere but information that requires linguistic processing is transferred via the corpus callosum to the left 'dominant' hemisphere. Similarly, signals presented in the right visual field (RVF) are transmitted directly to the left hemisphere. Hence words and other linguistic material exposed in the RVF are more efficiently perceived than similar material presented to the LVF. Conversely, some non-verbal stimuli are more efficiently handled by the LVF-right hemisphere combination.

The results of experimental studies of this kind are by no means unambiguous but they suggest that functional asymmetries are more marked in the male (e.g. Hannay and Malone, 1976; Lake and Bryden, 1976; Bradshaw, Gates and Nettleton, 1977; Pirozzolo and Rayner, 1977); and it is possible that the sex difference in perceptual asymmetry is more marked on spatial than on linguistic tasks (see McGlone and Davidson, 1973). In the developmental context, one study of tactual shape recognition in two hundred children suggests that boys show evidence of right hemisphere specialisation for this type of spatial ability as early as six years of age, whereas girls do not show comparable hemispheric asymmetries until the age of thirteen (Witelson, 1976).

There are also data from patients with cerebral lesions that support the hypothesis of sex differences in cerebral organisation. The data were first derived from studies of the effects of unilateral temporal lobectomy, a surgical operation involving resection of the temporal lobe in order to relieve certain types of intractable focal epilepsy. Removal of tissue from the left or from the right temporal lobe is followed by a lowering of performance on verbal and on non-verbal memory tasks respectively (Milner, 1958; Meyer, 1959; Milner, 1970). Sex-dependent effects of this operation were first detected by Lansdell

Figure 8.1: Schematic Diagram of the Human Visual Pathway

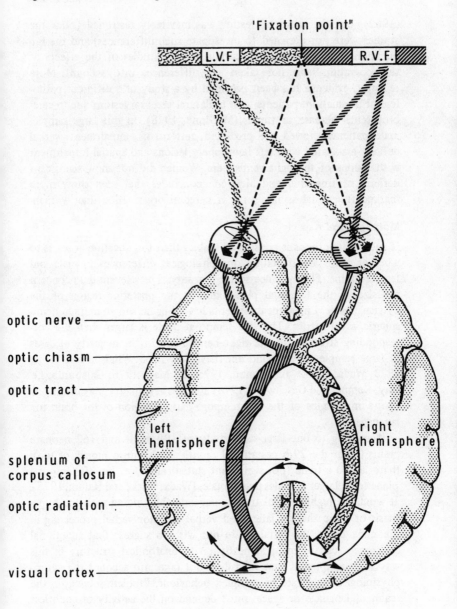

Stimuli to the side of the fixation point are transmitted initially to the posterior part of the contralateral hemisphere. The posterior parts of the brain are reciprocally connected across the corpus callosum.

(1962), but the range of testing was inevitably restricted (since the studies were not designed to investigate such differences) and the implications correspondingly uncertain. Other studies of the effects of this operation have not taken sex differences into account. More recently, evidence has been provided by a study of a different pathological population, patients with unilateral cerebral lesions due to cerebrovascular disease or tumor (McGlone, 1978). In this large sample, male patients showed the predicted pattern of impairment: verbal deficits associated with left hemisphere lesions and spatial impairment with lesions of the right hemisphere. Women did not show significant deficits of this kind and McGlone concludes that men show more marked functional asymmetries of cerebral organisation than women.

Morphological Aspects

If such a hypothesis is considered viable, then the question arises as to whether there are structural, morphological differences in male and female brains. The evidence so far is scanty. The relevant data concern the size of the temporal plane, that is the posterior region of the Sylvian fissure. Linear measurements have thus far shown marked hemispheric asymmetries. The left temporal plane is larger than the corresponding structure in the right hemisphere in the majority of cases in large samples (Geschwind and Levitsky, 1968; Witelson and Pallie, 1973; Wada, Clarke and Hamm, 1975; Le May, 1976; Galaburda, Le May, Kemper and Geschwind, 1978) and this asymmetry may be related to the importance of the left temporo-parietal region of the brain for language.

According to one large-scale study of 100 adult and 162 neonate brains (from the 29th gestational month to the third month of life), there is also a trend (not significant statistically) for the left temporal plane to be larger in males than females (Wada, Clarke and Hamm, 1975). It would be highly speculative to associate this finding with the hypothesis of more sharply lateralised verbal and non-verbal processing in the male brain. We certainly do not wish to suggest that functional differences can be mapped neatly on to anatomical structure in this way. Cartography of that kind does not take into account the neurophysiological substrate of complex behaviour. Problem-solving, in the realm of language or space, must depend on the activity of countless neurones, of which the trigger and the pattern cannot as yet be specified.

Genetic and Cultural Aspects

The biochemical and neurophysiological background to sex differences in non-sexual behaviour has been briefly mentioned. The role of genetic factors has not yet been considered. It is of special interest in relation to spatial ability. There is some support for the hypothesis of a sex-linked recessive gene from studies (Stafford, 1961; Hartlage, 1970) correlating the performance of father and daughters and of mothers and sons on spatial tasks. The higher correlations for these pairs than for same-sex pairings constitute the evidence. An additional and different source of evidence is to be found in a study of monozygotic and dizygotic twins (Vandenberg, Stafford and Brown, 1968): test scores showed a high 'heritability ratio' for boys on spatial subtests, especially those involving visualisation in three-dimensional space.

The genetic factor is clearly but one of a number of variables influencing the development of spatial ability. The role of culture and environment must obviously be considered but it has not yet been comprehensively explored. Some consistent sex differences on maze tasks (in the expected direction) have been found across a wide variety of cultures, including groups from Africa, Australia and India (see Harris, 1978). Similarly, male subjects tend to surpass females on spatial tasks (Embedded Figures and Rod-and-Frame) in groups from France, Italy, Hong Kong, The Netherlands and the United Kingdom.

There is, however, one widely quoted study of spatial ability in three different cultural groups that is taken to reflect the effect of culture (Berry, 1966). This study addressed the question of 'the relationship between the cultural and ecological characteristics of a society and the perceptual skills developed by members of that society.' Its author studied perceptual and spatial performance in members of the Temne tribe of Africa and the Canadian Eskimo. Two groups with a wide age range were taken from each culture, an isolated rural group and a sample from a port and trading station, assumed to be susceptible to cross-cultural, 'Western' influences. Their performance on spatial tasks was compared with Scottish samples from the city of Edinburgh and from a village, both samples being matched with the experimental groups for age (but not years of education).

The author's main predictions — namely, that spatial skills would be better developed in urban, more 'Westernised' samples and would be related to educational opportunity — were supported.[3] While he had no explicit hypothesis regarding sex differences, he 'suspected that the Eskimo might exhibit minimal sex differences on spatial tests, while the Temne might show them somewhat more.' His rationale for this expectation was that 'Eskimo women and children are in no way treated as dependent in the society' whereas 'the Temne. . .exercise strong control over wives and children, producing, as we have seen, field-dependent characteristics in the society as a whole.' In fact, significant sex differences on spatial tasks were found in the Temne and in the Scottish samples: no significant differences were found in the Eskimo samples. Unfortunately the raw data are not reported and the *extent* of the differences is not given for the Eskimo samples. Moreover, it is not clear whether the pattern of results is attributable to differences in culture ('field-dependence' — whatever that may be) or geographical environment, or a combination of these and other factors.

Hypotheses

In summary, the weight of evidence points to the existence of sex differences in cognitive ability. In addition, some recent experiments suggest that there may be striking differences in mode of processing information (Coltheart, Hull and Slater, 1975). Two simple tasks (counting, under time pressure, the number of upper case letters of the alphabet that are curved, and the number of letters that rhyme with /b/) were used to investigate sex differences in university undergraduates. Men made fewer errors in the former task and more errors on the latter task than women.

The authors then investigated the possibility that such differences were not restricted to tasks involving imagery. Tests included cancellation (crossing out all the 'e's in a prose passage) and lexical-decision tasks (responding 'yes' or 'no' to homophonic words (e.g. suite), homophonic non-words (e.g. throo) and non-homophonic, non-words (e.g. thron). On the cancellation task, there were no group differences in the detection of pronounced targets (e.g. the 'e' in 'let') but women omitted significantly more of the unpronounced targets (e.g. the 'e' in 'late'). A possible interpretation of this result is that women rely more on verbal analysis, and hence phonological coding, whereas men make more use of visual analysis, a more effective strategy for the cancellation task.

On the lexical decision tasks, there was further support for this interpretation. Women took significantly longer to reject a non-word if it sounded like an English word. Therefore, it is inferred that they make more use than men of a phonological access to the internal lexicon.

If phonological access is completed before visual access more often in women than in men (for example, because women are more efficient or faster than men at applying phonological rules to letter sequences), the sound of words will have more effect on women than on men; as was the case.

The authors stress that relatively 'pure' verbal and visual tasks of this kind are required to find out whether similar patterns of sex difference exist in young children. It would also be interesting to find out whether greater reliance on phonological coding in the female is associated with more efficient performance in auditory discrimination tasks not limited to linguistic material.

There have been other suggestions of sex differences in *mode* of processing, not so tightly related to experimental data. One of the more ingenious is that of Book (1932) who reported nearly half a century ago that males were superior at maze and block-counting tasks and females at clerical tasks. She suggested that these results were related to underlying neurophysiological differences, based on different conductivity rates. She associated the longer refractory periods of the male with the capacity for a sustained, analytic attitude and the shorter refractory periods of the female with a more flexible, adaptable approach, sensitive to detail. Speculations of this kind pose a fairly intractable challenge to experiment.

Coda

On a descriptive level, it is likely that genuine sex differences in cognitive skill are reflected in choice of career and professional achievement. The absence of women among the ranks of great composers and mathematicians, master chess players and famous architects is interesting. It can hardly be attributed solely to cultural prescription. It is difficult to believe that young girls are discouraged from playing chess in the USSR but we have yet to hear of a master. In contrast, in the field of literature, the achievement of women is unequivocal. Nevertheless, women were not encouraged to write novels in the early nineteenth century but in this small island they include Jane Austen, George Eliot (note the pseudonym) and the Brontë sisters. A tentative suggestion is that they tend to excel at novel-writing. They have not yet made a mark among the great poets (with very few and notable exceptions like Sappho). If this is so, is there something about verse form — its reliance on visual imagery and its elegant economy of expression — that makes it a less appropriate medium for the female author?

So far we have discussed group differences. A minority of individuals within these groups will clearly emerge with exceptional and perhaps uncharacteristic talents. The explanation may depend on a number of factors: overlap in the normal distribution of ability in groups of men and women; genetic and endocrine factors; and environmental stimulation. But there is no doubt in our mind that cognitive differences exist. They probably shape the patterns of choice in work and leisure and they might even be an advantage rather than a handicap for the evolution of the species. Two experiments are usually better than one.

Notes

1. Recent intelligence testing of a sample of over nine hundred people in Oxfordshire showed a consistent trend for men to obtain higher scores than women on both verbal and non-verbal tasks (Newcombe, Ratcliff, Carrivick, Hiorns, Harrison and Gibson, 1975).

2. This applies to virtually all right-handed subjects. About one third of left-handed subjects do not conform to this pattern and use their right hemisphere to a greater extent in language processing.

3. Problems of selectional bias are, however, difficult to avoid in this type of research.

Bibliography

Berry, J. 'Temne and Eskimo perceptual skills'. *International Journal of Psychology*, vol. 1 (1966), 207-29.

Book, H.M. 'A psychophysiological analysis of sex differences'. *Journal of Social Psychology*, Vol. 3 (1932), 434-61.

Bradshaw, J.L., Gates, A., and Nettleton, N.C. 'Bihemispheric involvement in lexical decisions: handedness and a possible sex difference'. *Neuropsychologia*, Vol. 15 (1977), 277-86

Canavan, D. (1969), cited by L. J. Harris, 'Sex differences in spatial ability: possible environmental, genetic, and neurological factors', *Hemispheric Asymmetries of Function*, M. Kinsbourne (ed.). Cambridge, Cambridge University Press, 1978

Clark, M.M. *Reading Difficulties in Schools*. Harmondsworth, Penguin, 1970

Coltheart, M., Hull, E., and Slater, D. 'Sex differences in imagery and reading'. *Nature*, Vol. 253 (1975), pp. 438-40

Corkin, S. 'The role of different cerebral structures in somesthetic perception' in *Handbook of Perception*, E.C. Carterette and M.P. Friedman (eds.). New York, Academic Press, 1977

Critchley, M. *Developmental Dyslexia*. London, William Heinemann Medical Books, 1964

Darwin, C., 'A biographical sketch of an infant'. *Mind*, Vol. 2 (1877), 285-94

De Renzi, E. 'Asimmetrie emisferiche nella rappresentazione di talune funzioni nervose superiori non verbali'. *Atti del XVI Congresso Nazionale di Neurologia* (Rome 23-26 October 1967), Vol. 1 (1967), 371-430

Fairweather, H. 'Sex differences in cognition', *Cognition* Vol. 4 (1976), 231-80.

Galaburda, A.M., LeMay, M., Kemper, T.L. and Geschwind, N. 'Right-left asymmetries in the brain'. *Science*, Vol. 199 (1978), 852-6

Garai, J.E., and Scheinfeld, A. 'Sex differences in mental and behavioural traits'. *Genetic Psychology Monograph*, Vol. 77 (1968), 169-299

Geschwind, N., and Levitsky, W. 'Left-right asymmetries in temporal speech region'. *Science*, Vol. 161 (1968), 186-7

Gesell, A. *The First Five Years of Life*. London, Methuen, 1942

Goldman, P.S., Crawford, H.T., Stokes, L.P., Galkin, T.W., and Rosvold, H.E. 'Sex-dependent behavioural effects of cerebral cortical lesions in the developing rhesus monkey', *Science*, Vol. 186 (1974), 540-2

Goldman, P.S. 'Maturation of the mammalian nervous system and the ontogeny of behaviour' in *Advances in the Study of Behaviour*, J.S. Rosenblatt, R.A. Hinde, E. Shaw and C. Beer (eds.), Vol. 7. New York, Academic Press, 1976, pp. 1-90

Gray, J.A. 'Sex differences in emotional behaviour in mammals including man: endocrine bases'. *Acta Psychologica*, Vol. 35 (1971), 29-46

Gray, J.A., and Buffery, A.W.H. 'Sex differences in emotional and cognitive behaviour in mammals including man: adaptive and neural bases'. *Acta Psychologica*, Vol. 35 (1971), 89-111

Hannay, H.J., and Malone, D.R. 'Visual field effects and short-term memory for verbal material'. *Neuropsychologia*, Vol. 14 (1976), 203-9

Harris, L.J. 'Sex differences in the growth and use of language' in *Women: a psychological perspective*, E. Donelson and J. Gullahorn (eds.). New York, John Wiley and Sons, Inc., 1977

Harris, L.J. 'Sex differences in spatial ability: possible environmental genetic, and neurological factors' in *Hemispheric Asymmetries of Function*, M. Kinsbourne (ed.). Cambridge, Cambridge University Press, 1978

Hartlage, L.C. 'Sex-linked inheritance of spatial ability'. *Perceptual and Motor Skills*, Vol. 31 (1970), 610

Hutt, C. 'Neuroendocrinological, behavioural, and intellectual aspects of sexual differentiation in human development' in *Gender Differences: Their Ontogeny and Significance*, C. Ounsted and D.C. Taylor. London, Churchill Livingstone, 1972

Ingram, T.T.S. 'Developmental disorders of speech' in *Handbook of Clinical Neurology*, Vol. 4, P.J. Vinken and G.W. Bruyn (eds.). Amsterdam, North Holland, 1969

Ingram, T.T.S. 'Speech disorders in childhood' in *Foundations of Language Development: A Multidisciplinary Approach*, E.H. Lenneberg and E. Lenneberg (eds.), Vol. 2. New York, Academic Press, 1975

Kimura, D. 'Right temporal-lobe damage'. *Archives of Neurology (Chic.)*, Vol. 8 (1963), 264-71

Lake, D.A., and Bryden, M.P. 'Handedness and sex differences in hemispheric asymmetry'. *Brain and Language*, Vol. 3 (1976), 266-82

Lansdell, H. 'A sex difference in effect of temporal-lobe neurosurgery on design preference'. *Nature*, Vol. 194 (1962), 852-4

Lansdell, H. 'Effect of extent of temporal lobe ablations on two lateralized deficits'. *Physiology and Behaviour*, Vol. 3 (1968), 271-273

LeMay, M. 'Morphological cerebral asymmetries of modern man, fossil man, and nonhuman primate'. Annals N.Y. Academy of Science, in *Origins and Evolution of Language and Speech*, S.R. Harnad, H.D. Steklis and J. Lancaster (eds.), 1976

Lenneberg, E.H. *Biological Foundations of Language*, New York, John Wiley, 1967

Lewis, C.S. *Prince Caspian*. London, Collins, 1951

Maccoby, E.E., and Jacklin, C.N. *The Psychology of Sex Differences*. Oxford, Oxford University Press, 1975

McGlone, J. 'Sex differences in functional brain asymmetry'. *Cortex*, 1978 (in press.

McGlone, J., and Davidson, W. 'The relation between cerebral speech laterality and spatial ability with special reference to sex and hand preference'. *Neuropsychologia*, Vol. 11 (1973), 105-13

Meier, M.J., and French, L.A. 'Lateralized deficits in complex visual discrimination and bilateral transfer of reminiscence following unilateral temporal lobectomy'. *Neuropsychologia*, Vol. 3, (1965), 261-72

Mellone, M.A. 'A factorial study of picture tests for young children'. *British Journal of Psychology*, Vol. 35 (1944), 9-16

Meyer, V. 'Cognitive changes following temporal lobectomy for relief of temporal lobe epilepsy'. *Archives of Neurology and Psychiatry, (Chic.)*, Vol. 81 (1959), 299-309

Milner, B. 'Psychological defects produced by temporal-lobe excision'. *Research Publications of the Association for Research in Nervous and Mental Disease (New York)*, Vol. 36 (1958), 244-57

Milner, B. 'Visual recognition and recall after right temporal-lobe excision in man'. *Neuropsychologia*, Vol. 6 (1968), 191-209

Milner, B. 'Memory and the medial temporal regions of the brain' in *Biology of Memory*, K.H. Pribram and D.E. Broadbent (eds.). New York, Academic Press, 1970

Moscovitch, M. 'Information processing and the cerebral hemispheres' in *Handbook of Behavioural Neurobiology*, M.S. Gazzaniga (ed.). New York, Plenum, 1978

Newcombe, F.G., Ratcliff, G.G., Carrivick, P.J., Hiorns, R.W., Harrison, G.A., and Gibson, J.B. 'Hand preference and I.Q. in a group of Oxfordshire villages'. *Annals of Human Biology*, Vol. 2 (1975) 235-42

Newcombe, F., and Russell, W.R. 'Dissociated visual perceptual and spatial deficits in focal lesions of the right hemisphere'. *Journal of Neurology, Neurosurgery and Psychiatry*, Vol. 32 (1969) 73-81

Ounsted, C., and Taylor, D.C. *Gender Differences: Their Ontogeny and Significance.* London, Churchill Livingstone, 1972

Pirozzolo, F.J., and Rayner, K. 'Hemispheric specialization in reading and word recognition'. *Brain and Language*, Vol. 4 (1977), 248-261

Ratcliff, G.G. 'Aspects of Disordered Space Perception'. Unpublished D.Phil. thesis, Oxford University, 1970

Ratcliff, G.G., and Newcombe, F. 'Spatial orientation in man: effects of left, right, and bilateral posterior cerebral lesions'. *Journal of Neurology, Neurosurgery and Psychiatry*, Vol. 36 (1973), 448-54

Reynell, J.K. *Reynell Developmental Language Scales.* Windsor, England, National Foundation for Educational Research, 1969

Rutter, M., Tizard, J., and Whitmore, K. *Education, Health and Behaviour.* London, Longman, 1970

Sandstrom, C.I. 'Sex differences in localization and orientation'. *Acta Psychologica*, Vol. 9 (1953), 82-96

Semmes, J., Weinstein, S., Ghent, L., and Teuber, H.–L. 'Spatial orientation in man after cerebral injury: 1. Analyses by locus of lesion'. *Journal of Psychology*, Vol. 39 (1955), 227-44

Shankweiler, D. 'Developmental dyslexia: a critique and review of recent evidence'. *Cortex*, Vol. 1 (1964), 53-62

Stafford, R.E. 'Sex differences in spatial visualization as evidence of sex-linked inheritance'. *Perceptual and Motor Skills*, Vol. 13 (1961) 428

Stein, D.G. 'Some variables influencing recovery of function after central nervous system lesions in the rat', in *Plasticity and Recovery of Function*

In the Central Nervous System, D.G. Stein, J.J. Rosen and N. Butters (eds.). New York, Academic Press, 1974

Tapley, S.M., and Bryden, M.P. 'An investigation of sex differences in spatial ability: mental rotation of three-dimensional objects'. *Canadian Journal of Psychology*, Vol. 31 (1977), 122-30

Tuddenham, R.D. 'Theoretical regularities and individual idiosyncracies' in *Measurement and Piaget*, D.R. Green, M.P. Ford and G.B. Flamer (eds.). New York, McGraw-Hill, 1971

Vandenberg, S.G., Stafford, R.E., and Brown, A. 'The Louisville Twin Study' in *Progress in Human Behaviour Genetics*, S.G. Vandenberg (ed.), Baltimore, Johns Hopkins, 1968

Wada, J.A., Clarke, R., and Hamm, A. 'Cerebral hemispheric asymmetry in humans'. *Archives of Neurology*, Vol 32 (1975), 239-46.

Warrington, E.K., and James, M. 'Disorders of visual perception in patients with unilateral cerebral lesions'. *Neuropsychologia*, Vol. 5 (1967), 253-66

Warrington, E.K., and Taylor, A.M. 'The contribution of the right parietal lobe to object recognition'. *Cortex*, Vol. 9 (1973), 152-64

Wechsler, D., *The Measurement and Appraisal of Adult Intelligence*, 4th Ed. Baltimore, Williams and Wilkins, 1958

Witelson, S.F. 'Sex and the single hemisphere: specialisation of the right hemisphere for spatial processing'. *Science*, Vol. 193 (1976) 425-7

Witelson, S.F., and Pallie, W. 'Left hemisphere specialization for language in the newborn'. *Brain*, Vol. 96 (1973) 641-6

9 HAREMS AND OVERLORDS: BIOSOCIAL MODELS AND THE FEMALE

Hilary Callan

... we know well that, both *de facto* and *de jure,* the emergence of culture will remain a mystery to man. Such a mystery will remain until he succeeds in determining, on the biological level, the modifications of the structure and functioning of the brain of which culture was at one and the same time the natural result and the social mode of apprehension, and which at the same time created the intersubjective milieu indispensable to further transformations (C. Lévi-Strauss, *The Scope of Anthropology,* 1967, pp. 24-5).

Introduction

This series of papers was planned with terms of reference which include exploration of the limits of the category 'woman'. The central dilemma of my own contribution is thereby rendered inescapable from the start. Current claims and counter-claims about the influence (as it is often phrased) of 'biological givens' on 'cultural responses' in relation to women frequently rest on a quite unwarranted assumption of the categorical equivalence of biological and cultural femaleness. By this I mean not that either side of the debate treats these as the same category (that is, confuses 'sex' with 'gender': a now quite unoriginal though valid objection[1]) but that they typically treat them as the same *kind* of category and hence as standing in a straightforwardly knowable mutual relationship. Because I believe that this assumption is premature and probably wrong, I shall argue that we have not yet reached a position where debate about 'facts' can begin. We are in a set of theoretical Chinese boxes, except that it is as if each box were made of a different material and existed in a different space. In developing my argument I shall certainly be making reference to 'facts' and theories about 'facts'; but it should be borne in mind that I am really trying to get to grips with what seems to me the more urgent task: that of characterising and drawing attention to one or two of the boxes which mediate, perhaps inescapably, a 'scientific' account of femaleness.

The Model and Its Sources

The possibility of a biosocial model in anthropology is itself of course a highly controversial issue. Seven or eight years ago, certainly, the question could not have been raised in quite this manner. In the mainstream British anthropology of that period, the institutional blocks against any search for biological processes in culture were so pervasive and so ill-recognised that it is no wonder if the intellectual barriers to such an encounter were misconceived at the time the effort began to be made. I refer here to the most recent effort, for the history of attempts to link biology with culture is a long and (in places) disreputable one. A number of forces converged in the mid-sixties to stimulate interest in a new *rapprochement* between biological and social science. Many people were diffusely involved in this movement; but it is fair to say that it first acquired the character of an 'official' debate in British social anthropology with Tiger and Fox's (1966) article, 'The zoological perspective in social science'. By 1973 the movement had acquired enough influence to occupy one session of the Special Decennial Conference of the Association of Social Anthropologists at Oxford. The resulting volume, *Biosocial Anthropology*, was published in 1975 with a Theoretical Introduction by Robin Fox. Brief quotations from these two papers will indicate the basis of the programmatic claims made then and currently for a biosocial model:

> sociological findings, in this perspective, provide data for a more comprehensive, zoological approach to the evolution of man as a gregarious organism. In consequence the study of human social behaviour becomes a sub-field of the comparative zoology of animal behaviour and is broadly subject to the same kind of analysis and explanation. No special theory other than the Darwinian is necessary to explain the development and persistence of more general features of human social organization (Tiger and Fox, 1966, p.76).

> Biosocial anthropology is strictly a branch of evolutionary biology — as are ethology, population genetics, physical anthropology etc. It is 'neo-Darwinian' and 'evolutionary' in that, within the framework of the neo-Darwinian synthesis, it accepts as its premiss the role of mutation and natural selection as the major factors determining the evolution of form and function in all species including our own. And it accepts this as the main point of departure for the analysis of anything concerning the life processes of any species. It views social behaviour, then, as the outcome of an evolutionary

process and analyses it as such; culture itself being an outcome of the same process and only understandable in these terms. It incorporates the data of comparative sociology (social anthropology) but analyses them in a different framework of assumptions from those of the prevailing 'superorganic' or Durkheimian positions (Fox in Fox (ed.), 1975, p. 2).

For a number of reasons, the quest for a biosocial synthesis could not and did not attempt to confine itself to the domain of academic social science. In part this is attributable to historical accident. Many of the early attempts to state the case appeared in a context of popular and often slipshod and sensational writing about the relation of biology to culture. There are, however, indications of a deeper inevitability which it would be well worth someone's time to trace. For the world-view within which the greater part of our shared vision of man's place in nature was constructed seems inherently predisposed to sustain debate about the 'ought' as well as the 'is' and the 'can be' of the human condition. If a present-day playwright such as Ardrey with a knack for catchy phrases can now cash in on the public appeal of animal stories and instant solutions to the human dilemma, this takes place fairly and squarely within the anecdotal tradition of early writers such as Romanes and, in places, Darwin himself.

With hindsight this is not difficult to see. Yet there was a time, recent enough to be within the experience of my own generation of anthropologists, when it was possible to view the moral and political component of the biosocial debate as superimposition, 'trappings', 'froth'. For the anthropologist (and I assume also for the biologist) it seemed possible to separate the issues from the trappings: to point out if necessary where intellectual sloppiness or sheer ignorance distorted the picture (as in Desmond Morris's assumption (1967) that non-monogamous societies are 'evolutionary failures') but to retain belief in the accessibility of 'evidence' bearing on a state of the world in which biological factors under this or that description do or do not enter into the causation of human social patterns. If, now, we can with greater maturity share Robert Young's perception that 'not only [is] science pressed into service to justify models of political and economic behaviour, but. . . these models are constitutive of the [very] project of enquiring into human nature and society' (1973), then we have a more difficult, but perhaps a more important, task in hand. Granting the likelihood of the biologists' case that material reality (in the form of selection and adaptation) enters into the determination of human social experience, and granted also the certainty that this same reality is simultaneously filtered and interpreted by the very experience which it determines, our problem is to state the material and logical relations between the two in a way which carries meaning and is, preferably, true. To say this is not to take up any position on the quite separate issue of 'commitment' and whether all social science has to be 'committed' social science. It is, however, to raise the elusive dilemma of the mind's capacity to confront the material constituents of its own operations.

The Feminist Challenge

Perhaps the sharpest and most sustained public critique of the developing biosocial approach has been a feminist one. By an historical coincidence the rise of the new feminism more or less coincided with that of the biosocial movement; yet it was not, surely, logical necessity which set the two on a collision course. It was natural no doubt that the pioneering biosocial writers should try their hand early in the game at the sexual division, widely taken for granted as the most fundamental axis of biological and social classification; and no less natural that this should scandalise feminist opinion. Yet it is not obvious why the feminist critics should have felt obliged to deny, unconvincingly, the very possibility of there being a biological infrastructure to certain human relationships rather than expose real weaknesses in the concepts and assumptions within which the biosocial hypotheses were framed. No doubt the answer lies in diffuse ramifications of the politico-intellectual struggles of our times; in particular the self-polarising force of the great opposition between nativist and 'blank-sheet' views of the nature of man. Someone some day will doubtless trace these currents in detail, and it is not my purpose to do so here. But it is worth saying, *en passant,* that this particular debate seems to me to have taken several early wrong turns, and to have degenerated into a sterility quite as tedious as that of the old nature-nurture battle at which it is currently fashionable to sneer. If, for example, we have reached a position where Goldberg, in his recently republished *The Inevitability of Patriarchy* (1977) can consider all feminist positions as equivalent *by definition* to ones of extreme environmentalism, then I am surely not alone in feeling that the argument is no longer worth pursuing on this ground.

Hazards of Theorising

It may or may not be another coincidence that, independently of the illusion that evolutionary and feminist analyses represent intrinsically

opposed modes of thought about the social, the presence of females on
the social scene presents a fairly sharp challenge to the developing biosocial model. Quite apart from our primary interest in women, we can
put to the test the model's claim to offer a potentially comprehensive
account of the social, through the strategy of examining its capacity
to handle female action. But first it is necessary to comment generally
on the biosocial model as revealed in the programmatic statements such
as those I quoted earlier. Unless these are to be interpreted as rhetoric,
a first reaction might be one of surprise at the apparent rashness of
undertaking to defend a position which views 'culture' as subject to
analysis within a single theoretical frame, and treats the 'data' of social
science as out there, ripe for redistribution within the new/old categories. One might almost imagine that there were the remotest prospect
of agreement within the social sciences about what their data actually
are. Rates of marriage and divorce? Totems? Mothers' brothers? Beyond this we can discern the outlines of a deeper problem: an in-
decisiveness in the programme reflecting a profound incoherence in the
biosocial model currently on offer.

A central difficulty is that those formulating the biosocial programme have felt called upon to specify *in advance* the nature of the relationship between 'biological givens' and 'cultural responses'. The
paradigm, whether conscious or not, is a theory of causation: natural
processes are seen as determining and limiting the cultural options
available to the species man. Now biology and culture are not of
course solely related as independent to dependent variables. Not only
do they as branches of enquiry share a history of at least a hundred
years of different sorts of mutual attraction and repulsion, but in both
areas 'facts' are embedded within distinctive conceptual and linguistic
structures. It may indeed turn out that the more enduring and interesting linkages between biological and social science lie at the level of
the structures of perception and reality engendered within each. But
the rather simple-minded theory of causation with which some of the
biosocial writers have burdened themselves has deposited them on the
horns of a particularly nasty dilemma. If certain biological factors in
mankind's present or past (such as the hunting transition or female
lactation) are seen to possess some general congruence with human
social arrangements, then you may well feel pushed towards a degree of
reductionism and determinism in your theory of society. But if (and
here comes the other horn) you do not want to be a simple-minded
biological reductionist, then you are reduced to vagary because your
theory of causation affords you no alternative way of formulating

the relationship between biology and culture. Thus Fox, in the passage I quoted, refers to social behaviour and culture respectively as 'the' and as 'an' *outcome* of an evolutionary process. I do not think he wants, or very often wants, this to mean that the entire study of culture and social relations could be reduced to a set of evolutionary hypotheses if one only knew enough about human prehistory. Yet if he does not mean this, what does he mean? Time and again in the writings of the biosocial programme-planners we find them flirting with a theoretical stance whose empiricist, 'scientific', linguistic echoes afford their work much of its air of self-assurance and whose apparent reductionist and determinist implications call down on them the wrath of other kinds of social scientists. Yet on the brink their nerve seems to fail, and we are given passages of extended imagery on the theme of programming, bio-grammars and 'what's in the wiring'. Nowhere, it seems, are we told how to interpret the model. What epistemological status do we assign to these analogies (or are they homologies?) from computer science, linguistics and household electrical circuitry?

A second general difficulty is more directly relevant to the capacity of a biosocial model to handle women. It can be traced to an oddly persistent tendency on the part of the bridge-builders to confuse argument about the limits of what *is* with argument about the limits of what *can be* in living systems. When Tiger and Fox published their 1966 paper I was in broad sympathy with their position, but worried about their apparent contentment with a method which would use detailed study of cultural *variation* as indicator of the extent of cultural *variability*, or (as they put it) the 'limits of plasticity' of cultures. I can only say that, ten years later, I was still worried. In *The Imperial Animal* (1971) Tiger and Fox again move without apparent stress from noting the cultural universality of a sexual division of labour to claiming that:

> Women have to be in on the economy. But a basic element of the biogrammar here seems to be that they have to be in on only special-ly defined terms: there appears to be a tendency to define some work as female and some as male, and to maintain the distinction whatever the content and whatever the cost. This is the same prin-ciple of male-bond-female-exclusion that, in politics, so rudely circumscribed the female role. In economic matters, since females cannot be excluded totally, at least they can be segregated into some set of specific activities (Tiger and Fox, 1971, p. 144).

Two years later, Fox writing alone gives us the following:

> [Man] is what he is because he has adapted successfully to changing environments and selection pressures. There is a range of behaviour that is natural to him, and that, if thwarted, will produce detrimental results. For this range to become clear, all the varieties of social order that man has produced must be carefully looked at (Fox, 1973, p.17).

And on the very same page:

> With this battery of information the range of possible behaviour and social orders that were recognizably human could be established. Outside this range would be those behaviours and organizations that were clearly forced on the creature — not part of his pattern of adaptedness (ibid.).

The confusions in this thinking scarcely require comment. My own inclination would be to turn the argument on its head. The sheer paucity of material at observational level on females, plus the relative novelty of the theoretical focus on them, indicate that we have barely begun to explore the possibility of a scientific account of female action. Nor would this move be without technical justification. It was apparently John Bowlby who pointed out that an account of the circumstances under which a structure or a behaviour evolves sets no automatic limit to that structure's plasticity, which is subject to a quite separate set of constraints.

Hazards of Observation

At a programmatic level, then, the dominant biosocial theorising of the period in question (mid-sixties to mid-seventies) is open to criticism on general grounds which subsume the problems it has in accounting for women in other than a purely negative way. There is at least one more level of inadequacy. The attempt to pinpoint this brings us up against the epistemology of the observer-observed relationship, and layers of intellectual function where social and behavioural scientists may well experience a parallel philosophical unease. Part of the matter is not difficult to discern. For its empirical base the biosocial model has depended heavily on the findings and methods of ethology (the biological study of behaviour), and there has been considerable *naiveté* and unconscious subjectivity in the work of certain ethologists as data-gatherers. This is most obvious in the writings of some of the early or 'classical' ethologists, and may be traceable to their failure to perceive the non-objective and non-elemental components of the 'behaviour' they thought they were recording (see E. Ardener, 1973 and 1977). Earlier ethological monographs – including many on the sub-human primates – tend to present the female segment of an animal society (often the numerical majority) as mere background to the dramas played out by the males; or at most as *objects* of competition, domination and possession. Social and political structures are to a large degree unconsciously equated with male relationships, social hierarchy with male dominance. Indeed, the females are often 'not there' in these monographs in a sense very close to that in which women are 'not there' in anthropological writings of a comparable period (comparable, that is, in a sense of equivalent phase in the moral career of the discipline). When in 'Belief and the Problem of Women' (1972) Ardener speaks of the presence of women in these anthropologies as being rather like that of their chickens or the cows of the Nuer – they move about, they 'behave', they are 'observed' ('a mere bird-watching indeed') but they do not enter into the model-making process – the image is more apt than perhaps even he was aware.

Hazards of Language

So far the imbalance is a procedural one and can be rectified as such – as is, happily, beginning to be done in the most recent primate studies. The same broadly goes for the evolutionary dimension, the second main strand of the biosocial fabric. The emphasis on the hunting transition as the evolutionary source of the alleged maleness of intrasexual bonding, of bargaining, risk-taking and of political competence leaves out of account the elements of coalition, initiative and conscious commitment of resources to selected options which attach to the gathering side of a hunting-gathering economy. In principle the gap can be – and, happily, is beginning to be – filled. A re-examination of the traditional (e.g. the Weberian) concepts of power, authority and legitimacy in the light of the parts actually played by females in the articulation of social relations could bring a much enriched appreciation of the biological infrastructure of politics including a focus on the political life-cycle (already present embryonically in the biosocial programme) and a capacity to examine such interesting questions as the political potential of old women.

A more intractable point is that there are respects in which language itself seems to impose its structures on the data-gatherers, and so to compromise any claim to a spurious objectivity. I award to a linguistic pre-ordering of experience the role which Robert Young and others have assigned to a political one. I do this not from doubt that he is right in many cases, nor through failure to perceive that the two are connected, but because I know from close association with ethologists that they are no more likely than anyone else to be contaminated by social or political prejudice. Linguistic structures by contrast – the unexamined kind in particular – dominate us all. The point in any case is the same; to enter as observer into relationship with animals and then to report on the relationship is an explicitly human, therefore social, therefore language-linked, thing to do.

M.R.A. Chance is an ethologist whose many theoretical and field-studies have given him a deservedly prominent reputation and position, and whose findings have been extensively drawn on by biosocial theorists. His gift for coining memorable terms lends his work particularly clearly to illustration of the epistemological state of affairs I am trying to indicate. In his early writings (for example, 1963) on social bonds among non-human primates, Chance depicted the male hierarchy as a central structural core of the typical baboon/macaque society, and noted a relative indeterminacy and tenuousness in female social bonds compared to those of males. In his book *Social Groups of Monkeys, Apes and Men* (1970, written with Clifford Jolly) he admittedly assigns importance to groupings of females and young as one component of the 'stem structure' of primate societies. In his discussion, however, the female bonds emerge as important primarily at the level of one-to-one (e.g. female-infant) relationships. Yet we know, and we knew in 1970 (though possibly not much earlier than that) that among the most important principles of internal social organisation in both monkey and ape societies are groupings and long-term alliances of biological kin, often spanning several generations and centred (obviously) on females. By 1975, and Chance's contribution to *Biosocial Anthropology* ('Social Cohesion and the Structure of Attention') the following have been well and truly assimilated as technical terms into the descriptive language of primatology: *cohorts* of adult males, *assemblies* of adult females and young, and *clusters* of juveniles. In addition the terms *harem* and *overlord* are accepted currency in studies of the rather atypical social organisation of the hamadryas baboon. At least one of these terms seems to have originated with Chance – although I must in honesty note that Wolfgang Wickler (for example, *The Sexual Code*, 1969) prefers 'pasha' to 'overlord' throughout. I leave the reader to reflect not only on the military – even Romanoid – associations of the term 'cohort'; but also on the placing of the three-term sequence cohort/assembly/cluster on what looks like a diminishing scale of activeness and intentionality in social participation. By contrast the terms 'harem' and 'overlord' have associations of sultanates and Eastern promise. Perhaps there is an unconscious connection with the Middle Eastern habitat of the hamadryas baboon.

It is emphatically no part of my purpose to single out, criticise or tease any individual ethologist unfairly. I seek only to point to the oddity that such semantic flights of fancy should appear in the writings of those who also claim adherence to an empiricist creed. It would take me too far from my theme to recommend a way out of this impasse for ethology, except to suggest that it might take the form of a partial 'paradigm shift' such as Harré, Hudson and others have advocated for other behavioural sciences. In this, explicit recognition might be given to the subjective streak which has (I maintain) been implicitly present in ethology from its beginnings. My theoretical purpose in this chapter so far has been to demonstrate that the efforts of current biosocial theories to offer an account of the female human condition have been doubly, perhaps multiply, hampered by incoherent treatment of material drawn from an ethology whose empiricist claims themselves seem, in certain areas, due for some re-evaluation.

It would be naive to suppose that niceties and quibbles like the foregoing have had any influence on the development of biosocial thinking. It has taken, rather, the debates between the biosocial writers and their feminist critics to demonstrate to all concerned that there exists for biosocial anthropology a 'problem of women'. As elsewhere, the 'problem' may turn out to be a spurious artefact of inadequacies in the 'conceptual toolbag' (containing such terms as 'dominance', 'hierarchy', 'status', 'control', 'possession', 'exchange', even 'politics') which, for want of any better, the biosocial theorists have used when constructing their model. As recently as the late 1960s it was possible to set this out schematically as a purely biological problem, in the form of an outline model in which the 'problem' resulted from the co-presence in a social system of a male-dominated social structure and sustained individual sexual bonds (Callan, 1970). A derived hypothesis was that a built-in ambiguity or equivocality in the females' relationship to the system's core might be a distinctive primate, and possibly human, adaptation. As a biological model this can be seen in retrospect to suffer from most of the drawbacks I have been complaining of. One can no longer so naively assume that, if females show an indefiniteness in their relations with a structure whose description has been arrived at chiefly by looking at males, these are grounds for considering their relationships intrinsically indefinite. As an avowedly anthropological model, in which the core of the system becomes something like 'the "official" version of reality' (one of the 'dominant structures' explored by Ardener (1975) and others) it might have more mileage. But to cut the model adrift in such a fashion leaves us with the problem of explaining the alleged universality of such a pattern, and hence leads us inexorably back to the task of deciding on the admissibility of any form of biological account.

Some Current Treatments

Recognition has indeed been growing in recent years that, as things stand, a problem exists, and that at the very least it is tactically unwise for biosocial anthropologists to continue to theorise about women in the face of a gross lack, even at observational level, of material on modes of female participation in non-human and human society. Accordingly, some recent writers have turned their attention to the capacity of biological and evolutionary models to interpret general features of women's social experience. I want to comment briefly on two of these works: Tiger and Shepher's *Women in the Kibbutz* (1976) and Reynolds' *The Biology of Human Action* (1976).[2] My purpose is not to offer a detailed commentary or critique of these works, but to use them to stake out an area of ground from which to start developing the suggestions I want to make later in this chapter.

The status of the kibbutz movement as a kind of natural experiment, a test case for a number of theories of human nature, is frequently asserted or assumed and (to judge by recent media presentations) has come to be accepted in general public awareness. Theories of incest avoidance and of women are among those widely held to be put to crucial test by the kibbutzim. In both of these cases, the central issue, recognised or not, is the explicitly biosocial one of the relationship between biological predispositions to act in certain ways, and cultural prescriptions of such action: between 'behaviour' (so-called) and the systems of rules and values surrounding it. I do not think we yet have a satisfactory statement of this relationship. In the case of incest it is claimed that boys and girls reared together during a critical period of infancy seldom or never become 'sexually bonded' to one another. This is placed alongside data on incest barriers in primates and other animals to form the basis of a biosocial theory of incest avoidance in man whose operating mechanism is the 'cue' of infant intimacy. Freud's objection to such an explanation (why ban incest if people don't want to commit it anyway?) remains to be dealt with. According to one view (Bischof, 1975) the answer is that the *rules* are related to the *behaviour* as *name* to *named*. Rules about incest avoidance serve to label patterns which would in any case tend to occur. Now I do not doubt, on the evidence, that incest barriers exist in animals and are a part of the natural world, and on grounds of parsimony alone it is highly likely that comparable mechanisms are present in man. The difficulty is to account for the rule-like character of incest rules, and the fact that (ignoring problems of definition) societies pick on incest, rather than some other avoided behaviour, to have rules about.

The case of women is parallel in this respect. The evidence, including that on the kibbutz, may well suggest a built-in tendency to sexual differentiation in certain departments of life, such as mathematical attainment, work preference, style of political action and relations with children. But as far as I know we have not yet been offered a statement of the nature-culture transformation which allows any account to be given of the way 'culture' treats these 'natural' statistical distributions, assigning to some of them a binding moral force. And yet, if such treatment is as humanly universal as its biological infrastructure, it ought to be within the purview of a comprehensively biosocial model.

If I may illustrate briefly from my own current field-work among British female nurses, even superficial observation makes it clear that many nurses have difficulties over the handling of authority. By this I mean, not that they cannot handle authority as givers or as takers, but that they frequently experience a tension between pressures towards supportive and towards hierarchical modes of action and self-perception. There is of course a popular mythology about the battle-axe nurse who achieves authority by renouncing femininity. There is another one about the angel of mercy who does the reverse. The co-existence of these two mythologies may express the same tension or dissonance in society. Real nurses experience this as one of a number of areas of indeterminacy or ambiguity in their situation and self-definition. They gather in neutral corners to mutter about staff nurses who 'flap about', or they may see it as a training problem: 'Nurses are taught nursing. They are not taught management.'

Now a simple biosocial theory might say that women are 'by nature' less well fitted for authority than men — perhaps because, as Tiger and Fox suggested (1971) they do not emit the attention-binding signals that release 'followership behaviour' in others. Tiger and Shepher found evidence of a special uneasiness surrounding kibbutz women in authority over others (especially men) which seems to incline them to this view. It is easy enough to see hierarchical arrangements in female or largely female groups — women's services, girls' schools, nurses —

as pale and none too competent imitations of male structures. But to take this view is to close rather than open the doors of enquiry. Moreover it does not help me at all in my field-work. The nurses' problem — and mine as ethnographer — is that the capacities and handicaps they may have *qua* biological females are manifested and mapped on to a terrain of experience which includes (among many other things) the existence of traditional male authority patterns (which may or may not be an authentic model for women) as well as the relevant parts of the profession's own encapsulated history. Further, these forces are linked not merely as cause to effect, but as simultaneities. A truly explanatory biosocial theory should have the capacity to handle events over this range, precisely because what needs explaining is the interpenetration of 'natural' and 'cultural' forces. Incidentally, it seems likely that public response to the type of biosocial theory of sex differences set out in books like *Men in Groups* (Tiger, 1969) and *The Imperial Animal* (Tiger and Fox, 1971) will itself affect the reality under investigation in much the same way as Liam Hudson (1972) has claimed that general knowledge of the work of Masters and Johnson has altered for ever the nature of sex among the educated classes.

To return to Tiger and Shepher's work: notwithstanding what I have said, the kibbutz movement is an important source of evidence on both 'incest' and 'woman' problems, and for the same reason. If there are both biological and cultural pressures towards sexual differentiation and avoidance of 'sibling' incest,[3] and if they usually act in the same direction, then the kibbutz on the face of it offers a case where they don't. A conscious ideology, it seems, has directed all social pressure towards complete sexual equality in all except reproduction, and set up marriage within the kibbutz as a positive ideal. If, then, the kibbutz is a true test case, it should provide us with a rather precise measure of the strength of those in-built patterns which are resistant to all the forces of a pioneering ideology. One can cast legitimate doubt on the capacity of three generations of self-conscious innovation to obliterate the influence of a historical and a surrounding Semitic culture to whose value-structure sexual polarisation is particularly central. Tiger and Shepher do deal in part with this objection, under the labels 'socialization argument' and 'external influences argument' (pp. 264-9). One could pursue the debate no doubt, and reach the predictable conclusion that no truly rigorous test case can be envisaged. Avoiding this tedious exercise, common ground might be that in an imprecise field the kibbutz experience provides as near an approximation to a true test case as we are likely to find. (Another possible candidate might be the progressive co-educational boarding school.) Hence the kibbutz findings on stubborn patterns of sexual differentiation, if themselves rigorously arrived at, are suggestive of what the biological infrastructure of certain social relations in our species is likely to be. Certainly no theory can afford to ignore them. In sharp contrast to the incoherence of earlier models on the issue of causation, Tiger and Shepher's position now is a logically very interesting one which includes both 'programming' and human choice, because human motives become a part of what is programmed. The coherence of this version is perhaps best left to philosophers to evaluate.

I want to move briefly to a theoretical posture – that of Vernon Reynolds in *The Biology of Human Action* (1976) – which while recognising the presence of innate factors in the human extra-reproductive sexual make-up denies that these have determining jurisdiction over social forms. Reynolds refers often to sex and gender in developing his integrated picture of the collaboration of evolutionary, genetic, somatic, developmental and cultural processes in producing the human actor. A true 'human sciences' text, this work is an excellent source of ready information on the biological ingredients of the human (including sexual) make-up. Yet Reynolds, unlike other writers in the field, is a sceptic as regards the determinative influence of 'nature' on 'culture'. In denying that the variability of cultural forms is in any way constrained by their evolved infrastructure, he retreats to an explicitly existentialist position with appeal to the principle that *l'existence précède l'essence*. G.H.Mead and Berger and Luckmann are among those invoked by Reynolds in asserting the human capacity for unrestrained self-construction, subject only to the limitations of the body itself.

This view might seem well designed to placate both evolutionary anthropologists and defenders of the autonomy of culture. Yet the retreat, if such it be, leaves yet another issue stranded and gasping: that of universality. For if man is free to construct himself, and he does so always and everywhere in broadly the same way, then if inbuilt predispositions are ruled out, what status are we to assign to these 'human universals' and what is the point of looking for them in the first place? Now one can quite well argue that there are non-trivial human universals, or that particular alleged cases are illusory products of biased expectations and loaded concepts, or as Crick (1975) has recently done, that the discovery of human universals does not justify a search for biological causes. My own view is that the whole question of human universals has been remarkably ill-handled in the past, and that if any such are found we should not necessarily expect them to be found at the level of the statistical distribution of surface events. In any case it is surely premature to retreat from the question just when it is beginning to look interesting, and when, as I shall suggest, we are beginning to see how to set about distinguishing 'universalism' from universality.

A Way Forward?

Throughout the entire debate, what seems to be conspicuously and embarrassingly missing is a satisfactory conceptual framework within which the relation of nature to culture can be specified, as a precondition for coming to grips with any particular problem of women. This may be no more than a naive re-statement of what many would deem the central problem of anthropology itself. Yet it is surprising how little direct attention it has received from the very biosocial writers who must in the long run rest their case on its satisfactory resolution. I have referred to the entrapment of earlier writings within an implicit theory of causation. Once more there may be non-academic reasons why the question of determination is still a prominent one. Tiger and Shepher and Reynolds, as we have seen, differ sharply on the issue of determination, but their difference is one-dimensional. They disagree about the strength of the influence wielded by biological predispositions on concrete cultural arrangements: a difference formalised in attempts to designate 'strong' and 'weak' types of biosocial theory. This is of course a perfectly valid source of disagreement; yet to be content with it is to restrict unnecessarily our conception of the nature-culture relationship. Needless to say, I have nothing so grand to offer as a theory on the subject, but one or two thoughts might be helpful.

'Nature' is not related to 'culture' solely as cause to effect, whether weakly or strongly. The self-perceiving and self-defining qualities of culture are enough to ensure that if nature intrudes into culture in important ways, the reverse is simultaneously true. Nature and culture as objects of knowledge contain each other, and are likely to do so many times over at different orders of reality. Yet the relationship is not thereby made arbitrary, nor is it idle to search for a biological infrastructure to human patterns of relationship. Overlaying any evolved general predispositions to certain modes of action there may be equally general, perhaps evolved, predispositions for these to be culturally construed in specific ways. 'Programming' (to borrow the language of the biogrammarians) may happen at many levels, and these may act on each other with the greatest complexity to produce the regularities we may observe at the surface level of events. We can on occasion make an inspired guess about the direction such manipulations may consistently take. It may be, for example, that what 'nature' provides at one level in the form of mere predispositions and outlines, 'culture' at another perversely exaggerates and hardens, transforming *distributions* into *categories* by the force of its own (evolved?) thirst for classification.[4] The regularities of sexual differentiation in society which Tiger and Shepher soberly, and Goldberg contentiously, seek to demonstrate may, despite their apparent reality, reflect 'programmes' at many levels from the neuro-endocrinal to the theological. 'Programmes' thus regarded may cancel each other in some places, summate in others, and are unpredictably subject to the modifying power of human cognition.

Against this background, we can tentatively suggest the outlines of a possible evolutionary hypothesis about the basis of extra-reproductive sexual differentiation in human society. Without needing for the moment to specify what these differences are I proceed as if their existence on the ground were to have been established. The apparent existence of areas of consistent sexual difference in human life beyond the narrowly reproductive becomes, then, a problem requiring explanation by whatever theoretical apparatus is appropriate and to hand. The hypothesis, although it owes much to works such as those I have discussed, is no more than an outline and is doubtless not the only one possible. But it seems to fit whatever 'facts' are known. At least it attempts to accommodate the ways in which 'reality' affects and is affected by social perceptions and interpretations of itself.

The hypothesis would rest on two major assumptions: that a self-conscious ordering of society appeared early enough in human pre-history to have played an active role in hominid evolution; and that if 'programmes' and predispositions can evolve at multiple levels, they can do so in such a way as to become *conditional* on one another. There is nothing intrinsically novel in either of these assumptions. Respecting the first, a convincing theory was long ago put forward by Kummer, Chance and others that social order itself furnished the selective impetus for the elaboration of the primate brain (see, e.g., Kummer, 1971). Regarding the second, there is apparently reason to think that even at gene level, the manifestation of a programme may be conditional on the local environment in which the gene finds itself (see e.g. Eisenberg 1973). In applying both to the present case, we need to suppose that not only social order itself but its self-conscious dimension go back far enough in some form, perhaps to Pithecanthropine times, to have been subject to evolutionary pressures and also to have engaged in conditional interplay with other kinds of programme within the evolutionary process. We can then imagine that ecological and morphological changes making for a sexual division of labour (e.g. the hunting transition, prolonged infant dependency, widening of the female pelvis to accommodate the enlarged infant skull, and corresponding relative immobilisation of the female) take place in the context of a developing world structure,[5] or collective perception of reality, which is coming to expect and anticipate precisely these differences. We can further imagine that such interchanges between programmes at different levels might lead to a present-day situation in which men and women are indeed 'predisposed' to perform differently in certain respects, but this predisposition is itself calibrated to a certain range of 'world structures'.

All the details remain to be filled in, of course. I said that the theory was no more than an outline: an attempt to suggest how we might set about opening up the debate so as to take account of the complexities of the real world, while retaining a legitimate evolutionary and biosocial interest. To choose a semantically crude example, suppose it were to be rigorously established that men everywhere tend statistically to adopt a 'dominant' posture towards women. Then suppose this finding to be backed by hard neurological and endocrinal evidence. Far from compelling us to admit that patriarchy in any form is inescapable, this could be interpreted as the outcome of an interplay of programmes such that men are indeed predisposed in this direction, but only if exposed — perhaps at some critical period of growth — to a structure which in some way provides for it. In a different sort of structure, one lacking the crucial expectations, we do not know what would happen, nor do we know what range of structures is potentially available. Naturally some patterns will be more resistant than others to changes in the programme at societal level; the kibbutz evidence may point to hard cases of this kind. But it should be obvious why the view I am suggesting we take of evolved predispositions to sexual differentiation is an essentially agnostic one, at least for the present: we know next to nothing about the boundary conditions governing any of the programmes.

This agnostic stance by no means entails a retreat from our present interest in the nature-culture interchange and its implications for human sexual identity and destiny. What needs to be recognised is that a satisfactory biosocial model must accommodate the essential openness of the key questions which would follow from acceptance of the outline view I have suggested. This openness applies at both theoretical and ethnographic levels of enquiry. Our own overall brief, that of exploring the categories 'man' and 'woman', would thus come to the forefront of such an improved biosocial programme, as would Tiger and Shepher's accurately phrased 'search for the ethnographic female'. Hence, although naturally I make no attempt to pre-empt any of the ground covered by my fellow contributors to this volume, some of what I have said points towards their material and will be enriched by it. Earlier biosocial writings showed an unfortunate tendency to leap to impulsive and premature claims about human universals, especially those governing women. The present view would allow — indeed necessitate — a descent from these heights of universalism to a kind of 'intermediate technology' of theory and field-work within which bounded segments of female action, each within its own social reality, can be analysed against the background of an enduring biosocial concern. By thus abandoning a false universal*ism*, we may paradoxically approach a true *universality*.

Tiger and Shepher have led the way here (although they might well not accept my placing of their work within the frame of my own argument). Despite great differences in method, I conceive my own current field-work among nurses as an exercise along similar lines. Nursing as a women's occupation has often been characterised by feminist writers as a kind of aberration, a capitulation to male power (see, for example, Ehrenreich and English, 1976) — a view which itself capitulates oddly to the 'male models' supposedly under attack. The documented history of nursing from the time of the Nightingale reforms and earlier reveals a sustained dialogue between changing perceptions of nursing as a system of knowledge, value and action — a 'world structure' of a kind — and changing perceptions of the 'nature' of women.[6] Nurses, of course, have views of their own. My own participant field-study among British nurses is in its early stages, and no firm findings can be appropriately presented here. But, to conclude, here is an example of the quality of material which can emerge from even preliminary work at ground level. A recently qualified staff-nurse was describing to me the inner conflicts which resulted from being expected to handle authority and responsibility on the ward, yet switch to a 'feminine' style of behaviour with her boy-friend when off duty. In the effort to express herself she began to stammer, and produced an extended *lapsus linguae* of reverberative significance for our theme: 'I . . . I . . . sometimes don't know what I am . . . I feel like a . . . what do you call it . . . eunuch . . . unique . . . unicorn . . .'

It is at such levels of intensity, detail and symbolic *richesse*, I submit, that we need to seek for documentation of a validly biosocial account of women.

Notes

1. See, for example, Oakley, 1972.

2. I do not here prejudge Reynolds's willingness or otherwise to be termed a 'biosocial anthropologist'. I include him as an anthropologist with a biological background and expertise, who has interests in common with those of the avowedly 'biosocial' writers.

3. I avoid, for the sake of brevity, unpacking these arguments fully.

4. This move places the determinist boot squarely on an unaccustomed foot — a point also made by Reynolds in a different way.

5. This usage is borrowed from E.W. Ardener (see, for example, 1975).

6. Abel-Smith, for example, quotes an 1871 source:

Waiving the question whether women might or might not be made capable with man's advantages of doing man's work, it surely will not be denied that a sphere of action would be preferable in which she would not have to compete with him, but in which her own peculiar endowments would give her a special advantage. And here is an opportunity for showing how a woman's work may complement man's in the true order of nature. Where does the character of the 'help-mate' come out so strikingly as in the sickroom, where the quick eye, the soft hand, the light step, and the ready ear, second the wisdom of the physician, and execute his behests better than he himself could have imagined? (Haddon, quoted in Abel-Smith, 1960, p. 18)

Bibliography

Abel-Smith, Brian. *A History of the Nursing Profession.* London, Heinemann, 1960

Ardener, E.W. 'Belief and the Problem of Women', 1972. Republished in S. Ardener (ed.), 1975

——. 'Behaviour: a social anthropological criticism'. *J. Anth. Soc. Oxford,* 4 (1973), 152-4

——. 'Language and the Social Anthropologist as Translator of Culture'. Paper presented to the Wenner-Gren Symposium on *Dilemmas of Focus in Linguistics,* 1977 (forthcoming)

Ardener, S. (ed.). *Perceiving Women.* London, Dent/Malaby; New York, Halsted, 1975

Ardrey, Robert. *The Social Contract.* London, Collins, 1970

Bischof, N. 'Comparative Ethology of Incest Avoidance', 1975, in Fox (ed.), 1975

Callan, H. *Ethology and Society.* London, Oxford University Press, 1970

Chance, M.R.A. 'The Nature and Special Features of the Instinctive Social Bond of the Primates'. *Primates,* 4 (ed.) (1963)

——. 'Social Cohesion and the Structure of Attention', 1975, in Fox (ed.),1975

Chance, M.R.A., and Jolly, C. *Social Groups of Monkeys, Apes and Men.* London, Cape, 1970

Crick, M. 'Ethology, Language and the Study of Human Action'. *J. Anth. Soc. Oxford* 6 (1975), 106-18

Ehrenreich, B., and English, D. *Witches, Midwives and Nurses: A History of Women Healers.* London, Writers and Readers Co-operative, 1973

Fox, R. *Encounter with Anthropology.* Harmondsworth, Peregrine, 1973

—— (ed.), *Biosocial Anthropology.* London, Malaby, 1975

Eisenberg, Leon. 'The "Human" Nature of Human Nature'' in Ashley Montagu (ed.). *Man and Aggression.* New York, Oxford University Press, 1973 (first published 1968)

Goldberg, Steven. *The Inevitability of Patriarchy*. London, Temple Smith, 1977

Harré, Rom. 'The Shift to an Anthropomorphic Model of Man'. *J. Anth. Soc. Oxford* 2, 1 (1971)

—— and Secord, P. *The Explanation of Social Behaviour*. Oxford, Blackwell, 1972

Hudson, L. *The Cult of the Fact*. London, Cape, 1972

Kummer, H. *Primate Societies*. Chicago, Aldine, 1971

Lévi-Strauss, C. *The Scope of Anthropology*. London, Cape, 1967

Morris, Desmond. *The Naked Ape*. London, Cape, 1967

Oakley, Ann. *Sex, Gender and Society*. London, Temple Smith, 1972

Reynolds, V. *The Biology of Human Action*. Reading and San Francisco, Freeman, 1976

Tiger, L. *Men In Groups*. London, Nelson, 1969

—— and Fox, R. 'The Zoological Perspective in Social Science'. *Man*, n.s., 1 (1966), 75-81

——. *The Imperial Animal*. London, Secker and Warburg, 1971

Tiger, L., and Shepher, J. *Women in the Kibbutz*. London, Peregrine, 1976

Wickler, Wolfgang. *The Sexual Code: The Social Behaviour of Animals and Men*. London, Weidenfeld, 1969

Young, R. 'The Human Limits of Nature' in J. Benthall (ed.), *The Limits of Human Nature*. London, Allen Lane, 1973

INDEX

Compiled by Diana Burfield

SUBJECT INDEX